An
AUTOBIOGRAPHY
Of
GENERAL CUSTER

An
AUTOBIOGRAPHY
Of
GENERAL CUSTER

Newly Edited and Introduced by Stephen Brennan

SKYHORSE PUBLISHING

Skyhorse Publishing books may be purchased in bulk at special discounts for sales promotion, corporate gifts, fund-raising, or educational purposes. Special editions can also be created to specifications. For details, contact the Special Sales Department, Skyhorse Publishing, 307 West 36th Street, 11th Floor, New York, NY 10018 or info@skyhorsepublishing.com.

Skyhorse® and Skyhorse Publishing® are registered trademarks of Skyhorse Publishing, Inc.®, a Delaware corporation.

www.skyhorsepublishing.com

10 9 8 7 6 5 4 3 2 1

Library of Congress Cataloging-in-Publication Data
Custer, George A. (George Armstrong), 1839-1876.
[My life on the plains]
An autobiography of General Custer / newly edited and introduced by Stephen Brennan.
    p. cm.
ISBN 978-1-62087-075-4
1. Custer, George A. (George Armstrong), 1839-1876. 2. Indians of North America--Wars--1866-1895. 3. Indians of North America--Wars--Great Plains. 4. Washita Campaign, 1868-1869. 5. Generals--United States--Biography. 6. United States. Army--Military life--History--19th century. 7. United States. Army. Cavalry, 7th. 8. Great Plains--Description and travel. 9. West (U.S.)--Description and travel. I. Brennan, Stephen Vincent. II. Title.

E83.866.C96A3 2012
973.8'2092--dc23
[B]

                                        2012030478

Printed in the United States of America

Table of Contents

Introduction

"Our hearts so stout have got us fame
For soon 'tis known from whence we came
Where'er we go they fear the name
Of Garryowen in glory."
—Traditional
(Battle Song of Custer's Seventh Cavalry)

We are schizophrenic about our heroes. No sooner do we raise one up than we pull him down. First the paean, then the hoot. So it is with George Armstrong Custer, who from the beginning of his military life right up until the present day, has come in for way more than his fair share of blame, trivialization, and overwrought, fulsome praise. Even George Washington, *the* true American icon, is subject to all manner of outrage at the hands of reevaluators, rehabilitators and revisers. First President, Father of the Country, and—oh yes, you know he had lousy teeth. First the cuddle, then the slap. All right, we know this is only human nature. No one likes to see somebody grow too big for his trouser size. And there is something about hero worship itself that's like to bring the acolyte up short, with a guilty shudder, often awakening an opposite and negative reaction. After all, worship is for God, and we understand too well that beneath their patina of glory, idols are often clay-footed. More than that, the verdicts of history can be brutal, and various, as each generation is quick to cavil, to take issue with the settled assessment of its forebears.

So what are we to think? Who was George Armstrong Custer? Or better yet, which Custer was the real Custer? Was he a gifted and talented commander of cavalry, or merely the "lucky Custer" sourly described by so many of his contemporaries? Was he the dashing and be-ringleted "Boy General" of the popular press, or just a relentless self-promoter? Was he a noble warrior doing dangerous and difficult work out on the nation's frontier, or only a callous and bloodthirsty agent of the genocide of our native peoples? And, in his last fight at the Little Big Horn, must he be forever counted a fool who sacrificed the lives of his command on the altar of an outsized ego, or was he instead a canny and capable leader of men, employing classic cavalry tactics, who had the misfortune to run into something that was simply way, way too big for him? One or the other, which is it to be? Was he, or was he not . . . man or monster, hero or antihero? This is history's whipsaw effect, and the best antidote for this kind of pain in the neck is autobiography.

The plain facts of Custer's life are not in dispute. Born (1839) in New Rumley, Ohio, of Anglo-German stock, into what we would these days call a middle-class family—his father was a small-time farmer and blacksmith—young George Armstrong lived a life straight out of Tom Sawyer, with plenty of hunting, fishing, and other rambles in the wilds surrounding his small town. Often noted in the reminiscences of his contemporaries was the boy's propensity for pranks and other tests of the limits of authority. It may have been this sort of thing that got young Autie (nickname) packed off to live with his half-sister and her husband in Michigan, where he attended school. In 1858 Custer began his studies at West Point, graduating in 1861 (at the bottom of his class) just in time to fight at the first Battle of Bull Run. In the following years of the Civil War, Custer's achievements were remarkable. He fought in seven great battles, served in four major campaigns, married the beautiful and intelligent Elizabeth Bacon—his beloved Libbie (nickname)—and finished the war with a brevet (temporary) rank of Major General. In the last decade of his life he served in various western commands, occasionally fighting, but most often chasing down and otherwise harrying the Tribes onto reservations, until the meeting at the Little Big Horn in 1876.

If you find—as I do—the bald recital of names and dates ultimately unsatisfying, then I suggest you turn to this *Autobiography*. Here is the man himself, his own story, told in his own words. The writing is excellent. We know from his official reports and correspondence that Custer wrote a clear and colorful prose, but in these stories Custer takes an almost novelistic approach. There is plenty of detail about military life on post and in the field, as well as much attention to descriptions of character and of landscape. As in the best kind of novel, you feel as though you are present. Some of this may be due to the influence of Mrs. Custer. Of an evening, on post and during his various leaves, Custer would sit at the dining room table with his beloved Libbie, and together they would compose the various stories of his exploits that would eventually become the book *My Life On the Plains,* which was a bestseller in its time, and from which *An Autobiography of General Custer* is largely taken.

Custer's narration begins shortly following the Civil War, when having gained a reputation as a bold and inventive leader of Cavalry, he is given command of an expedition to help subjugate various native peoples of the Great Plains and to force them onto reservations. His story touches on his own court martial and subsequent reinstatement to command. It ends shortly before he is to embark upon the campaign that is to lead to the Battle of the Little Big Horn and "Custer's Last Stand."

As Custer was unable to write about this, his most famous battle, the *Autobiography* concludes with an 1880s newspaper account of an interview with Sitting Bull, after his escape to Canada, in which the great chief looks back on the battle and offers his own point of view.

The illustrations are contemporaneous. The chapter headings are my own.

Stephen Brennan,
West Cornwall, CT

With Hancock's Expedition

CHAPTER 1

With General Hancock's Expedition—In Pursuit of the Indians—My First Buffalo Hunt—Indian Attack?—False Alarm—The Box Family Story

Under the most auspicious circumstances, and in time of peace with the Indians, the life of an army officer on the Plains or along our frontier is at best one involving no little personal discomfort, and demanding the sacrifice of many of the luxuries and benefits which he could obtain were he located within the limits of civilization. To many officers, service in the West amounts almost to social exile. Some can have their families with or near them. There is a limited opportunity for social intercourse; travel from the States, to and across the Plains, either for business or pleasure, is uninterrupted, and mail facilities with friends and relations in the States are maintained. An Indian war changes all this. The troops must prepare to take the field.

Provided with but few comforts, necessarily limited in this respect by the amount of transportation, which on the Plains is narrowed down to the smallest practicable, the soldier bids adieu—often a final one—to the dear ones of home, and with his comrades in arms sets out, no matter how inclement the season, to seek what? Fame and glory? How many military men have reaped laurels from their Indian campaigns? Does he strive to win the approving smile of his countrymen? That is indeed, in this particular instance, a difficult task. For let him act as he may in conducting or assisting in a campaign against the Indians, if he survives the campaign he can feel assured of this fact, that one half of his fellow citizens at home will revile him for his zeal and pronounce his success, if he achieves any, a massacre of poor, defenceless, harmless Indians; while the other half, if his efforts to chastise the common enemy are not crowned with satisfactory results, will cry, "Down with him. Down with the regular army and give us brave volunteers who can serve the government in other ways besides eating rations and drawing pay."

An unsuccessful campaign, under which head nineteen out of twenty may reasonably be classed, satisfies no portion of the public, and greatly dissatisfies that portion of the Western population whose knowledge of the murders and depredations committed by the Indians is, unlike that of the people of the States further east, of too recent origin to be swept away by false notions of clemency. During the continuance of the campaign both officers and soldiers are generally cut off from all communication with the friends left behind. Couriers, sent as bearers of a few despatches and letters, are sometimes under cover of the night enabled to make their way back to the forts; but even these fail sometimes. I now recollect the circumstance of two trusty scouts being sent with despatches and a small mail, to make their way from the southern portion of Kansas to Fort Dodge on the Arkansas River. When we saw them again, we beheld their lifeless, mangled remains, their bodies pierced with numerous arrows, and mutilated almost beyond recognition—our letters scattered here and there by the savages, who had torn open the little canvas mailbag in search of plunder. The Indians had surrounded these faithful fellows within about ten miles of the end of their perilous journey. The numerous empty cartridge shells which lay around and near the bodies of the two men proved how persistently and bravely they had struggled for their lives.

The opening of an Indian campaign is also the signal for the withdrawal of all privileges and enjoyments, such as leaves of absence, visits from Eastern friends, hunting and pleasure parties of all kinds. The reception from the East of all luxuries and delicacies for the table and of all current literature, such as the numerous railroads being constructed in the West, particularly the two Pacifics render easy of procurement, ceases; and not only the private soldier but the officer is limited in his mess fare to an indifferent portion of the ordinary ration. Is it probable or reasonable that these objects and results, the principal ones generally, so far as the army as individuals is concerned, would be considered sufficient to render either officers or soldiers "eager to get up an Indian war"? I have yet to make the acquaintance of that officer of the army who, in time of undisturbed peace, desired a war with the Indians. On the contrary, the army is the Indian's best friend, so long as the latter desires to maintain friendship. It is pleasant at all times, and always interesting, to have a village of peaceable Indians locate their lodges near our frontier posts or camps. The daily visits of the Indians, from the most venerable chief to the strapped pappoose, their rude interchange of civilities, their barterings, races, dances, legends, strange customs, and fantastic ceremonies, all combine to render them far more agreeable as friendly neighbors than as crafty, bloodthirsty enemies.

Of the many important expeditions organized to operate in the Indian country, none, perhaps, of late years has excited more general and unfriendly comment, considering the slight loss of life inflicted upon the Indians, than the expedition organized and led in person by Major-General Hancock in the spring of 1867. The clique generally known as the "Indian ring" were particularly malevolent and bitter in their denunciations of General Hancock for precipitating, as they expressed it, an Indian war. This expedition was quite formidable in appearance, being made up of eight troops of cavalry, seven companies of infantry, and one battery of light artillery, numbering altogether about 1,400 men. As General Hancock at the time and since has been so often accused of causelessly bringing on an Indian war, a word in explanation may not be amiss.

Being in command of the cavalry connected with the expedition, I had ample and frequent opportunities for learning the true purposes and objects of the march into the heart of the Indian country.

It may be asked: "What had the Indians done to make this incursion necessary?" They had been guilty of numerous thefts and murders during the preceding summer and fall, for none of which had they been called to account. They had attacked the stations of the overland mail route, killed the employees, burned the station, and captured the stock. Citizens had been murdered in their homes on the frontier of Kansas; murders had been committed on the Arkansas route. The principal perpetrators of these acts were the Cheyennes and Sioux. The agent of the former, if not a party to the murder on the Arkansas, knew who the guilty persons were, yet took no steps to bring the murderers to punishment. Such a course would have interfered with his trade and profits. It was not to punish for these sins of the past that the expedition was set on foot, but rather by its imposing appearance and its early presence in the Indian country to check or intimidate the Indians from a repetition of their late conduct. This was deemed particularly necessary from the fact that the various tribes from which we had greatest cause to anticipate trouble had, during the winter through their leading chiefs and warriors, threatened that as soon as the grass was up in spring a combined outbreak would take place along our entire frontier, and especially against the main routes of travel. To assemble the tribes for the desired council, word was sent early in March to the agents of those tribes whom it was desirable to meet. The agents sent runners to the villages inviting them to meet us at some point near the Arkansas River.

General Hancock, with the artillery and six companies of infantry, reached Fort Riley, Kansas, from Fort Leavenworth by rail the last week in March; here he was joined by four companies of the Seventh Cavalry and an additional company of the Thirty-Seventh Infantry. It was at this point that I joined the expedition. And as a very fair sample of the laurels which military men may win in an Indian campaign by a zealous discharge of what they deem their duty, I will here state, in parenthesis, that after engaging in the expedition, some of the events of which I am about to relate, and undergoing fatigue, privations, and dangers equal to those of a campaign during the Rebellion, I found myself at the termination of the campaign again at Fort Riley *in arrest*. This is not mentioned in a fault-finding spirit. I have no fault to find. It is said that blessings sometimes come in disguise. Such proved to be true in this instance, although I must say the disguise for some little time was most perfect.

From Fort Riley we marched to Fort Harker, a distance of ninety miles, where our force was strengthened by the addition of two more troops of cavalry. Halting only long enough to replenish our supplies, we next directed our march toward Fort Larned, near the Arkansas, about seventy miles to the southeast. A march from the 3rd to the 7th of April brought us to Fort Larned. The agent for the Comanches and Kiowas accompanied us. At Fort Larned we found the agent of the Cheyennes, Arapahos, and Apaches; from the latter we learned that he had, as requested, sent runners to the chiefs of his agency inviting them to the council, and that they had agreed to assemble near Fort Larned on the 10th of the month, requesting that the expedition would remain there until that date. To this request General Hancock acceded.

On the 9th of April, while encamped awaiting the council, which was to be held the following day, a terrible snowstorm occurred, lasting all day until late in the evening. It was our good fortune to be in camp rather than on the march; had it been otherwise, we could not well have escaped without loss of life from the severe cold and blinding snow. The cavalry horses suffered seriously, and were only preserved by doubling their ration of oats, while to prevent their being frozen during the intensely cold night which followed, the guards were instructed to keep passing along the picket lines with a whip, and to keep the horses moving constantly. The snow was eight inches deep. The council, which was to take place the next day, had to be postponed until the return of good weather. Now began the display of a kind of diplomacy for which the Indian is peculiar. The Cheyennes and a band of the Sioux were encamped on Pawnee Fork, about thirty miles above Fort Larned. They neither desired to move nearer to us nor have us approach nearer to them. On the morning of the 11th they sent us word that they had started to visit us, but discovering a large herd of buffalo near their camp, they had stopped to procure a supply meat. This message was not received with much confidence, nor was a buffalo hunt deemed of sufficient importance to justify the Indians in breaking their engagement. General Hancock decided, however, to delay another day, when, if the Indians still failed to come in, he would move his command to the vicinity of their village and hold the conference there.

Orders were issued on the evening of the 12th for the march to be resumed on the following day. Later in the evening two chiefs of the "Dog Soldiers," a band composed of the most warlike and troublesome Indians on the Plains, chiefly made up of Cheyennes, visited our camp. They were accompanied by a dozen warriors, and expressed a desire to hold a conference with General Hancock, to which he assented. A large council fire was built in front of the General's tent, and all the officers of his command assembled there. A tent had been erected for the accommodation of the chiefs a short distance from the General's. Before they could feel equal to the occasion, and in order to obtain time to collect their thoughts, they desired that supper might be prepared for them, which was done. When finally ready they advanced from their tent to the council fire in single file, accompanied by their agent and an interpreter. Arrived at the fire, another brief delay ensued. No matter how pressing or momentous the occasion, an Indian invariably declines to engage in a council until he has filled his pipe and gone through with the important ceremony of a smoke. This attended to, the chiefs announced that they were ready "to talk." They were then introduced to the principal officers of the group, and seemed much struck with the flashy uniforms of the few artillery officers who were present in all the glory of red horsehair plumes, aigulets, etc. The chiefs seemed puzzled to determine whether these insignia designated chieftains or medicine men. General Hancock began the conference by a speech, in which he explained to the Indians his purpose in coming to see them, and what he expected of them in the future. He particularly informed them that he was not there to make war, but to promote peace. Then expressing his regret that more of the chiefs had not visited him, he announced his intention of proceeding on the morrow with his command to the vicinity of their village and there holding a council with all of the chiefs. Tall Bull, a fine, warlike-looking chieftain, replied to General Hancock, but his speech contained nothing important, being made up of allusions to the growing scarcity of the buffalo, his love for the white man, and the usual hint that a donation in the way of refreshments would be highly acceptable; he added that he would have nothing new to say at the village.

Rightly concluding that the Indians did not intend to come to our camp as they had at first agreed to, it was decided to move nearer to their village. On the morning following the conference held with the two chiefs of the "Dog Soldiers," our entire force therefore marched from Fort Larned up Pawnee Fork in the direction of the main village, encamping the first night about twenty-one miles from the fort. Several parties of Indians were seen in our advance during the day, evidently watching our movements; while a heavy smoke, seen to rise in the direction of the Indian village, indicated that something more than usual was going on. This smoke we afterwards learned arose from the burning grass. The Indians, thinking to prevent us from encamping in their vicinity, had set fire to and burned all the grass for miles in the direction from which they expected us. Before we arrived at our camping-ground we were met by several chiefs and warriors belonging to the Cheyennes and Sioux. Among the chiefs were Pawnee Killer of the Sioux and White Horse of the Cheyennes. It was arranged that these chiefs should accept our hospitality and remain with us during the night, and in the morning all the chiefs of the two tribes then in the village were to come to General Hancock's headquarters and hold a council. On the morning of the 14th Pawnee Killer left our camp at an early hour, for the purpose, as he said, of going to the village to bring in the other chiefs to the council. Nine o'clock had been agreed upon as the hour at which the council should assemble. The hour came, but the chiefs did not. Now an Indian council is not only often an important but always an interesting occasion. And, somewhat like a famous recipe for making a certain dish, the first thing necessary in holding an Indian council is to get the Indian. Half-past nine o'clock came, and still we were lacking this one important part of the council. At this juncture Bull Bear, an influential chief among the Cheyennes, came in and reported that the chiefs were on their way to our camp, but would not be able to reach it for some time. This was a mere artifice to secure delay. General Hancock informed Bull Bear that as the chiefs could not arrive for some time, he would move his forces up the stream nearer to the village, and the council could be held at our camp that night. To this proposition Bull Bear gave his assent.

At 11 AM we resumed the march, and had proceeded but a few miles when we witnessed one of the finest and most imposing military displays, prepared according to the Indian art of war, which it has ever been my lot to behold. It was nothing more nor less than an Indian line of battle drawn directly across our line of march; as if to say, "Thus far and no further." Most of the Indians were mounted; all were bedecked in their brightest colors, their heads crowned with the brilliant war-bonnet, their lances bearing the crimson pennant, bows strung, and quivers full of barbed arrows. In addition to these weapons, which with the hunting knife and tomahawk are considered as forming the armament of the warrior, each one was supplied with either a breech-loading rifle or revolver, sometimes with both—the latter obtained through the wise foresight and strong love of fair play which prevails in the Indian Department, which, seeing that its wards are determined to fight, is equally determined that there shall be no advantage taken, but that the two sides shall be armed alike; proving, too, in this manner the wonderful liberality of our government, which not only is able to furnish its soldiers with the latest improved style of breech-loaders to defend it and themselves, but is equally able and willing to give the same pattern of arms to their common foe. The only difference is, that the soldier, if he loses his weapon, is charged double price for it; while to avoid making any such charge against the Indian, his weapons are given him without conditions attached. In the line of battle before us there were several hundred Indians, while further to the rear and at different distances were other organized bodies acting apparently as reserves. Still further were small detachments who seemed to perform the duty of couriers, and were held in readiness to convey messages to the village. The ground beyond was favorable for an extended view, allowing the eye to sweep the plain for several miles. As far as the eye could reach small groups or individuals could be seen in the direction of the village; these were evidently parties of observation, whose sole object was to learn the result of our meeting with the main body and hasten with the news to the village.

For a few moments appearances seemed to foreshadow anything but a peaceful issue. The infantry was in the advance, followed closely by the artillery, while my command, the cavalry, was marching on the flank. General Hancock, who was riding with his staff at the head of the column, coming suddenly in view of the wild fantastic battle array, which extended far to our right and left and not more than half a mile in our front, hastily sent orders to the infantry, artillery, and cavalry to form line of battle, evidently determined that if war was intended we should be prepared. The cavalry, being the last to form on the right, came into line on a gallop, and, without waiting to align the ranks carefully, the command was given to "draw sabre." As the bright blades flashed from their scabbads into the morning sunlight, and the infantry brought their muskets to a carry, a most beautiful and wonderfully interesting sight was spread out before and around us, presenting a contrast which, to a military eye, could but be striking. Here in battle array, facing each other, were the representatives of civilized and barbarous warfare. The one, with but few modifications, stood clothed in the same rude style of dress, bearing the same patterned shield and weapon that his ancestors had borne centuries before; the other confronted him in the dress and supplied with the implements of war which the most advanced stage of civilization had pronounced the most perfect. Was the comparative superiority of these two classes to be subjected to the mere test of war here? Such seemed the prevailing impression on both sides. All was eager anxiety and expectation. Neither side seemed to comprehend the object or intentions of the other; each was waiting for the other to deliver the first blow. A more beautiful battleground could not have been chosen. Not a bush or even the slightest irregularity of ground intervened between the two lines which now stood frowning and facing each other. Chiefs could be seen riding along the line as if directing and exhorting their braves to deeds of heroism.

After a few moments of painful suspense, General Hancock, accompanied by General A. J. Smith and other officers, rode forward, and through an interpreter invited the chiefs to meet us midway, for the purpose of an interview. In response to this invitation Roman Nose, bearing white flag, accompanied by Bull Bear, White Horse, Gray Beard, and Medicine Wolf on the part of the Cheyennes, and Pawnee Killer, Bad Wound, Tall Bear that Walks under the Ground, Left Hand, Little Bear, and Little Bull on the part of the Sioux, rode forward to the middle of the open space between the two lines. Here we shook hands with all of the chiefs, most of them exhibiting unmistakable signs of gratification at this apparently peaceful termination of our rencounter. General Hancock very naturally inquired the object of the hostile attitude displayed before us, saying to the chiefs that if war was their object we were ready then and there to participate. Their immediate answer was that they did not desire war, but were peacefully disposed. They were then told that we would continue our march toward the village, and encamp near it, but would establish such regulations that none of the soldiers would be permitted to approach or disturb them. An arrangement was then effected by which the chiefs were to assemble at General Hancock's headquarters as soon as our camp was pitched. The interview then terminated, and the Indians moved off in the direction of their village, we following leisurely in rear.

A march of a few miles brought us in sight of the village, which was situated in a beautiful grove on the banks of the stream up which we had been marching. The village consisted of upwards of three hundred lodges, a small fraction over half belonging to the Cheyennes, the remainder to the Sioux. Like all Indian encampments, the ground chosen was a most romantic spot, and at the same time fulfilled in every respect the requirements of a good camping ground; wood, water, and grass were abundant. The village was placed on a wide, level plateau, while on the north and west, at a short distance off, rose high bluffs, which admirably served as a shelter against the cold winds which at that season of the year prevail from these directions. Our tents were pitched within half a mile of the village. Guards were placed between to prevent intrusion upon our part. A few of the Indian ponies found grazing near our camp were caught and returned to them, to show that our intentions were at least neighborly. We had scarcely pitched our tents when Roman Nose, Bull Bear, Gray Beard, and Medicine Wolf, all prominent chiefs of the Cheyennes, came into camp, with the information that upon our approach their women and children had all fled from the village, alarmed by the presence of so many soldiers and imagining a second Chivington massacre to be intended. General Hancock insisted that they should all return, promising protection and good treatment to all; that if the camp was abandoned he would hold it responsible. The chiefs then stated their belief in their ability to recall the fugitives, could they be furnished with horses to overtake them. This was accordingly done, and two of them set out mounted on two of our horses. An agreement was also entered into at the same time that one of our interpreters, Ed. Gurrier, a half-breed Cheyenne who was in the employ of the government, should remain in the village and report every two hours as to whether any Indians were leaving the village. This was about seven o'clock in the evening. At half past nine the half-breed returned to headquarters, with the intelligence that all the chiefs and warriors were saddling up to leave, under circumstances showing that they had no intention of returning, such as packing up such articles as could be carried with them, and cutting and destroying their lodges, this last being done to obtain small pieces for temporary shelter.

I had retired to my tent, which was located some few hundred yards from that of General Hancock, when a messenger from the latter awakened me with the information that General Hancock desired my presence at his tent. Imagining a movement on the part of the Indians, I made no delay in responding to the summons. General Hancock briefly stated the situation of affairs, and directed me to mount my command as quickly and as silently as possible, surround the Indian village, and prevent the departure of its inhabitants. Easily said, but not so easily done. Under ordinary circumstances, silence not being necessary, I could have returned to my camp, and by a few blasts from the trumpet placed every soldier in his saddle almost as quickly as it has taken time to write this sentence. No bugle calls must be sounded; we were to adopt some of the stealth of the Indian—how successfully remains to be seen. By this time every soldier, officers as well as men, was in his tent sound asleep. How to awaken them and impart to each the necessary order? First going to the tent of the adjutant and arousing him, I procured an experienced assistant in my labors. Next the captains of companies were awakened and orders imparted to them. They in turn transmitted the order to the first sergeant, who similarly aroused the men. It has often surprised me to observe the alacrity with which disciplined soldiers, experienced in campaigning, will hasten to prepare themselves for the march in an emergency like this. No questions are asked, no time is wasted. A soldier's toilet, on an Indian campaign, is a simple affair, and requires little time for arranging. His clothes are gathered up hurriedly, no matter how, so long as he retains possession of them. The first object is to get his horse saddled and bridled, and until this is done his own toilet is a matter of secondary importance, and one button or hook must do the duty of half a dozen. When his horse is ready for the mount the rider will be seen completing his own equipment; stray buttons will receive attention, arms be overhauled, spurs restrapped; then, if there still remain a few spare moments, the homely black pipe is filled and lighted, and the soldier's preparation is completed.

The night was all that could be desired for the success of our enterprise. The air was mild and pleasant; the moon, although nearly full, kept almost constantly behind the clouds, as if to screen us in our hazardous undertaking. I say hazardous, because there were none of us who imagined for one moment that if the Indians discovered us in our attempt to surround them and their village, we would escape without a fight—a fight, too, in which the Indians, sheltered behind the trunks of the stately forest trees under which their lodges were pitched, would possess all the advantage. General Hancock, anticipating that the Indians would discover our approach, and that a fight would ensue, ordered the artillery and infantry under arms, to await the result of our moonlight venture. My command was soon in the saddle and silently making its way toward the village. Instructions had been given forbidding all conversation except in a whisper. Sabres were so disposed of as to prevent clanging. Taking a campfire which we could see in the village as our guiding point, we made a detour so as to place the village between ourselves and the infantry. Occasionally the moon would peep out from behind the clouds and enable us to catch a hasty glance at the village. Here and there under the thick foliage we could see the white conical-shaped lodges. Were their inmates slumbering, unaware of our close proximity, or were their dusky defenders concealed, as well they might have been, along the banks of the Pawnee, quietly awaiting our approach, and prepared to greet us with their well-known war-whoop? These were questions that were probably suggested to the mind of each individual of my command. If we were discovered approaching in the stealthy, suspicious manner which characterized our movements, the hour being midnight, it would require a more confiding nature than that of the Indian to assign a friendly or peaceful motive to our conduct. The same flashes of moonlight which gave us hurried glimpses of the village enabled us to see our own column of horsemen stretching its silent length far into the dim darkness, and winding its course, like some huge anaconda about to envelop its victim.

The method by which it was determined to establish a cordon of armed troopers about the fated village was to direct the march in a circle, with the village in the centre, the commanding officer of each rear troop halting his command at the proper point, and deploying his men similarly to a line of skirmishers—the entire circle, when thus formed, facing toward the village, and distant from it perhaps a few hundred yards. No sooner was our line completely formed than the moon, as if deeming darkness no longer essential to our success, appeared from behind her screen and lighted up the entire scene. And a beautiful scene it was. The great circle of troops, each individual of which sat on his steed silent as a statue, the beautiful and in some places dense foliage of the cotton trees sheltering and shading the bleached, skin-clad lodges of the red man, while in the midst of all murmured undisturbedly in its channel the little stream on whose banks the village was located, all combined to produce an artistic effect, as beautiful as it was interesting. But we were not there to study artistic effects. The next step was to determine whether we had captured an inhabited village, involving almost necessarily a fierce conflict with its savage occupants, or whether the red man had again proven too wily and crafty for his more civilized brothers.

Directing the entire line of troopers to remain mounted with carbines held at the "advance," I dismounted, and taking with me Gurrier, the half-breed, Dr. Coates, one of our medical staff, and Lieutenant Moylan, the adjutant, proceeded on our hands and knees toward the village. The prevailing opinion was that the Indians were still asleep. I desired to approach near enough to the lodges to enable the half-breed to hail the village in the Indian tongue, and if possible establish friendly relations at once. It became a question of prudence with us, which we discussed in whispers as we proceeded on our "Tramp, tramp, tramp, the boys are creeping," how far from our horses and how near to the village we dared to go. If so few of us were discovered entering the village in this questionable manner, it was more than probable that, like the returners of stolen property, we should be suitably rewarded and no questions asked. The opinions of Gurrier, the half-breed, were eagerly sought for and generally deferred to. His wife, a full-blooded Cheyenne, was a resident of the village. This with him was an additional reason for wishing a peaceful termination to our efforts. When we had passed over two-thirds of the distance between our horses and the village, it was deemed best to make our presence known. Thus far not a sound had been heard to disturb the stillness of the night. Gurrier called out at the top of his voice in the Cheyenne tongue. The only response came from the throats of a score or more of Indian dogs which set up a fierce barking. At the same time one or two of our party asserted that they saw figures moving beneath the trees. Gurrier repeated his summons, but with no better result than before.

A hurried consultation ensued. The presence of so many dogs in the village was regarded by the half-breed as almost positive assurance that the Indians were still there. Yet it was difficult to account for their silence. Gurrier in a loud tone repeated who he was, and that our mission was a friendly one. Still no answer. He then gave it as his opinion that the Indians were on the alert, and were probably waiting in the shadow of the trees for us to approach nearer when they would pounce upon us. This comforting opinion induced another conference. We must ascertain the truth of the matter; our party could do this as well as a large number, and to go back and send another party in our stead could not be thought of.

Forward was the verdict. Each one grasped his revolver, resolved to do his best, whether it was in running or fighting. I think most of us would have preferred to take our own chances at running. We had approached near enough to see that some of the lodges were detached some distance from the main encampment. Selecting the nearest of these, we directed our advance on it.

Cautiously approaching, on all fours, to within a few yards of the nearest lodge, occasionally halting and listening to discover evidence as to whether the village was deserted or not, we finally decided that the Indians had fled before the arrival of the cavalry, and that none but empty lodges were before us. This conclusion somewhat emboldened as well as accelerated our progress. Arriving at the first lodge, one of our party raised the curtain or mat which served as a door, and the doctor and myself entered. The interior of the lodge was dimly lighted by the decaying embers of a small fire built in the centre. All around us were to be seen the usual adornments and articles which constitute the household effects of an Indian family. Buffalo robes were spread like carpets over the floor; head-mats, used to recline upon, were arranged as if for the comfort of their owners; parfleches, a sort of Indian bandbox, with their contents apparently undisturbed, were to be found carefully stowed away under the edges or borders of the lodge. These, with the doormats, paint-bags, rawhide ropes, and other articles of Indian equipment, were left as if the owners had only absented themselves for a brief period. To complete the picture of an Indian lodge, over the fire hung a camp-kettle, in which, by means of the dim light of the fire, we could see what had been intended for the supper of the late occupants of the lodge. The doctor, ever on the alert to discover additional items of knowledge, whether pertaining to history or science, snuffed the savory odors which arose from the dark recesses of the mysterious kettle. Casting about the lodge for some instrument to aid him in his pursuit of knowledge, he found a horn spoon, with which he began his investigation of the contents, finally succeeding in getting possession of a fragment which might have been the half of a duck or rabbit, judging merely from its size. "Ah!" said the doctor, in his most complacent manner, "Here is the opportunity I have long been waiting for. I have often desired to test and taste of the Indian mode of cooking. What do you suppose this is?" holding up the dripping morsel. Unable to obtain the desired information, the doctor, whose naturally good appetite had been sensibly sharpened by his recent exercise *à la quadrupède*, set to with a will and ate heartily of the mysterious contents of the kettle. "What can this be?" again inquired the doctor. He was only satisfied on one point, that it was delicious—a dish fit for a king. Just then Guerrier, the half-breed, entered the lodge. He could solve the mystery, having spent years among the Indians. To him the doctor appealed for information. Fishing out a huge piece, and attacking it with the voracity of a hungry wolf, he was not long in determining what the doctor had supped so heartily upon. His first words settled the mystery: "Why, this is dog." I will not attempt to repeat the few but emphatic words uttered by the heartily disgusted member of the medical fraternity as he rushed from the lodge.

Nothing was gleaned from our search of the village which might indicate the direction of the flight. General Hancock, on learning the situation of affairs, despatched some companies of infantry to the deserted village, with orders to replace the cavalry and protect the village and its contents from disturbance until its final disposition could be determined upon. Starting my command back to our camp near General Hancock's headquarters, I galloped on in advance to report the particulars to the General. It was as then decided that with eight troops of cavalry I should start in pursuit of the Indians at early dawn on the following morning (April 15). There was no sleep for my command the remainder of the night, the time being fully occupied in preparation for the march, neither the extent nor direction of which was known.

Mess kits were overhauled, and fresh supplies of coffee, sugar, flour, and the other articles which go to supply the soldier's larder, were laid in. Blankets were carefully rolled so as to occupy as little space as possible; every useless pound of luggage was discarded, for in making a rapid pursuit after Indians, much of the success depends upon the lightness of the order of march. Saratoga trunks and their accompaniments are at a discount. Never was the old saying that "in Rome one must do as Romans do" more aptly illustrated than on an Indian campaign. The Indian, knowing that his safety either on offensive or defensive movements depends in a great measure upon the speed and endurance of his horse, takes advantage of every circumstance which will favor either the one or the other. To this end he divests himself of all superfluous dress and ornament when preparing for rapid movements. The white man, if he hopes for success, must adopt the same rule of action and encumber his horse as little as possible. Something besides well-filled mess chests and carefully rolled blankets is necessary in preparing for an Indian campaign. Arms must be reexamined, cartridge-boxes refilled, so that each man should carry about one hundred rounds of ammunition "on his person," while each troop commander must see that in the company wagon there are placed a few boxes of reserve ammunition. Then, when the equipment of the soldier has been attended to, his horse, without whose assistance he is helpless, must be looked after; loose shoes are tightened by the driving of an additional nail, and to accomplish this one may see the company blacksmith. So energetic had everybody been that before daylight everything was in readiness for the start. In addition to the regularly organized companies of soldiers which made up the pursuing column, I had with me a detachment of white scouts or Plainsmen, and one of friendly Indians, the latter belonging to the tribe of Delawares, once so famous in Indian wars. Of the Indians one only could speak English; he acted as interpreter for the party. Among the white scouts were numbered some of the most noted of their class. The most prominent man among them was "Wild Bill," whose highly varied career was made the subject of an illustrated sketch in one of the popular monthly periodicals a few years ago. Wild Bill was a strange character, just the one which a novelist might gloat over. He was a Plainsman in every sense of the word, yet unlike any other of his class. In person he was about six feet one in height, straight as the straightest of the warriors whose implacable foe he was; broad shoulders, well-formed chest and limbs, and a face strikingly handsome; a sharp, clear, blue eye, which stared you straight in the face when in conversation; a finely-shaped nose, inclined to be aquiline; a well-turned mouth, with lips only partially concealed by a handsome moustache. His air and complexion were those of the perfect blond. The former was worn in uncut ringlets falling carelessly over his powerfully formed shoulders. Add to this figure a costume blending the immaculate neatness of the dandy with the extravagant taste and style of the frontiersman, and you have Wild Bill, then as now the most famous scout on the Plains. Whether on foot or on horseback, he was one of the most perfect types of physical manhood I ever saw. Of his courage there could be no question; it had been brought to the test on too many occasions to admit of a doubt. His skill in the use of the rifle and pistol was unerring; while his deportment was exactly the opposite of what might be expected from a man of his surroundings. It was entirely free from all bluster or bravado. He seldom spoke of himself unless requested to do so. His conversation, strange to say, never bordered either on the vulgar or blasphemous. His influence among the frontiersmen was unbounded, his word was law; and many are the personal quarrels and disturbances which he has checked among his comrades by his simple announcement that "this has gone far enough," if need be followed by the ominous warning that when persisted in or renewed the quarreller "must settle it with me." Wild Bill is anything but a quarrelsome man; yet no one but himself can enumerate the many conflicts in which he has been engaged, and which have almost invariably resulted in the death of his adversary. I have a personal knowledge of at least half a dozen men whom he has at various times killed, one of these being at the time a member of my command. Others have been severely wounded, yet he always escapes unhurt. On the Plains every man openly carries his belt with its invariable appendages, knife and revolver, often two of the latter. Wild Bill always carried two handsome ivory-handled revolvers of the large size; he was never seen without them. Where this is the common custom, brawls or personal difficulties are seldom if ever settled by blows. The quarrel is not from a word to a blow, but from a word to the revolver, and he who can draw and fire first is the best man. No civil law reaches him; none is applied for. In fact there is no law recognized beyond the frontier but that of "might makes right." Should death result from the quarrel, as it usually does, no coroner's jury is impanelled to learn the cause of death, and the survivor is not arrested. But instead of these old-fashioned proceedings, a meeting of citizens takes place, the survivor is *requested* to be present when the circumstances of the homicide are inquired into, and the unfailing verdict of "justifiable," " self-defence," etc., is pronounced, and the law stands vindicated. That justice is often deprived of a victim there is not a doubt. Yet in all of the many affairs of this kind in which Wild Bill has performed a part, and which have come to my knowledge, there is not a single instance in which the verdict of twelve fair-minded men would not be pronounced in his favor. Guerrier, the half-breed, also accompanied the expedition as guide and interpreter.

Everything being in readiness to move, the column began its march, and reached the vicinity of the village before day had fully dawned. Here a brief halt was necessary, until the light was sufficient to enable our scouts to discover the trail of the Indians.

In pursuit of the Indians

When they finally set to discover this, their method was highly interesting, and resembled not a little the course of a thorough sportsman, who, with a well-trained pointer or setter, thoroughly "ranges" and "beats" the ground in search of his coveted game. The Indians had set out on their flight soon after dark the preceding night; a heavy frost covered the ground and rendered it difficult to detect the trail from the many pony tracks which are always found in the vicinity of a village. We began to grow impatient at the delay, when one of the Indians gave the "halloo" as the signal that the trail was discovered, and again the column marched forward. Our order of march was for the Indian and white scouts to keep a few hundred paces in advance of the troops, so that momentary delays upon the part of those watching and following the trail should not extend to the troops. The Indians on leaving the village had anticipated pursuit and had adopted measures to mislead us. In order to prevent their trail from being easily recognizable, they had departed in as many detachments or parties almost as there were families or lodges in the village, each party taking a different direction from the others, having personally agreed, of course, upon the general direction and place of reuniting. Once being satisfied that we were on the right trail, no difficulty was found in following it as rapidly as our horses could walk. The Indians "had a nearly twelve-hours the start of us" but being encumbered by their families, we hoped to overhaul them before many days. Our first obstacle was encountered when we struck Walnut Creek, a small stream running east and west some thirty miles north of the Arkansas at that point. The banks were so high and abrupt that it was impossible to reach the water's edge, let alone clamber up the opposite bank. A few of the Indians had been able to accomplish this feat, as was shown by the tracks on the opposite side; but the main band had moved upstream in search of a favorable crossing, and we were compelled to do likewise. Here we found that the Indians had called a halt, built fires, and cooked their breakfast. So rapidly had we gained upon them that the fires were burning freshly, and the departure of the Indians had been so abrupt that they left several ponies with their packs tied to trees. One of the packs belonged to a famous chief, Roman Nose, who was one of those who met us at the grand gathering just before we reached their village a few days before. One of our Delawares who made the capture was very proud of the success, and was soon seen ornamenting his head-dress with the bright crimson feathers taken from the wardrobe of Roman Nose. Encouraged by our progress, we continued the pursuit as rapidly as a due regard for our horses would permit. Thus far, neither myself nor any of the soldiers had caught sight of any Indians; but our Delaware scouts, who were constantly in the advance and on our flanks, taking advantage of the bluffs to reconnoitre, frequently reported that they saw small parties of Indians observing our movements from a distance. From positive evidences, we were convinced that we were rapidly gaining upon the Indians. The earth upturned by the feet of their ponies and by the ends of the trailing lodge-poles, was almost as damp and fresh as that disturbed by the horses of the command. Soon we discovered additional signs of encouragement. The route now became strewn with various lodge-poles and other obstacles peculiar to an Indian's outfit, showing that they were lightening up so as to facilitate their escape. Would darkness intervene to disappoint us? We must imitate the example of the Indians, and disembarrass ourselves of everything tending to retard our speed. The troops would march much faster, if permitted to do so, than the rate at which our wagons had forced themselves along. It was determined to leave the wagons, under escort of one squadron, to follow our trail as rapidly as they could, while the other three squadrons pushed on in pursuit. Should darkness settle down before overtaking the Indians, the advantage was altogether against us, as we would be compelled to await daylight to enable us to follow the trail, while the Indians were free to continue their flight, sheltered and aided by the darkness. By three o'clock PM we felt that we were almost certain to accomplish our purpose. No obstacle seemed to stand in our way; the trail was broad and plain, and apparently as fresh as our own. A half hour, or an hour at furthest, seemed only necessary to enable us to dash in upon our wily enemy. Alas for human calculations! The Indians, by means of the small reconnoitring parties observed by our scouts, had kept themselves constantly informed regarding our movements and progress. They had first risked their safety upon the superior speed and endurance of their ponies—a safe reliance when favored by the grass season, but in winter this advantage was on our side. Failing in their first resource, they had a second and better method of eluding us. Again dividing his tribe, as when first setting out from the village, into numerous small parties, we were discouraged by seeing the broad well-beaten trail suddenly separate into hundreds of indistinct routes, leading fan-shape in as many different directions. What was to be done?

The general direction of the main trail, before dissolving into so many small ones, had been nearly north, showing that if undisturbed in their flight the Indians would strike the Smoky Hill overland route, cross it, then pursue their way northward to the headwaters of the Solomon or Republican River, or further still, to the Platte River. Selecting a central trail, we continued our pursuit, now being compelled often to halt and verify our course. The trail gradually grew smaller and smaller, until by five o'clock it had become so faint as to be followed with the greatest difficulty. We had been marching exactly twelve hours without halting, except to water our horses. Reluctantly we were forced to go into camp and await the assistance of daylight. The Delaware scouts continued the pursuit six miles further, but returned without accomplishing anything. The Indians, after dividing up into small parties, kept up communication with each other by means of columns of signal smoke. These signal smokes were to be seen to the west, north, and east of us, but none nearer then ten miles. They only proved to us that we were probably on the trail of the main body, as the fires were in front and on both sides of us. We had marched over thirty-five miles without a halt. The Delawares having determined the direction of the trail for six miles, we would be able next morning to continue that far at least unaided by daylight. Our wagons overtook us a few hours after we reached camp. Reveille was sounded at two o'clock the next morning, and four o'clock found us again in the saddle, and following the guidance of our friendly Delawares. The direction of our march took us up the valley and almost dry bed of a small stream. The Delawares thought we might find where the Indians had encamped during the night, by following the upward course of the stream, but in this we were disappointed. The trail became more and more indistinct, until it was lost in the barren waste over which we were then moving. To add to our annoyance, the watercourse had become entirely dry, and our guides were uncertain as to whether water could be procured in one day's march in any direction except that from which we had come. We were, therefore, forced to countermarch after reaching a point thirteen miles from our starting-place in the morning, and retrace our steps until the uncertain stream in whose valley we then were would give us water enough for our wants.

Here I will refer to an incident entirely personal, which came very near costing me my life. When leaving our camp that morning I felt satisfied that the Indians, having travelled at least a portion of the night, were then many miles in advance of us, and there was neither danger nor probability of encountering any of them near the column. We were then in a magnificent game country, buffalo, antelope, and smaller game being in abundance on all sides of us. Although an ardent sportsman, I had never hunted the buffalo up to this time, consequently was exceedingly desirous of tasting of its excitement. I had several fine English greyhounds, whose speed I was anxious to test with that of the antelope, said to be—which I believe—the fleetest of animals. I was mounted on a fine large thoroughbred horse. Taking with me but one man, the chief bugler, and calling my dogs around me, I galloped ahead of the column as soon as it was daylight, for the purpose of having a chase after some antelope which could be seen grazing nearly two miles distant. That such a course was rashly imprudent I am ready to admit. A stirring gallop of a few minutes brought me near enough to the antelope, of which there were a dozen or more, to enable the dogs to catch sight of them. Then the chase began, the antelope running in a direction which took us away from the command. By availing myself of the turns in the course, I was able to keep well in view of the exciting chase, until it was evident that the antelope were in no danger of being caught by the dogs, which latter had become blown from want of proper exercise. I succeeded in calling them off, and was about to set out on my return to the column. The horse of the chief bugler, being a common-bred animal, failed early in the race, and his rider wisely concluded to regain the command, so that I was alone. How far I had travelled from the troops I was trying to determine, when I discovered a large, dark-looking animal grazing nearly a mile distant. As yet I had never seen a wild buffalo, but I at once recognized this as not only a buffalo, but a very large one. Here was my opportunity. A ravine near by would enable me to approach unseen until almost within pistol range of my game. Calling my dogs to follow me, I slowly pursued the course of the ravine, giving my horse opportunity to gather himself for the second run. When I emerged from the ravine I was still several hundred yards from the buffalo, which almost instantly discovered me, and set off as fast as his legs could carry him. Had my horse been fresh the race would have been a short one, but the preceding long run had not been without effect. How long or how fast we flew in pursuit, the intense excitement of the chase prevented me from knowing. I only knew that even the greyhounds were left behind, until finally my good steed placed himself and me close alongside the game. It may be because this was the first I had seen, but surely of the hundreds of thousands of buffaloes which I have since seen, none have corresponded with him in size and lofty grandeur. My horse was above the average size, yet the buffalo towered even above him. I had carried my revolver in my hand from the moment the race began. Repeatedly could I have placed the muzzle against the shaggy body of the huge beast, by whose side I fairly yelled with wild excitement and delight, yet each time would I withdraw the weapon, as if to prolong the enjoyment of the race. It was a race for life or death, yet how different the award from what could be imagined. Still we sped over the springy turf, the high breeding and mettle of my horse being plainly visible over that of the huge beast that struggled by his side. Mile after mile was traversed in this way, until the rate and distance began to tell perceptibly on the bison, whose protruding tongue and labored breathing plainly betrayed his distress. Determined to end the chase and bring down my game, I again placed the muzzle of the revolver close to the body of the buffalo, when, as if divining my intention, and feeling his inability to escape by flight, he suddenly determined to fight, and at once wheeled, as only a buffalo can, to gore my horse. So sudden was this movement, and so sudden was the corresponding veering of my horse to avoid the attack, that to retain my control over him I hastily brought up my pistol hand to the assistance of the other. Unfortunately as I did so my finger, in the excitement of the occasion, pressed the trigger, discharged the pistol, and sent the fatal ball into the very brain of the noble animal I rode. Running at full speed he fell dead in the course of his leap. Quick as thought I disengaged myself from the stirrups and found myself whirling through the air over and beyond the head of my horse. My only thought, as I was describing this trajectory, and my first thought on reaching *terra firma* (solid earth), was, "What will the buffalo do with me?" Although at first inclined to rush upon me, my strange procedure seemed to astonish him. Either that, or pity for the utter helplessness of my condition, inclined him to alter his course and leave me alone to my own bitter reflections.

In a moment the danger into which I had unluckily brought myself stood out in bold relief before me. Under ordinary circumstances the death of my horse would have been serious enough. I was strongly attached to him; had ridden him in battle during a portion of the late war; yet now his death, expect in its consequences, was scarcely thought of. Here I was, alone in the heart of the Indian country, with warlike Indians known to be in the vicinity. I was not familiar with the country. How far I had travelled, or in what direction from the column, I was at a loss to know. In the excitement of the chase I had lost all reckoning. Indians were liable to pounce upon me at any moment. My command would not note my absence probably for hours. Two of my dogs overtook me, and with mute glances first at the dead steed, then at me, seemed to inquire the cause of this strange condition of affairs. Their instinct appeared to tell them that we were in misfortune. While I was deliberating what to do, the dogs became uneasy, whined piteously, and seemed eager to leave the spot. In this desire I sympathized with them, but whither should I go? I observed that their eyes were generally turned in one particular direction; this I accepted as my cue, and with one parting look at my horse, and grasping a revolver in each hand, I set out on my uncertain journey. As long as this body of my horse was visible above the horizon, I kept referring to it as my guiding point, and in this way contrived to preserve my direction. This resource soon failed me, and I then had recourse to weeds, buffalo skulls, or any two objects I could find on my line of march. Constantly my eyes kept scanning the horizon, each moment expecting, and with reason too, to find myself discovered by Indians.

I had travelled in this manner what seemed to me about three or four miles, when far ahead in the distance I saw a column of dust rising. A hasty examination soon convinced me that the dust was produced by one of three causes: white men, Indians, or buffalo. Two to one in my favor at any rate. Selecting a ravine where I could crawl away undiscovered should the approaching body prove to be Indians, I called my dogs to my side and concealed myself as well as I could to await developments. The object of my anxious solicitude was still several miles distant. Whatever it was, it was approaching in my direction, as was plainly discernible from the increasing columns of dust. Fortunately I had my field-glass slung across my shoulder, and if Indians I could discover them before they could possibly discover me. Soon I was able to see the heads of mounted men running in irregular order. This discovery shut out the probability of their being buffaloes, and simplified the question to white men or Indians. Never during the war did I scan an enemy's battery or approaching column with half the anxious care with which I watched the party then approaching me. For a long time nothing satisfactory could be determined, until my eye caught sight of an object which, high above the heads of the approaching riders, told me in unmistakable terms that friends were approaching. It was the cavalry guidon, and never was the sight of stars and stripes more welcome. My comrades were greatly surprised to find me seated on the ground alone and without my horse. A few words explained all. A detachment of my men, following my direction, found my horse and returned with the saddle and other equipments.

In retracing our steps later in the day, in search of water sufficient for camping purposes, we marched over nine miles of our morning route, and at 2 PM of April 16 we went into camp. From this point I wrote a despatch to General Hancock and sent it back by two of my scouts, who set out on their journey as soon as it was dark. It was determined to push on and reach the Smoky Hill route as soon as possible, and give the numerous stage stations along that route notice of the presence of warlike Indians. Resting our animals from 2 until 7 PM we were again in the saddle and setting out for a night march, our only guide being the north star. We hoped to strike the stage route near a point called Downie's Station. After riding all night we reached and crossed about daylight the Smoky Hill River, along whose valley the stage route runs. The stations were then from ten to fifteen miles apart; if Indians had crossed this line at any point the station men would be informed of it. To get information as to this, as well as to determine where we were, an officer with one company was at once despatched on this mission. This party had scarcely taken its departure and our pickets been posted, before the entire command of tired, sleepy cavalrymen, scouts, and Delawares had thrown themselves on the ground and were wrapped in the deepest slumber. We had slept perhaps an hour or more, yet it seemed but a few moments, when an alarm shot from the lookout and the startling cry of "Indians!" brought the entire command under arms.

Although in search of Indians and supposed to be always prepared to encounter them, yet the warning shot of the sentry, followed as it was by his cry of "Indians!" could not but produce the greatest excitement in camp. Where all had been quiet before—men sleeping and resting after their long night march, animals grazing unsuspectingly in the midst of the wagons and tents which thickly dotted the Plain here and there—all was now bustle if not confusion. Herders and teamsters ran to their animals to conduct them inside the limits of camp. The troopers of one platoon of each company hastened to secure the cavalry horses and provide against a stampede, while those of the remaining platoons were rapidly marshalled under arms by their troop officers, and advanced in the direction from which the lookout reported the enemy to be approaching.

All this required but a few moments of time. Recovering from the first shock of surprise, we endeavored, one and all, to discover the number and purpose of the foes who had in so unceremonious a manner disturbed our much-needed slumbers.

Daylight had just dawned, but the sun was not yet high enough to render a satisfactory view of the country possible. This difficulty was aggravated, too, by a dull heavy mist, which hung like a curtain near the horizon. Yet in spite of all these obstructions we could clearly perceive, at a distance of perhaps a mile, the dim outlines of numerous figures—horsemen evidently—approaching our camp, not as if simply on the march, but in battle array. First came a deployed line of horsemen, followed in rear, as we could plainly see, by a reserve, also mounted and moving in compact order.

It required no practised eye to comprehend that be they who or what they might, the parties advancing in this precise and determined manner upon us were doing so with hostile purpose, and evidently intended to charge into our camp unless defeated in their purpose. No time was to be lost. Dispositions to meet the coming attack were rapidly made. To better observe the movements and determine the strength of the approaching parties, an officer ascended the knoll occupied by the lookout.

We had often heard of the high perfection of some of the Indian tribes in military evolutions and discipline, but here we saw evidences which went far to convince us that the red man was not far behind his more civilized brother in the art of war. Certainly no troops of my command could have advanced a skirmish line or moved a reserve more accurately than was done in our presence that morning.

As yet we had no means of determining to what tribe the attacking party belonged. We were satisfied they must be in either Sioux or Cheyennes, or both; in either case we should encounter troublesome foes. But for the heavy mist we could have comprehended everything. Soon we began receiving reports from the officer who had ascended the lookout. First, there were not more than eighty horsemen to be seen. This number we could easily dispose of. Next, the attacking parties seemed to have changed their plan; a halt was ordered, and two or three horsemen seemed to be advancing to the front as if to parley, or reconnoitre our position. Then the skirmishers were suddenly withdrawn and united with the reserve, when the entire party wheeled about and began to move off. This was mystifying in the extreme, but a couple of young cavalry officers leaped into their saddles and taking a few mounted troopers with them dashed after our late enemies, determined to learn more about them than they seemed willing we should.

A brisk gallop soon cleared away the mystery, and furnished another proof of the deceptive effects produced by the atmosphere on the Plains. Those who have read the preceding article will remember that at the termination of the night march which brought us to our present camp, an officer was despatched with one troop of cavalry to find the nearest stage station on the overland route, near which we knew we must then be. Our camp lay on the Smoky Hill River. The stage better route, better known as the "Smoky Hill route," was known to be but a few miles north of us. To determine our exact locality, as we had been marching by compass over a wild country and in the night-time, and to learn something regarding the Indians, this officer was sent out. He was selected for this service because of his professed experience on and knowledge of the Plains. He had set out from our camp an hour or more before daylight, but losing his bearings had marched his command in a semicircle until daylight found him on the side of our camp opposite that from which he had departed. The conical Sibley tent used in my command, resembling the Indian lodge from which it was taken, seen through the peculiar and uncertain morning atmosphere of that region, had presented to his eyes and to those of his men the appearance of an Indian village. The animals grazing about our camp might well have been taken for the ponies of the Indians. Besides, it was well known that large encampments of Indians were in the part of the country over which we were marching. The bewilderment of this detachment, then, was not surprising considering the attending circumstances. Had the officer in command been young and inexperienced, his mishap might have been credited to these causes; but here was an officer who had grown gray in the service, familiar with the Plains and with Indians, yet so completely misled by appearances as to mistake his camp, which he had left but an hour before, for an Indian village.

Few officers laboring under the same impression would have acted so creditably. He and his men imagined they had discovered the camp of the Indians whom we had been pursuing, and although believing their enemies outnumbered them ten to one, yet their zeal and earnestness prompted them—instead of sending to their main camp for reinforcements, thereby losing valuable time and probable opportunities to effect a surprise—to make a dash at once into the village. And it was only the increasing light of day that enabled them to discover their mistake and saved us from a charge from our own troopers. This little incident will show how necessary experienced professional guides are in connection with all military movements on the Plains. It was a long time before the officer who had been so unlucky as to lose his way heard the last of it from his brother officers.

The remainder of his mission was completed more successfully. Aided by daylight, and moving nearly due north, he soon struck the well-travelled overland route, and from the frightened employés at the nearest station he obtained intelligence which confirmed our worst fears as to the extent of the Indian outbreak. Stage stations at various points along the route had been attacked and burned, and the inmates driven off or murdered. All travel across the Plains was suspended, and an Indian war with all its barbarities had been forced upon the people of the frontier.

As soon as the officer ascertaining these facts had returned to camp and made his report, the entire command was again put in motion and started in the direction of the stage route, with the intention of clearing it of straggling bands of Indians, reopening the main line of travel across the Plains, and establishing if possible upon the proper tribes the responsibility for the numerous outrages recently committed. The stage stations were erected at points along the route distant from each other from ten to fifteen miles, and were used solely for the shelter and accommodation of the relays of drivers and horses employed on the stage route. We found, in passing over the route on our eastward march, that only about every fourth station was occupied, the occupants of the other three having congregated there for mutual defence against the Indians, the latter having burned the deserted stations.

From the employés of the company at various points we learned that for the few preceding days the Indians had been crossing the line, going toward the north in large bodies. In some places we saw the ruins of the burned stations, but it was not until we reached Lookout Station, a point about fifteen miles west of Fort Hays, that we came upon the first real evidences of an Indian outbreak. Riding some distance in advance of the command, I reached the station only to find it and the adjacent buildings in ashes, the ruins still smoking. Near by I discovered the bodies of the three station-keepers, so mangled and burned as to be scarcely recognizable as human beings. The Indians had evidently tortured them before putting an end to their sufferings. They were scalped and horribly disfigured. Their bodies were badly burned, but whether before or after death could not be determined. No arrow, or other article of Indian manufacture, could be found to positively determine what particular tribe was the guilty one. The men at other stations had recognized some of the Indians passing as belonging to the Sioux and Cheyennes, the same we had passed from the village on Pawnee Fork.

Continuing our march, we reached Fort Hays, from which point I despatched a report to General Hancock, on the Arkansas, furnishing him all the information I had gained concerning the outrages and movements of the Indians.

Here was positive evidence from the agents themselves that the Indians against whom we were operating were guilty, and deserving of severe punishment. The only conflicting portion of the testimony was as to which tribe was most guilty. Subsequent events proved, however, that all of the five tribes named, as well as the Sioux, had combined for a general war throughout the Plains and along our frontier. Such a war had been threatened to our post commanders along the Arkansas on many occasions during the winter. The movement of the Sioux and Cheyennes toward the north indicated that the principal theatre of military operations during the summer would be between the Smoky Hill and Platte Rivers. General Hancock accordingly assembled the principal chiefs of the Kiowas and Arapahos in council at Fort Dodge, hoping to induce them to remain at peace and observe their treaty obligations.

The most prominent chiefs in council were Satanta, Lone Wolf, and Kicking Bird of the Kiowas, and Little Raven and Yellow Bear of the Arapahos. During the council extravagant promises of future good conduct were made by these chiefs. So effective and convincing was the oratorical effort of Satanta, that at the termination of his address the department commander and staff presented him with the uniform coat, sash, and hat of a major-general. In return for this compliment Satanta, within a few weeks after, attacked the post at which the council was held, arrayed in his new uniform. This said chief had but recently headed an expedition to the frontier of Texas, where, among other murders committed by him and his band, was that known as the "Box massacre." The Box family consisted of the father, mother, and five children, the eldest a girl about eighteen, the youngest a babe. The entire family had been visiting at a neighbor's house, and were returning home in the evening, little dreaming of the terrible fate impending, when Satanta and his warriors dashed upon them, surrounded the wagon in which they were driving, and at the first fire killed the father and one of the children. The horses were hastily taken from the wagon, while the mother was informed by signs that she and her four surviving children must accompany their captors. Mounting their prisoners upon led horses, of which they had a great number stolen from the settlers, the Indians prepared to set out on their return to the village, then located hundreds of miles north. Before departing from the scene of the massacre, the savages scalped the father and child, who had fallen as their first victims. Far better would it have been had the remaining members of the family met their death in the first attack. From the mother, whom I met when released from her captivity, after living as a prisoner in the hands of the Indians for more than a year, I gathered the details of the sufferings of herself and children.

No pen can describe the painful tortures of mind and body endured by this unfortunate family. They remained as captive in the hands of the Indians for more than a year, during which time the eldest daughter, a beautiful girl just ripening into womanhood, was exposed to a fate infinitely more dreadful than death itself. She first fell to one of the principal chiefs, who, after robbing her of that which was more precious than life, and forcing her to become the victim of his brutal lust, bartered her in return for two horses to another chief; he again, after wearying of her, traded her to a chief of a neighboring band; and in that way this unfortunate girl was passed from one to another of her savage captors, undergoing a life so horribly brutal that, when meeting her upon her release from captivity, one could only wonder how a young girl, nurtured in civilization and possessed of the natural refinement and delicacy of thought which she exhibited, could have survived such degrading treatment.

The mother and second daughter fared somewhat better. The youngest, however separated from mother and sisters, and thrown among people totally devoid of all kind feeling, spent the time in shedding bitter tears. This so enraged the Indians that, as a punishment as well preventive, the child was seized and the soles of her naked feet exposed to the flames of the lodge fire until every portion of the cuticle was burned therefrom. When I saw this little girl a year afterward, her feet were from this cause still in a painful and unhealed condition. These poor captives were reclaimed from their bondage through the efforts of officers of the army, and by the payment of a ransom amounting to many hundreds of dollars.

As soon as General Hancock had terminated his council with the Kiowas and Arapahos, he marched with the remaining portion of the expedition across from the Arkansas to Fort Hays, where my command was then encamped, arriving there on the third of May. Here, owing to the neglect or delay of the officers of the Quartermaster's Department in forwarding the necessary stores, the cavalry was prevented from undertaking any extensive movement, but had to content itself for the time being in scouting the adjacent country.

The time, however, was well employed in the preparation of men and animals for the work which was to be assigned them. Unfortunately, desertions from the ranks became so frequent and extensive as to cause no little anxiety.

To produce these, several causes combined. Prominent among them was the insufficiency and inferior quality of the rations furnished the men. At times the latter were made the victims of fraud, and it was only by the zealous care and watchfulness of the officers immediately over them, that their wants were properly attended to.

Dishonest contractors at the receiving depots further east had been permitted to perpetrate gross frauds upon the government, the result of which was to produce want and suffering among the men. For example, unbroken packages of provisions shipped from the main depot of supplies, and which it was impracticable to replace without loss of time, were when opened discovered to contain huge stones for which the government had paid so much per pound according to contract price. Boxes of bread were shipped and issued to the soldiers of my command, the contents of which had been baked in 1861, yet this was in 1867. It is unnecessary to state that but little of this bread was eaten, yet there was none at hand of better quality to replace it. Bad provisions were a fruitful cause of bad health. Inactivity led to restlessness and dissatisfaction. Scurvy made its appearance, and cholera attacked neighboring stations. For all these evils desertion became the most popular antidote. To such an extent was this the case, that in one year one regiment lost by desertion alone more than half of its effective force.

General Hancock remained with us only a few days before setting out with the battery for his headquarters at Fort Leavenworth. Supplies were pushed out and every preparation made for resuming offensive movements against the Indians. To find employment for the few weeks which must ensue before breaking up camp was sometimes a difficult task. To break the monotony and give horses and men exercise, buffalo hunts were organized, in which officers and men joined heartily. I know of no better drill for perfecting men in the use of firearms on horseback, and thoroughly accustoming them to the saddle, than buffalo-hunting over a moderately rough country. No amount of riding under the best of drill masters will give that confidence and security in the saddle, which will result from a few spirited charges into a buffalo herd.

The command, consisting of cavalry alone, was at last in readiness to move. Wagons had been loaded with reserve supplies, and we were only waiting the growth of the spring grass to set out on the long march which had previously been arranged. On the first of June, with about 350 men and a train of twenty wagons, I left Fort Hays and directed our line of march toward Fort McPherson, on the Platte River, distant by the proposed route 225 miles. The friendly Delawares accompanied us as scouts and trailers, but our guide was a young white man known on the Plains as Will Comstock. No Indian knew the country more thoroughly than did Comstock. He was perfectly familiar with every divide, water-course, and strip of timber for hundreds of miles in either direction. He knew the dress and peculiarities of every Indian tribe, and spoke the languages of many of them. Perfect in horsemanship, fearless in manner, a splendid hunter, and a gentleman by instinct, as modest and unassuming as he was brave, he was an interesting as well as valuable companion on a march such as was then before us. Many were the adventures and incidents of frontier life with which he was accustomed to entertain us when around the campfire or on the march. Little did he then imagine that his own life would soon be given as a sacrifice to his daring, and that he, with all his experience among the savages, would fall a victim of Indian treachery.

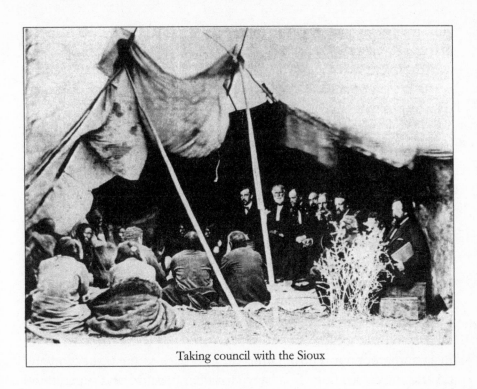

Taking council with the Sioux

Mrs. Custer's Adventure—Taking Council with the Sioux—General Sherman Arrives—Taking Council with the Sioux, Again—Rescue of Captain Hamilton—Rescue of the Wagon Train

It had been decided that my command should thoroughly scout the country from Fort Hays near the Smoky Hill River, to Fort McPherson, on the Platte; thence describe a semicircle to southward, touching the head waters of the Republican, and again reach the Platte at or near Fort Sedgwick, at which post we would replenish our supplies; then move directly south to Fort Wallace, on the Smoky Hill, and from there march down the overland route to our starting point at Fort Hays. This would involve a ride of upwards of one thousand miles.

As is usually the case, the first day's march was not to be a long one. The troops, under charge of the officer second in command, Colonel Wickliffe Cooper, left camp and marched up the valley of Big Creek a distance of eighteen miles, and there encamped. Two companies of cavalry and a small force of infantry were to constitute the garrison to remain behind. When the troops composing my command left, it became necessary to rearrange the camp and provide new dispositions for defence. My wife, who always accompanied me when in camp or on the march except when I was engaged in active pursuit of Indians, had rejoined me soon after my arrival at Fort Hays. She was accompanied by a young lady friend from the East, a schoolmate, who had been tempted by the novelties of wild Western life to make her a visit in camp. As there were other ladies in camp, wives of officers who were to remain with the garrison, my wife and friend decided to remain and await our return, rather than go back to the protection and luxuries of civilization. To arrange for their comfort and superintend the locating of their tents, I remained behind my command, intending to wait until after midnight, and then, guided by the moonlight, ride on and overtake my command before it should commence its second day's march. I retained with me two soldiers, one scout, and four of the Delawares.

As soon as the command moved, the portion to remain at Fort Hays was drawn in near the few buildings which constituted the fort. All of the cavalry and a portion of the infantry were to encamp in the valley and not far from the stream. For three-quarters of a mile on either side the valley consisted of a level unbroken plain; then a low bluff was encountered, succeeded by a second plain of less extent. This was bordered by a higher and more broken bluff than the first. Fortunately, in selecting the ground on which the tents intended for the ladies were to stand, I had chosen a little knoll, so small as to be scarcely perceptible, yet the only elevated ground to be found. It was within a few steps of the bank of the stream, while the main camp was located below and nearer the bluff. For safety a few soldiers were placed in camp a short distance above. In ordinary times the banks of Big Creek are at this point from twenty-five to forty feet above the water, and a person accustomed to the slow and gradual rise and fall which prevails along the beds of streams in the Eastern States, can with difficulty realize the suddenness with which the deep and narrow channels of watercourses on the Plains become filled to overflowing. In proportion to the surface of the country or the watersheds, the watercourses or channels are few, too few to accommodate the drainage necessities during the wet season. The bank on which the little knoll stood was, by actual measurement, thirty-six feet above ordinary water mark. The knoll was probably three or four feet above the level of the valley. Surely this location might be considered well enough protected naturally against the rainy season. So I thought, as I saw the working party putting the finishing touches to the bright white canvas house, which to all intents and purposes was to be to me, even in absence, my army home.

I confidently expected to return to this camp at the termination of my march. I will be pardoned if I anticipate events and terminate its history now. A few days after my command had marched, a heavy storm set in, the rain pouring down in a manner resembling a waterspout. The immediate effect of the heavy shower was not at once noticeable near the camp at Fort Hays, as the heaviest rainfall had occurred far above that point. But in the nighttime, after the entire camp except the guards had long since retired and fallen asleep, the stream, overcharged by the rushing volumes from above, soon became transformed from a mild and murmuring brook into an irresistible, turbulent torrent. So sudden and unexpected had been the rise, that before the alarm could be given the thirty-six feet which had separated the surface of the water from the top of the banks had been overcome, and in addition the water began now sweeping over the entire plain. After overflowing the natural banks of the creek, the first new channel ran in such a manner as to surround the tents occupied by the ladies as well as that occupied by the few soldiers stationed up the stream, but still leaving communication open between the main camp and the bluff toward the mainland. The soldiers, as well as the officers and their families in the main camp, hastened to the bluff to escape being swept down before the huge torrent which each instant became more fearful.

To add to the embarrassment of the situation, the blackest darkness prevailed, only relieved at times by vivid gleams of lightning, while the deep sullen roar of the torrent, increasing each moment in depth and volume, was only drowned at intervals by the fierce and more deafening uproar of the thunder, which sounded like the applause of some huge fury watching this struggle between the elements.

When Mrs. Custer and her young lady companion were awakened by the storm, they discovered that their tents were surrounded by the new channel, and that all efforts to reach the main camp would prove unavailing. They had with them at this time only a colored female servant. They did not even know the fate of the other portion of the camp. In the midst of this fearful scene, they heard the cries of men in despair near their tent. The cries came from the soldiers who had been in camp above them, but were now being carried off in the darkness by the rising current. No assistance could reach them. It is doubtful if they could have been saved even had they been found by daylight. There were seven in all. One of them, as he was being swept by the tent, contrived, through accident no doubt, to grasp the branch of a small bush which grew on the bank. It was from him that the cries of distress principally proceeded. Aided by the dim light of a camp lantern, the ladies were enabled to see this unfortunate man clinging, as it were, between life and death. With commendable presence of mind, considering the fate staring them in the face, a rope was procured, and after a few failures one end was thrown to the unfortunate man, and by the united strength of the two ladies and their servant he was pulled to shore and, for the time being at least, his life was saved. His six less fortunate companions were drowned.

Two of the officers, Brevet Major-General A. J. Smith, and his Adjutant-General, Colonel Weir, with a view to rescuing the ladies, had succeeded in making their way across the new channel made by the torrent to the knoll; but when attempting to return on horseback to the mainland, they found the current too deep and swift for them to succeed. They were compelled then to await their fate. The water continued to rise until the entire valley from the natural channel to the first bluff, a distance of a quarter of a mile, was covered by an unfordable river. The only point still free from water was the little knoll which I had been so fortunate as to select for the tents. But the rise in the water continued until it finally reached the edge of the tent. At this rate the tents themselves must soon be swept away. As a last resort, a Gatling gun which stood near the entrance of the tent, and which from its great weight would probably withstand the force of the current, was hauled closer to the tent and ropes securely attached to the wheels; by these ropes it was proposed to fasten the ladies and the servant to the gun, and in this way, should the streams not rise too high above the knoll, their lives might be saved.

The colored girl, Eliza, who was devoted to her mistress, and who had been amid scenes of great danger, was on this occasion invaluable. Eliza had quite a history before she visited the Plains. Formerly a slave, but set free by the war, she had accompanied me as cook during the last three years of the war. Twice taken prisoner by the Confederates, she each time made her escape and refound me. She was present at almost every prominent battle of the Army of the Potomac, accompanied my command on all the raids and winter marches, and upon more than one occasion during the progress of a battle Eliza might be seen near the front earnestly engaged in preparing a cup of coffee for the officers at headquarters, who but for her would have gone through the day dinnerless. I have seen her remain by her camp cook fire when the enemy's shells were bursting overhead, to such an extent that men who were similarly employed deserted their station and sought shelter in the rear. There were few officers or soldiers in the cavalry corps, from General Sheridan down, with whom Eliza was not a great favorite. All had a pleasant word for her, and few had not at some time or other cause to remember her kindness.

When the water finally approached close to the tent, Eliza marked its progress from time to time by placing small stakes at the water line. How anxiously the gradual rise of the torrent must have been watched. At last, when all hope seemed almost exhausted, the waters were stayed in their progress, and soon, to the great joy of the little party besieged, began to recede. It was still dark, but so rapidly did the volume of water diminish—as rapidly as it had accumulated—that a few hours after daylight a safe passage was effected to the mainland. With the exception of those of the six soldiers, no lives were lost, although many narrow escapes were made.

In the morning, daylight showed the post hospital, a stone building, surrounded by an unfordable stream, the water rushing through the doors and windows. The patients had managed to climb upon the roof, and could be seen by the officers and men on the mainland. No boats were to be had, but no class of men are so full of expedients as soldiers. The beds of some government wagons were hastily removed, the canvas covers were stretched under the bottoms, and in this way a temporary kind of pontoon was constructed which answered the desired purpose, and by means of which the beleaguered patients were soon released.

The officer in command of the infantry, Major Merriam, was occupying a tent with his wife near the main camp. Finding himself cut off from the main land, but before the water had attained its greatest depth, he took his wife in his arms and forded the stream which ran between his tent and the bluff, and in this manner reached a point of safety. It is remarkable, however, that within two years from the date of this occurrence, this same officer with his wife and child encountered a similar freshet in Texas, hundreds of miles from this locality, and that the watery grave which was so narrowly avoided in Kansas awaited the mother and child in Texas. Of the circumstances of the storm at Fort Hays I was necessarily ignorant until weeks later.

Soon after midnight, everything being in readiness, and my little party having been refreshed by a cup of good army coffee, it only remained to say adieu to those who were to remain behind, and we were ready for our moonlight gallop.

But little was said as we made our way rapidly over the plain in the direction taken by the command. Occasionally, as we dashed across a ravine, we would suddenly come upon a herd of antelopes or a few scattering buffaloes, startling them from their repose and causing them to wonder what was the occasion and who the strange parties disturbing the peaceful quiet of the night in this unusual manner. On we sped, our good steeds snuffing the early morning air and pressing forward as eagerly as if they knew their companions were awaiting them in the advance.

Daylight had given us no evidence of its coming, when, after a ride of nearly twenty miles, we found ourselves descending into a valley in which we knew the command must be encamped. The moon had disappeared below the horizon, and we were left to make our way aided by such light as the stars twinkling in a clear sky afforded us. Our horses gave us unmistakable evidence that camp was near. To convince us beyond all doubt, the clear ringing notes of the bugle sounding the reveille greeted our ears, and directed by the sound we soon found ourselves in camp.

Our second day's march brought us to the Saline River, where we encamped for the night. From our campground we could see on a knoll some two miles distant a platform or scaffold erected, which resembled somewhat one of our war signal stations. Curious to discover its purpose, I determined to visit it.

Taking with me Comstock and a few soldiers, I soon reached the point, and discovered that the object of my curiosity and surprise was an Indian grave. The body, instead of being consigned to Mother Earth, was placed on top of the platform. The latter was constructed of saplings, and was about twenty feet in height. From Comstock I learned that with some of the tribes this is the usual mode of disposing of the body after death. The prevailing belief of the Indian is that when done with this world the spirit of the deceased is transferred to the "happy hunting ground," where he is permitted to engage in the same pleasures and pursuits which he preferred while on earth. To this end it is deemed essential that after death the departed must be supplied with the same equipment and ornaments considered necessary while in the flesh. In accordance with this belief a complete Indian outfit, depending in extent upon the rank and importance of the deceased, is prepared, and consigned with the body to the final resting place.

The body found on this occasion must have been that of a son of some important chief; it was not full grown, but accompanied with all the arms and adornments usually owned by a warrior. There was the bow and quiver full of steel-pointed arrows, the tomahawk and scalping knife, and a red clay pipe with a small bag full of tobacco. In order that the departed spirit should not be wholly dependent upon friends after his arrival at the happy hunting-ground, he had been supplied with provisions, consisting of small parcels containing coffee, sugar, and bread. Weapons of modern structure had also been furnished him, a revolver and rifle with powder and ball ammunition for each, and a saddle, bridle, and lariat for his pony. Added to these was a supply of wearing apparel, embracing every article known in an Indian's toilet, not excepting the various colored paints to be used in decorating himself for war. A handsome buckskin scalping pocket, profusely ornamented with beads, completed the outfit. But for fear that white women's scalps might not be readily obtainable, and desiring no doubt to be received at once as a warrior, who in his own country at least was not without renown, a white woman's scalp was also considered as a necessary accompaniment, a letter of introduction to the dusky warriors and chieftains who had gone before. As the Indian of the Plains is himself only when on horseback, provision must be made for mounting him properly in the Indian heaven. To accomplish this, the favorite war pony is led beneath the platform on which the body of the warrior is placed at rest, and there strangled to death.

No signs indicating the recent presence of Indians were discovered by our scouts until we neared the Republican River, where the trail of a small war party was discovered running down one of the tributaries of the Republican. After following it far enough to determine the futility of pursuit, the attempt was relinquished. Upon crossing the Republican we suddenly came in full view of about a hundred mounted warriors, who, without waiting for a parley of any kind, set off as fast as their horses could carry them. One squadron was sent in pursuit, but was unable to overhaul the Indians. From the tracks we learned that the Indians were mounted on horses stolen from the stage company. These horses were of a superior quality, and purchased by the company at a price about double that paid by the government. This was the only occasion on which we saw Indians before reaching the Platte River.

Nothing occurred to break the monotony of our march until we reached Fort McPherson, on the Platte River. The country over which we had marched had been quite varied in its character, and as we neared the Platte it became very broken and abrupt. It was only by availing ourselves of Comstock's superior knowledge of the country that we found an easy exit from the deep cañons and rough defiles which were encountered.

At Fort McPherson we refilled our wagons with supplies of rations and forage. At the same time, in accordance with my instructions, I reported by telegraph my arrival to General Sherman, who was then further west on the line of the Union Pacific road. He did not materially change my instructions, further than to direct me to remain near Fort McPherson until his arrival, which would be in the course of a few days.

Moving my command about twelve miles from the fort, I arranged for a council with Pawnee Killer and a few other Sioux chiefs, who had arrived at the Platte about the same time my command had. My object was, if possible, to induce Pawnee Killer and his band, with such other Indians as might choose to join them, to bring their lodges into the vicinity of the fort, and remain at peace with the whites. Pawnee Killer and his chiefs met me in council and the subject was discussed, but with no positive conclusions. While protesting strongly in favor of preserving peaceful relations with us, the subsequent conduct of the chiefs only confirmed the suspicion that they had arranged the council not to perfect a friendly agreement with us, but to spy out and discover, if possible, our future plans and movements. In this they were disappointed. Their numerous inquiries as to where we intended proceeding when we resumed the march were unavailing. Desiring to

Genl. W. T. Sherman.

leave nothing undone to encourage a friendly attitude on their part, I gave the chiefs on parting with them liberal presents of coffee, sugar, and other articles gratifying to the taste of an Indian. They departed after giving utterance to the strongest expressions of their desire to live at peace with their "white brothers," and promised to collect their families and bring them in under protection of the fort, and thus avoid becoming entangled in the ravages of an Indian war which now promised to become general throughout the Plains. Pawnee Killer and his chiefs never attempted to keep their promises.

General Sherman arrived at my camp next day. He had no confidence in the faith of Pawnee Killer and his band, and desired that a party be sent in pursuit at once, and bring the chiefs back and retain a few of the prominent ones as hostages for the fulfilment of their agreement. This was decided to be impracticable. It was then judged best for me to move my command in a southwesterly direction to the forks of the Republican, a section of country usually infested by Indians, and there endeavor to find the village of Pawnee Killer, and compel him, if necessary, to move nearer to the fort, so that we might distinguish between those who were friendly and those who were not. Besides, it was known that the Cheyennes and Sioux, whom we had pursued from the Arkansas across the Smoky Hill River, had not crossed north of the Platte, and they were rightly supposed to be located somewhere near the forks of the Republican. I could reach this point in three days' marching after leaving the Platte River, on whose banks we were then encamped.

Owing to the rough and broken character of the bluffs which bound the valley of the Platte on the south side, it was determined to march up the men about fifteen miles from the fort and strike south through an opening in the bluffs known as Jack Morrow's cañon. General Sherman rode with us as far as this point, where, after commending the Cheyennes and Sioux to us in his expressive manner, he bade us good-by, and crossed the river to the railroad station on the north side. Thus far we had no real Indian warfare. We were soon to experience it, attended by all its frightful barbarities.

Before leaving the Platte I employed two additional interpreters who were familiar with the Sioux language. Both were white men, but, following the example of many frontiersmen, they had taken unto themselves Indian wives, and each had become the head of a considerable family of half-breeds.

Starting nearly due south from the Platte, and marching up the cañon, which forms a natural gateway through the otherwise almost impassable barrier of bluffs and deep ravines bordering the valley of the Platte River, we again set out in search of Indians. The latter are sought after so frequently and found so seldom, except when not wanted, that scouting parties, as a general thing, are not overburdened with confidence on beginning an expedition. Most of us, however, felt that we were destined to see Indians—an impression probably due to the fact that we had determined to accomplish our purpose, if hard riding and watchfulness could attain this result.

Our first day's march brought us to a small stream, a tributary of the Republican River, on whose banks we encamped for the night. Daylight the following morning found us in the saddle and ascending from the valley to the table-lands; we were still in the broken country. On reaching the plateau overlooking the valley we found ourselves enveloped in a dense fog, so dense that the sky was not visible, nor was an extended view of the country possible. Had the surface of the plain been, as usual, level and unbroken, we could have pursued our march guided by the unerring compass. But deep and impassable cañons divided the country in all directions and rendered our further progress impracticable. The sun, however, soon rose high enough to drive away the mist, and permitted us to proceed on what might be truly termed our winding way.

The afternoon of the fourth day we reached the forks of the Republican and there went into camp. We were then located about seventy-five miles southeast of Fort Sedgwick, and about the same distance northeast of Fort Wallace. Intending to scout the surrounding country thoroughly in search of Indians, we selected our camp with reference to a sojourn of several days, combining among its essentials wood, water, good grazing, and last, but not least, facilities for defence.

When I parted from General Sherman the understanding was, that after beating up the country thoroughly about the forks of the Republican River, I should march my command to Fort Sedgwick, and there I would either see General Sherman again or receive further instructions from him. Circumstances seemed to favor a modification of this plan, at least as to marching the entire command to Fort Sedgwick. It was therefore decided to send a trusty officer with a sufficient escort to Fort Sedgwick with my despatch, and to receive the despatches which might be intended for me. My proposed change of programme contemplated a continuous march, which might be prolonged twenty days or more. To this end additional supplies were necessary. The guides all agreed in the statement that we were then about equidistant from Fort Wallace on the south and Fort Sedgwick on the north, at either of which the required supplies could be obtained; but that while the country between our camp and the former was generally level and unbroken—favorable to the movement of our wagon train—that between us and Fort Sedgwick was almost impassable for heavily-laden wagons. The train then was to go to Fort Wallace under sufficient escort, be loaded with fresh supplies, and rejoin us in camp. At the same time the officer selected for that mission could proceed to Fort Sedgwick, obtain his despatch, and return.

Major Joel A. Elliot, a young officer of great courage and enterprise, was selected as bearer of despatches to Fort Sedgwick. As the errand was one involving considerable danger, requiring for the round trip a ride of almost two hundred miles, through a country which was not only almost unknown but infested by large numbers of hostile Indians, the Major was authorized to arrange the details in accordance with his own judgment.

Knowing that small detachments can move more rapidly than large ones, and that he was to depend upon celerity of movement rather than strength of numbers to evade the numerous war parties prowling in that vicinity, the Major limited the size of his escort to ten picked men and one of the guides, all mounted on fleet horses. To elude the watchful eyes of any parties that might be noting our movements, it was deemed advisable to set out from camp as soon as it was dark, and by making a rapid night ride get beyond the circle of danger. In this way the little party took its departure on the night of the 23rd of June.

On the same day our train of wagons set out for Fort Wallace to obtain supplies. Colonel West with one full squadron of cavalry was ordered to escort the train to Beaver Creek, about midway, and there halt with one of his companies, while the train, under escort of one company commanded by Lieutenant Robbins, should proceed to the fort and return—Colonel West to employ the interval in scouting up and down Beaver Creek. The train was under the special management of Colonel Cook, who on this occasion was acting in the capacity of a staff officer.

While at Fort McPherson, and when under the impression that my command upon arriving at Fort Wallace, after terminating the scouting expedition we were then engaged upon, would remain in camp for several weeks, I wrote to my wife at Fort Hays, advising her to meet me at Fort Wallace, provided that travel between the two posts was considered safe. I expected her to reach Fort Wallace before the arrival of the train and escort from my camp, and under this impression I sent a letter to her by Colonel Cook, asking her to come to our camp on the Republican under escort of the Colonel, who was an intimate friend of the family.

After the departure of the two detachments, which left us in almost opposite directions, our camp settled down to the dull and unexciting monotony of waiting patiently for the time when we should welcome our comrades back again, and listen to such items of news as they might bring to us.

Little did we imagine that the monotony of idleness was so soon and so abruptly to be broken. That night our pickets were posted as usual; the horses and mules, after being allowed to graze in the evening, were brought in and securely tethered close to our tents, and the "stable guards" of the different troops had been assigned to their stations for the night. At half-past eight the bugler at headquarters sounded the signal for "taps," and before the last note had died away every light, in obedience to this command, disappeared, and nothing remained to the eye, except here and there a faint glimpse of a white tent, to indicate the presence of our camp.

It was just that uncertain period between darkness and daylight on the following morning, and I was lying in my tent deep in the enjoyment of that perfect repose which only camp life offers, when the sharp, clear crack of a carbine nearby brought me to my feet. I knew in an instant that the shot came from the picket posted not far from the rear of my camp. At the same moment my brother, Colonel Custer, who on that occasion was officer of the day, and whose duties required him to be particularly on the alert, rushed past my tent, halting only long enough to show his face through the opening and shout, "They are here!"

Now I did not inquire who were referred to, or how many were included in the word "they," nor did my informant seem to think it necessary to explain. "They" referred to Indians, I knew full well. Had I doubted, the brisk fusillade which opened the next moment, and the wild war-whoop, were convincing evidences that in truth "they were here!"

My orderly, as was his custom, on my retiring had securely tied all the fastenings to my tent, and it was usually the work of several minutes to undo this unnecessary labor. I had no time to throw away in this manner. Leaping from my bed, I grasped my trusty Spencer, which was always at my side whether waking or sleeping, and with a

Attack on the wagon train.

single dash burst open the tent, and, hatless as well as shoeless, ran to the point where the attack seemed to be concentrated.

It was sufficiently light to see our enemies and be seen. The first shot had brought every man of my command from his tent, armed and equipped for battle. The Indians, numbering hundreds, were all around the camp, evidently intending to surround us, while a party of about fifty of their best mounted warriors had, by taking advantage of a ravine, contrived to approach quite close before being discovered. It was the intention of this party to dash through our camp, stampede all our horses, which were to be caught up by the parties surrounding us, and then finish us at their leisure.

The picket, however, discovered the approach of this party, and by firing gave timely warning, thus frustrating the plan of the Indians, who almost invariably base their hopes of success upon effecting a surprise.

My men opened on them such a brisk fire from their carbines that they were glad to withdraw beyond range. The picket who gave the alarm was shot down at his post by the Indians, the entire party galloping over his body, and being prevented from scalping him only by the fire from his comrades, who dashed out and recovered him. He was found to be badly though not mortally wounded by a rifle ball through the body.

The Indians, seeing that their attempt to surprise us and to stampede our horses had failed, then withdrew to a point but little over a mile from us, where they congregated, and seemed to hold a conference with each other. We did not fear any further attack at this time. They were satisfied with this attempt, and would await another opportunity.

It was desirable, however, that we should learn if possible to what tribe our enemies belonged. I directed one of our interpreters to advance midway between our camp and the Indians, and make the signal for holding a parley, and in this way ascertain who were the principal chiefs.

The ordinary manner of opening communication with parties known or supposed to be hostile is to ride toward them in a zigzag manner or to ride in a circle. The interpreter gave the proper signal, and was soon answered by a small party advancing from the main body of the Indians to within hailing distance. It was then agreed that I, with six of the officers, should come to the bank of the river, which was about equidistant from my camp and from the point where the Indians had congregated, and there be met by an equal number of the leading chiefs. To guard against treachery, I placed most of my command under arms and arranged with the officer left in command that a blast from the bugle should bring assistance to me if required.

Six of the officers and myself, taking with us a bugler and an interpreter, proceeded on horseback to the designated point. Dismounting, we left our horses in charge of the bugler, who was instructed to watch every movement of the Indians, and upon the first appearance of violence or treachery to sound the "advance." Each of us took our revolvers from their leather cases and stuck them loosely in our belts.

Descending to the river bank, we awaited the arrival of the seven chiefs. On one side of the river the bank was level and covered with a beautiful green sward, while on the opposite side it was broken and thickly covered by willows and tall grass. The river itself was at this season of the year, and at this distance from its mouth, scarcely deserving of the name. The seven chiefs soon made their appearance on its opposite bank, and, after removing their leggings, waded across to where we stood. Imagine our surprise at recognizing as the head chief Pawnee Killer, our friend of the conference of the Platte, who on that occasion had overwhelmed us with the earnestness of his professions of peace, and who, after partaking of our hospitality under the guise of friendship, and leaving our camp laden with provisions and presents, returned to attack and murder us within a fortnight. This, too, without the slightest provocation, for surely we had not trespassed against any right of theirs since the exchange of friendly greetings near Fort McPherson.

Pawnee Killer and his chiefs met us as if they were quite willing to forgive us for interfering with the success of their intended surprise of our camp in the morning. I avoided all reference to what had occurred, desiring if possible to learn the locality of their village and their future movements. All attempts, however, to elicit information on these points were skilfully parried. The chiefs in turn were anxious to know our plans, but we declined to gratify them. Upon crossing to our side of the river, Pawnee Killer and his companions at once extended their hands, and saluted us with the familiar "How." Suspicious of their intentions, I kept one hand on my revolver during the continuance of our interview.

When we had about concluded our conference a young brave, completely armed, as were all the chiefs, emerged from the willows and tall grass on the opposite bank and waded across to where we were, greeting us as the others had done. Nothing was thought of this act until a few moments after another brave did the same, and so on until four had crossed over and joined our group. I then called Pawnee Killer's attention to the conditions under which we met, and told him he was violating his part of the contract. He endeavored to turn it off by saying that his young men felt well disposed toward us, and came over only to shake hands and say "How." He was told, however, that no more of his men must come. The conversation was then resumed and continued until another party of the warriors was seen preparing to cross from the other side. The conduct of these Indians in the morning, added to our opinions in general as regards treachery, convinced us that it would be in the highest degree imprudent to trust ourselves in their power. They already outnumbered us, eleven to seven, which were as heavy odds as we felt disposed to give. We all felt convinced that the coming over of these warriors, one by one, was but the execution of a preconceived plan whereof we were to become the victims as soon as their advantage in numbers should justify them in attacking us.

Again reminding Pawnee Killer of the stipulations of our agreement, and that while we had observed ours faithfully, he had disregarded his, I told him that not another warrior of his should cross the river to our side. And calling his attention to the bugler, who stood at a safe distance from us, I told him that I would then instruct the bugler to watch the Indians who were upon the opposite bank, and, upon any of them making a movement as if to cross, to sound the signal which would bring my entire command to my side in a few moments. This satisfied Pawnee Killer that any further attempt to play us false would only end in his own discomfiture. He at once signalled to the Indians on the other side to remain where they were.

Nothing definite could be gleaned from the replies of Pawnee Killer. I was satisfied that he and his tribe were contemplating mischief. Their previous declarations of peaceful intent went for naught. Their attack on our camp in the morning proved what they would do if able to accomplish their purpose. I was extremely anxious, however, to detain the chiefs near my camp, or induce them to locate their village near us, and keep up the semblance at least of friendship. I was particularly prompted to this desire by the fact that the two detachments which had left my command the previous day would necessarily continue absent several days, and I feared that they might become the victims of an attack from this band if steps were not taken to prevent it. Our anxiety was greatest regarding Major Elliot and his little party of eleven. Our only hope was that the Indians had not become aware of their departure. It was fortunate that the Major had chosen night as the most favorable time for setting out. As to the detachment that had gone with the train to Fort Wallace we felt less anxious, it being sufficiently powerful in numbers to defend itself, unless attacked after the detachment became divided at Beaver Creek.

Finding all efforts to induce Pawnee Killer to remain with us unavailing, I told him that we would march to his village with him. This did not seem satisfactory.

Before terminating our interview, the chiefs requested me to make them presents of some sugar, coffee, and ammunition. Remembering the use they had made of the latter article in the morning, it will not appear strange if I declined to gratify them. Seeing that nothing was to be gained by prolonging the interview, we separated, the officers returning to our camp, and the Indians recrossing the river, mounting their ponies, and galloping off to the main body, which was then nearly two miles distant.

My command was in readiness to leap into their saddles, and I determined to attempt to follow the Indians, and, if possible, get near their village. They were prepared for this move on our part, and the moment we advanced toward them set off at the top of their speed. We followed as rapidly as our heavier horses could travel, but the speed of the Indian pony on this occasion, as on many others, was too great for that of our horses. A pursuit of a few hours proved our inability to overtake them, and we returned to camp.

Soon after arriving at camp a small party of Indians was reported in sight in a different direction. Captain Louis Hamilton, a lineal descendant of Alexander Hamilton, was immediately ordered to take his troop and learn something of their intentions. The Indians resorted to their usual tactics. There were not more than half a dozen to be seen—not enough to appear formidable. These were there as a decoy. Captain Hamilton marched his troop toward the hill on which the Indians had made their appearance, but on arriving at its crest found that they had retired to the next ridge beyond. This maneuver was repeated several times, until the cavalry found itself several miles from camp. The Indians then appeared to separate into two parties, each going in different directions. Captain Hamilton divided his troop into two detachments, sending one detachment, under command of my brother, after one of the parties, while he with twenty-five men continued to follow the other.

When the two detachments had become so far separated as to be of no assistance to each other, the Indians developed their scheme. Suddenly dashing from a ravine, as if springing from the earth, forty-three Indian warriors burst out upon the cavalry, letting fly their arrows and filling the air with their wild war-whoops. Fortunately Captain Hamilton was an officer of great presence of mind as well as undaunted courage. The Indians began circling about the troops, throwing themselves upon the sides of their ponies and aiming their carbines and arrows over the necks of their well-trained war-steeds. Captain Hamilton formed his men in order to defend themselves against the assaults of their active enemies. The Indians displayed unusual boldness, sometimes dashing close up to the cavalry and sending in a perfect shower of bullets and arrows. Fortunately their aim, riding as they did at full speed, was necessarily inaccurate.

All this time we who had remained in camp were in ignorance of what was transpiring. Dr. Coates had accompanied Captain Hamilton's command, but when the latter was divided the doctor joined the detachment of my brother. In some unexplained manner the doctor became separated from both parties, and remained so until the sound of the firing attracted him toward Captain Hamilton's party. When within half a mile of the latter, he saw what was transpiring; saw our men in the centre and the Indians charging and firing from the outside. His first impulse was to push on and endeavor to break through the line of savages, casting his lot with his struggling comrades. This impulse was suddenly nipped in the bud. The Indians, with their quick, watchful eyes, had discovered his presence, and half a dozen of their best mounted warriors at once galloped toward him.

Happily the doctor was in the direction of camp from Captain Hamilton's party, and, comprehending the peril of his situation at a glance, turned his horse's head toward camp, and applying the spur freely set out on a ride for life. The Indians saw this move, but were not disposed to be deprived of their victim in this way. They were better mounted than the doctor, his only advantage being in the start and the greater object to be attained. When the race began he was fully four miles from camp, the day was hot and sultry, the country rough and broken, and his horse somewhat jaded from the effects of the ride in the morning. These must have seemed immense obstacles in the eyes of a man who was riding for dear life. A false step, a broken girth, or almost any trifle, might decide his fate.

How often, if ever, the doctor looked back, I know not; his eyes more probably were strained to catch a glimpse of camp or of assistance accidentally coming to his relief. Neither the one nor the other appeared. His pursuers, knowing that their success must be gained soon if at all, pressed their fleet ponies forward until they seemed to skim over the surface of the green plain, and their shouts of exultation falling clearer and louder upon his ear told the doctor that they were surely gaining upon him. Fortunately our domestic horses, until accustomed to their presence, are as terrified by Indians as by a huge wild beast, and will fly from them if not restrained. The yells of the approaching Indians served no doubt to quicken the energies of the doctor's horse, and impelled him to greater efforts to escape.

So close had the Indians succeeded in approaching that they were almost within arrow range, and would soon have sent one flying through the doctor's body, when, to the great joy of the pursued and the corresponding grief of his pursuers, camp suddenly appeared in full view scarcely a mile distant. The ponies of the Indians had been ridden too hard to justify their riders in venturing near enough to provoke pursuit upon fresh animals. Sending a parting volley of bullets after the flying doctor, they turned about and disappeared. The doctor did not slacken his pace on this account, however; he knew that captain Hamilton's party was in peril, and that assistance should reach him as soon as possible. Without tightening rein or sparing spur, he came dashing into camp, and the first we knew of his presence he had thrown himself from his almost breathless horse, and was lying on the ground unable, from sheer exhaustion and excitement, to utter a word.

To the rescue of Capt. Hamilton.

The officers and men gathered about him in astonishment, eager and anxious to hear his story, for all knew that something far from any ordinary event had transpired to place the doctor in such a condition of mind and body. As soon as he had recovered sufficiently to speak, he told us that he had left Captain Hamilton surrounded by a superior force of Indians, and that he himself had been pursued almost to the borders of camp.

This was enough. The next moment the bugle rang out the signal "To horse," and in less time than would be required to describe it, horses were saddled and arms ready. Then "there was mounting in hot haste." A moment later the command set off at a brisk trot to attempt the rescue of their beleaguered comrades.

We had advanced probably two miles, when we discerned in the distance the approach of Captain Hamilton's party. They were returning leisurely to camp, after having succeeded in driving off their assailants and inflicting upon them a loss of two warriors killed and several wounded. The Indians could only boast of having wounded a horse belonging to Captain Hamilton's party.

This encounter with the Indians occurred in the direction taken by Major Elliot's detachment on leaving camp, and the Indians, after this repulse by Captain Hamilton, withdrew in that direction. This added to our anxiety concerning the safety of Major Elliot and his men. There was no doubt now that all Indians infesting the broad belt of country between the Arkansas and Platte Rivers were on the war path, and would seek revenge from any party so unfortunate as to fall in their way. The loss of the two warriors slain in the fight, and their wounded comrades, would be additional incentives to acts of hostility. If there had been any possible means of communicating with Major Elliot, and either strengthening or warning him, it would have been done. He left us by no travelled or defined route, and it was by no means probable that he would pass over the same trail in coming from Fort Sedgwick as in going to that point; otherwise reinforcements could have been sent out over his trail to meet him.

On the 27th our fears for the safety of the Major and his escort were dispelled by their safe return to camp.

Our anxiety became centred in the fate of the larger party which had proceeded with the train to Fort Wallace for supplies. The fact that Major Elliot had made his trip unmolested by Indians proved that the latter were most likely assembled south of us, that is, between us and Fort Wallace. Wherever they were, their numbers were known to be large. It would be impossible for a considerable force, let alone a wagon train, to pass from our camp to Fort Wallace and not be seen by the Indian scouting parties. They had probably observed the departure of the train and escort at the time, and, divining the object which occasioned the sending of the wagons, would permit to go to the fort unmolested, but would waylay them on their return, in the hope of obtaining the supplies they contained.

Looking at these probable events, I not only felt impelled to act promptly to secure the safety of the train and its escort, but a deeper and stronger motive stirred me to leave nothing undone to circumvent the Indians. My wife, who in answer to my letter, I believed was then at Fort Wallace, would place herself under the protection of the escort of the train and attempt to rejoin me in camp. One full squadron, well-mounted and armed, under command of Lieutenant-Colonel Myers, an officer of great experience in Indian affairs, left our camp at dark on the evening of the day that Captain Hamilton had his engagement with the Indians, and set out in the direction of Fort Wallace. His orders were to press forward as rapidly as practicable, following the trail made by the train. Written orders were sent in his care to Colonel West, who was in command of that portion of the escort which had halted at Beaver Creek, to join Colonel Myers's command with his own, and then to continue the march toward Fort Wallace until he should meet the returning train and escort. The Indians, however, were not to be deprived of this opportunity to secure scalps and plunder.

From our camp to Beaver Creek was nearly fifty miles. Colonel Myers marched his command without halting until he joined Colonel West at Beaver Creek. Here the two commands united, and under the direction of Colonel West, the senior officer of the party, proceeded toward Fort Wallace, following the trail left by the wagon train and escort. If the escort and Colonel West's forces could be united, they might confidently hope to repel any attack made upon them by Indians. Colonel West was an old Indian fighter, and too thoroughly accustomed to Indian tactics to permit his command to be surprised or defeated in any manner other than by a fair contest.

Let us leave them for a time and join the wagon train and its escort—the latter numbering, all told, as before stated, forty-eight men under the immediate command of Lieutenant Robbins.

Colonel Cook, whose special duty connected him with the train and its supplies, could also be relied upon for material assistance with the troops, in case of actual conflict with the enemy. Comstock, the favorite scout, a host in himself, was sent to guide the party to and from Fort Wallace. In addition to these were the teamsters, who could not be expected to do more than control their teams should the train be attacked.

The march from camp to Beaver Creek was made without incident. Here the combined forces of Colonel West and Lieutenant Robbins encamped together during the night. Next morning at early dawn Lieutenant Robbins's party, having the train in charge, continued the march toward Fort Wallace, while Colonel West sent out scouting parties up and down the stream to search for Indians.

As yet none of their party were aware of the hostile attitude assumed by the Indians within the past few hours, and Colonel West's instructions contemplated a friendly meeting between his forces and the Indians should the latter be discovered. The march of the train and escort was made to Fort Wallace without interruption. The only incident worthy of remark was an observation of Comstock's, which proved how thoroughly he was familiar with the Indian and his customs.

The escort was moving over a beautifully level plateau. Not a mound or hillock disturbed the evenness of the surface for miles in either direction. To an unpractised eye there seemed no recess or obstruction in or behind which an enemy might he concealed, but everything appeared open to the view for miles and miles, look in what direction one might. Yet such was not the case. Ravines of greater or less extent, though not perceptible at a glance, might have been discovered if searched for, extending almost to the trail over which the party was moving. These ravines, if followed, would be found to grow deeper and deeper, until, after running their course for an indefinite extent, they would terminate in the valley of some running stream. These were the natural hiding places of Indian war parties, waiting their opportunities to dash upon unsuspecting victims. These ravines serve the same purpose to the Indians of the timberless plains that the ambush did to those Indians of the Eastern States accustomed to fighting in the forests and everglades. Comstock's keen eyes took in all at a glance, and he remarked to Colonel Cook and Lieutenant Robbins, as the three rode together at the head of the column, that "If

the Injuns strike us at all, it will be just about the time we are comin'
along back over this very spot. Now mind what I tell ye all." We shall
see how correct Comstock's prophecy was.

Arriving at the fort, no time was lost in loading up the wagons
with fresh supplies, obtaining the mail intended for the command,
and preparing to set out on the return to camp the following day. No
late news regarding Indian movements was obtained. Fortunately, my
letter from Fort McPherson to Mrs. Custer, asking her to come to
Fort Wallace, miscarried, and she did not undertake a journey which
in all probability would have imperilled her life, if not terminated it in
a most tragic manner.

On the following morning Colonel Cook and Lieutenant Robbins
began their return march. They had advanced one half the distance
which separated them from Colonel West's camp without the slightest occurrence to disturb the monotony of their march, and had
reached the point where, on passing before, Comstock had indulged
in his prognostication regarding Indians; yet nothing had been seen to
excite suspicion or alarm.

Comstock, always on the alert and with eyes as quick as those of an
Indian, had been scanning the horizon in all directions. Suddenly he perceived, or thought he perceived, strange figures, resembling human heads,
peering over the crest of a hill far away to the right. Hastily levelling his
field glass, he pronounced the strange figures, which were scarcely perceptible, to be neither more nor less than Indians. The officers brought
into requisition their glasses, and were soon convinced of the correctness
of Comstock's report. It was some time before the Indians perceived
that they were discovered. Concealment then being no longer possible,
they boldly rode to the crest and exposed themselves to full view. At first
but twenty or thirty made their appearance; gradually their number became augmented, until about a hundred warriors could be seen.

It may readily be imagined that the appearance of so considerable
a body of Indians produced no little excitement and speculation in
the minds of the people with the train. The speculation was as to the
intentions of the Indians, whether hostile or friendly. Upon this subject all doubts were soon dispelled. The Indians continued to receive
accessions to their numbers, the reinforcements coming from beyond
the crest of the hill on which their presence was first discovered. Finally, seeming confident in their superior numbers, the warriors, all
of whom were mounted, advanced leisurely down the slope leading

in the direction of the train and its escort. By the aid of field glasses, Comstock and the two officers were able to determine fully the character of the party now approaching them. The last doubt was thus removed. It was clearly to be seen that the Indians were arrayed in full war costume, their heads adorned by the brilliantly colored war bonnets, their faces, arms, and bodies painted in various colors, rendering their naturally repulsive appearance even more hideous. As they approached nearer they assumed a certain order in the manner of their advance. Some were to be seen carrying the long glistening lance with its pennant of bright colors; while upon the left arm hung the round shield, almost bullet-proof, and ornamented with paint and feathers according to the taste of the wearer. Nearly all were armed with carbines and one or two revolvers, while many in addition to these weapons carried the bow and arrow. When the entire band had defiled down the inclined slope, Comstock and the officers were able to estimate roughly the full strength of the party. They were astonished to perceive that between six and seven hundred warriors were bearing down upon them, and in a few minutes would undoubtedly commence the attack. Against such odds, and upon ground so favorable for the Indian mode of warfare, it seemed unreasonable to hope for a favorable result. Yet the entire escort, officers and men, entered upon their defence with the determination to sell their lives as dearly as possible.

As the coming engagement, so far as the cavalry was concerned, was to be purely a defensive one, Lieutenant Robbins at once set about preparing to receive his unwelcome visitors. Colonel Cook formed the train in two parallel columns, leaving ample space between for the horses of the cavalry. Lieutenant Robbins then dismounted his men and prepared to fight on foot. The led horses, under charge of the fourth trooper, were placed between the two columns of wagons, and were thus in a measure protected from the assaults which the officers had every reason to believe would be made for their capture. The dismounted cavalrymen were thus formed in a regular circle enclosing the train and horses. Colonel Cook took command of one flank, Lieutenant Robbins of the other, while Comstock, who as well as the two officers remained mounted, galloped from point to point wherever his presence was most valuable. These dispositions being perfected, the march was resumed in this order, and the attack of the savages calmly awaited.

The Indians, who were interested spectators of these preparations for their reception, continued to approach, but seemed willing to delay their attack until the plain became a little more favorable for their operations. Finally, the desired moment seemed to have arrived. The Indians had approached to within easy range, yet not a shot had been fired, the cavalrymen having been instructed by their officers to reserve their fire for close quarters. Suddenly, with a wild ringing war-whoop, the entire band of warriors bore down upon the train and its little party of defenders.

On came the savages, filling the air with their terrible yells. Their first object, evidently, was to stampede the horses and draught animals of the train; then, in the excitement and consternation which would follow, to massacre the escort and drivers. The wagon-master in immediate charge of the train had been ordered to keep his two columns of wagons constantly moving forward and well closed up. This last injunction was hardly necessary, as the frightened teamsters, glancing at the approaching warriors and hearing their savage shouts, were sufficiently anxious to keep well closed upon their leaders.

The first onslaught of the Indians was made on the flank which was superintended by Colonel Cook. They rode boldly forward as if to dash over the mere handful of cavalrymen, who stood in skir-mishing order in a circle about the train. Not a soldier faltered as the enemy came thundering upon them, but waiting until the Indians were within short rifle range of the train, the cavalrymen dropped upon their knees, and taking deliberate aim poured a volley from their Spencer carbines into the ranks of the savages, which seemed to put a sudden check upon the ardor of their movements and forced them to wheel off to the right. Several of the warriors were seen to reel in there saddles, while the ponies of others were brought down or wounded by the effectual fire of the cavalrymen.

As the Indians were being driven back by the well-directed volley of the cavalrymen, the latter, overjoyed at their first success, became reassured, and sent up a cheer of exultation, while Comstock, who had not been idle in the fight, called out to the retreating Indians in their native tongue, taunting them with their unsuccessful assault.

The Indians withdrew to a point beyond the range of our carbines, and there seemed to engage in a parley. Comstock, who had closely watched every movement, remarked, "There's no sich good luck for us as to think them Injuns mean to give it up so. Six hundred red devils ain't agoin' to let fifty men stop them from gettin' at the coffee and sugar that is in these wagons. And they ain't agoin' to be satisfied until they get some of our scalps to pay for the bucks we popped out of their saddles a bit ago."

The officers passed along the line of skirmishers—for this in reality was all their line consisted of—and cautioned the men against wasting their ammunition. It was yet early in the afternoon, and should the conflict be prolonged until night, there was great danger of exhausting the supply of ammunition. The Indians seemed to have thought of this, and the change in their method of attack encouraged such a result.

But little time was spent at the parley. Again the entire band of warriors, except those already disabled, prepared to renew the attack, and advanced as before—this time, however, with greater caution, evidently desiring to avoid a reception similar to the first. When sufficiently near to the troops, the Indians developed their new plan of attack. It was not to advance *en masse*, as before, but fight as individuals, each warrior selecting his own time and method of attack. This is the habitual manner of fighting among all Indians of the Plains, and is termed "circling." First the chiefs led off, followed at regular intervals by the warriors, until the entire six or seven hundred were to be seen riding in single file as rapidly as their fleet-footed ponies could carry them. Preserving this order, and keeping up their savage chorus of yells, war-whoops, and taunting epithets, this long line of mounted barbarians was guided in such manner as to envelop the train and escort, and make the latter appear like a small circle within a larger one.

The Indians gradually contracted their circle, although maintaining the full speed of their ponies, until sufficiently close to open fire upon the soldiers. At first the shots were scattering and wide of their mark; but, emboldened by the silence of their few but determined opponents, they rode nearer and fought with greater impetuosity. Forced now to defend themselves to the uttermost, the cavalrymen opened fire from their carbines, with most gratifying results. The Indians, however, moving at such a rapid gait and in single file, presented a most uncertain target. To add to this uncertainty, the savages availed themselves of their superior—almost marvellous—powers of horsemanship. Throwing themselves upon the sides of their well-trained ponies, they left no part of their persons exposed to the aim of the troopers except the head and one foot, and in this posture they were

able to aim the weapons either over or under the necks of their ponies, thus using the bodies of the latter as an effective shield against
the bullets of their adversaries.

At no time were the Indians able to force the train and its escort to come to a halt. The march was continued at an uninterrupted
gait. This successful defence against the Indians was in a great measure due to the presence of the wagons, which, arranged in the order
described, formed a complete barrier to the charges and assaults of
the savages; and, as a last resort, the wagons could have been halted and used as a breastwork, behind which the cavalry, dismounted,
would have been almost invincible against their more numerous enemies. There is nothing an Indian dislikes more in warfare than to
attack a foe, however weak, behind breastworks of any kind. Any
contrivance which is an obstacle to his pony is a most serious obstacle
to the warrior.

The attack of the Indians, aggravated by their losses in warriors
and ponies, as many of the latter had been shot down, was continued
without cessation for three hours. The supply of ammunition of the
cavalry was running low. The "fourth troopers," who had remained in
charge of the led horses between the two columns of wagons, were
now replaced from the skirmishers, and the former were added to
the list of active combatants. If the Indians should maintain the fight
much longer, there was serious ground for apprehension regarding
the limited supply of ammunition.

If only night or reinforcements would come! was the prayerful
hope of those who contended so gallantly against such heavy odds.
Night was still too far off to promise much encouragement; while as
to reinforcements, their coming would be purely accidental—at least
so argued those most interested in their arrival. Yet reinforcements
were at that moment striving to reach them. Comrades were in the
saddle and spurring forward to their relief. The Indians, although
apparently turning all their attention to the little band inside, had omit-
ted no precaution to guard against interference from outside parties.
In this instance, perhaps, they were more than ordinarily watchful, and
had posted some of their keen-eyed warriors on the high line of bluffs
that ran almost parallel to the trail over which the combatants moved.
From these bluffs not only a good view of the fight could be obtained,
but the country for miles in either direction was also spread out beneath
them, and enabled the scouts to discern the approach of any hostile

party that might be advancing. The warriors on the lookout were not long in discovering something which occasioned them no little anxiety. Dismounting from their ponies and concealing the latter in a ravine, they prepared to investigate more fully the cause of their alarm.

That which they saw was as yet but a faint dark line on the surface of the plain, almost against the horizon. So faint was it that no one but an Indian or practised frontiersman would have observed it. It was fully ten miles from them and directly in their line of march. The ordinary observer would have pronounced it a break or irregularity in the ground, or perhaps the shadow of a cloud, and its apparent permanency of location would have dispelled any fear as to its dangerous character. But was it stationary? Apparently, yes. The Indians discovered otherwise. By close watching, the long faint line could be seen moving along, as if creeping stealthily upon an unconscious foe. Slowly it assumed a more definite shape, until what appeared to be a mere stationary dark line drawn upon the green surface of the plain developed itself to the searching eyes of the red man into a column of cavalry moving at a rapid gait toward the very point they were then occupying.

Convinced of this fact, one of the scouts leaped upon his pony and flew with almost the speed of the wind to impart this knowledge to the chiefs in command on the plain below. True, the approaching cavalry, being still several miles distant, could not arrive for nearly two hours; but the question to be considered by the Indians was, whether it would be prudent for them to continue their attack on the train— their ponies already becoming exhausted by the three hours' hard riding given them—until the arrival of the fresh detachment of the enemy, whose horses might be in condition favorable to a rapid pursuit, and thereby enable them to overtake those of the Indians whose ponies were exhausted. Unwilling to incur this new risk, and seeing no prospect of overcoming their present adversaries by a sudden or combined dash, the chiefs decided to withdraw from the attack and make their escape while the advantage was yet in their favor.

The surprise of the cavalrymen may be imagined at seeing the Indians, after pouring a shower of bullets and arrows into the train, withdraw to the bluffs, and immediately after continue their retreat until lost to view.

This victory for the troopers, although so unexpected, was nonetheless welcome. The Indians contrived to carry away with them their killed and wounded. Five of their bravest warriors were known to have been sent to the happy hunting ground, while the list of their wounded was much larger.

After the Indians had withdrawn and left the cavalrymen masters of the field, our wounded, of whom there were comparatively few, received every possible care and attention. Those of the detachment who had escaped unharmed were busily engaged in exchanging congratulations and relating incidents of the fight.

The approaching party was none other than Colonel West's detachment, hastening to the relief of the train and its gallant little escort. A few words explained all, and told the heroes of the recent fight, how it happened that reinforcements were sent to their assistance; and then was explained why the Indians had so suddenly concluded to abandon their attack and seek safety in quietly withdrawing from the field.

Deserters

Worry Over Kidder's Party—Deserters—Re-Supplying Fort Wallace—Death of Comstock

On the morning of the 28th the train, with its escort, returned to the main camp on the Republican. All were proud of the conduct of those detachments of the command which had been brought into actual conflict with the Indians.

The despatches brought by Major Elliott from General Sherman directed me to continue my march, as had been suggested, up the North Republican, then strike northward and reach the Platte again at some point west of Fort Sedgwick, near Riverside Station. This programme was carried out. Leaving our camp on the Republican, we marched up the north fork of that river about sixty miles, then turned nearly due north, and marched for the valley of the Platte.

The only incident connected with this march was the painful journey under a burning July sun, of sixty-five miles, without a drop of water for our horses or draught animals. This march was necessarily effected in one day, and produced untold suffering among the poor dumb brutes. Many of the dogs accompanying the command died from thirst and exhaustion. When the sun went down we were still many miles from the Platte. The moon, which was nearly full at the time, lighted us on our weary way for some time; but even this was only an aggravation, as it enabled us from the high bluffs bordering the Platte Valley to see the river flowing beneath us, yet many miles beyond our reach.

Taking Lieutenant Moylan, Dr. Coates, and one attendant with me, and leaving the command under temporary charge of Major Elliott, I pushed on, intending after arriving at the river to select as good camping ground as the darkness and circumstances would permit. We then imagined ourselves within four or five miles of the river, so near did it appear to us. Mile after mile was traversed by our tired horses, yet we apparently arrived no nearer to our journey's end. At last, at about eleven o'clock, and after having ridden at a brisk rate for nearly fifteen miles, we reached the river bank. Our first act was to improve the opportunity to quench our thirst and that of our horses. Considering the lateness of the hour, and the distance we had ridden since leaving the command, it was idle to expect the latter to reach the river before daylight. Nothing was left to us but to bivouac for the night. This we did by selecting a beautiful piece of sward on the river bank for our couch, and taking our saddle blankets for covering and our saddles for pillows. Each of us attached his horse by the halter-strap to the hilt of his sabre, and then forced the sabre firmly into the ground. Both horses and riders were weary as well as hungry. At first the horses grazed upon the fresh green pasture which grew luxuriantly on the river bank, but fatigue, more powerful than hunger, soon claimed the mastery, and in a few minutes our little group, horses and men, were wrapped in the sweetest of slumber.

Had we known that the Indians were then engaged in murdering men within a few minutes' ride of where we slept, and that when we awakened in the morning it would be to still find ourselves away from the command, our sleep would not have been so undisturbed.

Being the first to awake, I rose to a sitting posture and took a hasty survey of our situation. Within a few feet of us flowed the Platte River. Our group, horses and men, presented an interesting subject for a painter. To my surprise I discovered that a heavy shower of rain had fallen during the night, but so deep had been our slumber that even the rain had failed to disturb us. Each one of the party had spread his saddle blanket on the ground to serve as his couch, while for covering we had called into requisition the india-rubber poncho or rubber blanket which invariably forms an important part of the plainsman's outfit.

It was now becoming sufficiently light to enable us to see indistinctly for almost a mile in either direction, yet our eyes failed to reveal to us any evidence of the presence of the command. Here was fresh cause for anxiety, not only as to our own situation, but as to the whereabouts of the troops. Saddling up our horses, each person acting as his own groom, we awaited the clearing away of the morning mist to seek the main body. We had not long to wait. The light was soon sufficient to enable us to scan the country with our field glasses in all directions. Much to our joy we discovered the bivouac of the troops about three miles down the river. A brisk gallop soon placed us where we desired to be, and a few words explained how, in the darkness, the column had failed to follow us, but instead had headed for the river at a point below us, a portion not reaching the bank until near morning.

Breakfast disposed of, the next question was to ascertain our exact location and distance from the nearest telegraph station. Fortunately Riverside Station was near our camp, and from there we ascertained that we were then about fifty miles west of Fort Sedgwick. The party obtaining this information also learned that the Indians had attacked the nearest stage station west of camp the preceding evening, and killed three men. This station was only a few minutes' ride from the point on the river bank where myself and comrades had passed the night in such fancied security.

Believing that General Sherman must have sent later instructions for me to Fort Sedgwick than those last received from him, I sent a telegram to the officer in command at the fort, making inquiry to that effect. To my surprise I received a despatch saying that, the day after the departure of Major Elliott and his detachment from Fort Sedgwick with despatches, of which mention has been previously made, a second detachment of equal strength, viz., ten troopers of the Second United States Cavalry, under command of Lieutenant Kidder and guided by a famous Sioux chief Red Bead, had left Fort Sedgwick with important despatches for me from General Sherman, and that Lieutenant Kidder had been directed to proceed to my camp near the forks of the Republican, and failing to find me there he was to follow rapidly on my trail until he should overtake my command. I immediately telegraphed to Fort Sedgwick that nothing had been seen or heard of Lieutenant Kidder's detachment, and requested a copy of the despatches borne by him to be sent me by telegraph. This was done; the instructions of General Sherman were for me to march my command, as was at first contemplated, across the country from the Platte to the Smoky Hill River, striking the latter at Fort Wallace. Owing to the low state of my supplies, I determined to set out for Fort Wallace at daylight next morning.

Great anxiety prevailed throughout the command concerning Lieutenant Kidder and his party. True, he had precisely the same number of men that composed Major Elliott's detachment when the latter went upon a like mission, but the circumstances which would govern in the one case had changed when applied to the other. Major Elliott, an officer of experience and good judgment, had fixed the strength of his escort and performed the journey before it was positively known that the Indians in that section had entered upon the war path. Had the attack on the commands of Hamilton, Robbins, and Cook been made prior to Elliott's departure, the latter would have taken not less than fifty troopers as escort.

Anxiety for the fate of Kidder and his party was one of the reasons impelling me to set out promptly on my return. From our camp at the forks of the Republican to Fort Wallace was about eighty miles—but eighty miles of the most dangerous country infested by Indians. Remembering the terrible contest in which the command of Robbins and Cook had been engaged on this very route within a few days, and knowing that the Indians would in all probability maintain a strict watch over the trail to surprise any small party which might venture over it, I felt in the highest degree solicitous for the safety of Lieutenant Kidder and party. Even if he succeeded in reaching Fort Wallace unmolested, there was reason to apprehend that, impressed with the importance of delivering his despatches promptly, he would set out on his return at once and endeavor to find my command.

Let us leave him and his detachment for a brief interval, and return to events which were more immediately connected with my command, and which bear a somewhat tragic as well as personal interest.

Reference has been made to the state of dissatisfaction that had made its appearance among the enlisted men. This state of feeling had been principally superinduced by inferior and insufficient rations, a fault for which no one connected with the troops in the field was responsible, but which was chargeable to persons far removed from the theatre of our movements, persons connected with the supply departments of the army. Added to this internal source of disquiet, we were then on the main line of overland travel to some of our most valuable and lately discovered mining regions. The opportunity to obtain marvellous wages as miners and the prospect of amassing sudden wealth proved a temptation sufficiently strong to make many of the men forget their sworn obligations to their government and their duties as soldiers. Forgetting for the moment that the command to which they belonged was actually engaged in war, and was in a country infested with armed bodies of the enemy, and that the legal penalty of desertion under such circumstances was death, many of the men formed a combination to desert their colors and escape to the mines.

The first intimation received by any person in authority of the existence of this plot occurred on the morning fixed for our departure from the Platte. Orders had been issued the previous evening for the command to march at daylight. Upwards of forty men were reported as having deserted during the night. There was no time to send parties in pursuit, or the capture and return of a portion of them might have been effected.

The command marched southward at daylight. At noon, having marched fifteen miles, we halted to rest and graze the horses for one hour. The men believed that the halt was made for the remainder of the day, and here a plan was perfected among the disaffected by which upwards of one third of the effective strength of the command was to seize their horses and arms during the night and escape to the mountains. Had the conspirators succeeded in putting this plan into execution, it would have been difficult to say how serious the consequences might be, or whether enough true men would remain to render the march to Fort Wallace practicable. Fortunately it was decided to continue the march some fifteen miles further before night. The necessary orders were given and everything was being repacked for the march, when attention was called to thirteen soldiers who were then to be seen rapidly leaving camp in the direction from which we had marched. Seven of these were mounted and were moving off at a rapid gallop; the remaining six were dismounted, not having been so fortunate as their fellows in procuring horses. The entire party were still within sound of the bugle, but no orders by bugle note or otherwise served to check or diminish their flight. The boldness of this attempt at desertion took everyone by surprise. Such an occurrence as enlisted men deserting in broad daylight and under the immediate eyes of their officers had never been heard of. With the exception of the horses of the guard and a few belonging to the officers, all others were still grazing and unsaddled. The officer of the guard was directed to mount his command promptly and, if possible overtake the deserters. At the same time those of the officers whose horses were in readiness were also directed to join in the pursuit and leave no effort untried to prevent the escape of a single malcontent. In giving each party sent in pursuit instructions, there was no limit fixed to the measures that they were authorized to adopt in executing their orders. This, unfortunately, was an emergency which involved the safety of the entire command and required treatment of the most summary character.

It was found impossible to overtake that portion of the party which was mounted, as it was afterwards learned that they had selected seven of the fleetest horses in the command. Those on foot, when discovering themselves pursued, increased their speed, but a chase of a couple of miles brought the pursuers within hailing distance.

Major Elliott, the senior officer participating in the pursuit, called out to the deserters to halt and surrender. This command was several times repeated, but without effect. Finally, seeing the hopelessness of further flight, the deserters came to bay, and to Major Elliott's renewed demand to throw down their arms and surrender, the ringleader drew up his carbine to fire upon his pursuers. This was the signal for the latter to open fire, which they did successfully, bringing down three of the deserters, although two of them were worse frightened than hurt.

Rejoining the command with their six captive deserters, the pursuing party reported their inability to overtake those who had deserted on horseback. The march was resumed and continued until near nightfall, by which time we had placed thirty miles between us and our last camp on the Platte. While on the march during the day, a trusty sergeant, one who had served as a soldier long and faithfully, imparted the first information which could be relied upon as to the plot that had been formed by the malcontents to desert in a body. The following night had been selected as the time for making the attempt. The best horses and arms in the command were to be seized and taken away. I believed that the summary action adopted during the day would intimidate any who might still be contemplating desertion, and was confident that another day's march would place us so far in a hostile and dangerous country, that the risk of encountering war parties of Indians would of itself serve to deter any but large numbers from attempting to make their way back to the settlements. To bridge the following night in safety was the next problem. While there was undoubtedly a large proportion of the men who could be fully relied upon to remain true to their obligations and to render any support to their officers that might be demanded, yet the great difficulty at this time, owing to the sudden development of the plot, was to determine who could be trusted.

This difficulty was solved by placing every officer in the command on guard during the entire night. The men were assembled as usual for roll call at tattoo, and then notified that every man must be in his tent at the signal "taps," which would be sounded half an hour later; that their company officers, fully armed, would walk the company streets during the entire night, and any man appearing outside the limits of his tent between the hours of "taps" and reveille would do so at the risk of being fired upon after being once hailed.

The night passed without disturbance, and daylight found us in the saddle and pursuing our line of march toward Fort Wallace. It is proper to here record the fact that from that date onward desertion from that command during the continuance of the expedition was never attempted. It may become necessary in order "to perfect the record," borrowing a term from the War Department, to refer in a subsequent chapter to certain personal and official events which resulted partially from the foregoing occurrences.

Let us now turn our attention to Lieutenant Kidder and his detachment. The third night after leaving the Platte my command encamped in the vicinity of our former camp near the forks of the Republican. So far, nothing had been learned which would enable us to form any conclusion regarding the route taken by Kidder. Comstock, the guide, was frequently appealed to for an opinion which, from his great experience on the Plains, might give us some encouragement regarding Kidder's safety. But he was too cautious and careful a man, both in word and deed, to excite hopes that his reasoning could not justify. When thus appealed to he would usually give an ominous shake of the head and avoid a direct answer.

At daylight our column could have been seen stretching out in the direction of the Wallace trail. A march of a few miles brought us to the point of intersection. Comstock and the Delawares had galloped in advance, and were about concluding a thorough examination of the various tracks to be seen in the trail, when the head of the column overtook them. "Well, what do you find, Comstock?" was my first inquiry. "They've gone toward Fort Wallace, sure," was the reply; and in support of this opinion he added, "The trail shows that twelve American horses, shod all round, have passed at a walk, goin' in the direction of the fort; and when they went by this p'int they were all right, because their horses were movin' along easy, and there are no pony tracks behind 'em, as wouldn't be the case ef the Injuns had got an eye on 'em." He then remarked, as if in parenthesis, "It would be astonishin' ef that lootenint and his lay-out gits into the fort without a scrimmage. He may; but ef he does, it will be a scratch ef ever there was one, and I'll lose my confidence in Injuns."

The opinion expressed by Comstock as to the chances of Lieutenant Kidder and party making their way to the fort across eighty miles of danger unmolested was the concurrent opinion of all the officers. And now that we had discovered their trail, our interest and anxiety became immeasurably increased as to their fate. The latter could not remain in doubt much longer, as two days' marching would take us to the fort. Alas! we were to solve the mystery without waiting so long.

Pursuing our way along the plain, heavy trail made by Robbins and Cook, and directing Comstock and the Delawares to watch closely that we did not lose that of Kidder and his party, we patiently but hopefully awaited further developments. How many miles we had thus passed over without incident worthy of mention, I do not now recall. The sun was high in the heavens, showing that our day's march was about half completed, when those of us who were riding at the head of the column discovered a strange-looking object lying directly in our path, and more than a mile distant. It was too large for a human being, yet in color and appearance, at that distance, resembled no animal frequenting the Plains with which any of us were familiar. Eager to determine its character, a dozen or more of our party, including Comstock and some of the Delawares, galloped in front.

Before riding the full distance the question was determined. The object seen was the body of a white horse. A closer examination showed that it had been shot within the past few days, while the brand, U.S., proved that it was a government animal. Major Elliott then remembered that while at Fort Sedgwick he had seen one company of cavalry mounted upon white horses. These and other circumstances went far to convince us that this was one of the horses belonging to Lieutenant Kidder's party. In fact there was no room to doubt that this was the case.

Almost the unanimous opinion of the command was that there had been a contest with Indians, and this only the first evidence we should have proving it. When the column reached the point where the slain horse lay, a halt was ordered, to enable Comstock and the Indian scouts to thoroughly examine the surrounding ground to discover, if possible, any additional evidence, such as empty cartridge shells, arrows, or articles of Indian equipment, showing that a fight had taken place. All the horse equipments, saddle, bridle, etc., had been carried away, but whether by friend or foe could not then be determined.

The scouts being unable to throw any additional light upon the question, we continued our march, closely observing the ground as we passed along. Comstock noticed that instead of the trail showing that Kidder's party was moving in regular order, as when at first discovered, there were but two or three tracks to be seen in the beaten trail, the rest being found on the grass on either side.

We had marched two miles perhaps from the point where the body of the slain horse had been discovered, when we came upon a second, this one, like the first, having been killed by a bullet, and all of his equipments taken away. Comstock's quick eyes were not long in detecting pony tracks in the vicinity, and we had no longer any but the one frightful solution to offer: Kidder and his party had been discovered by the Indians—probably the same powerful and bloodthirsty band that had been resisted so gallantly by the men under Robbins and Cook—and against such overwhelming odds the issue could not be doubtful.

We were then moving over a high and level plateau, unbroken either by ravines or divides, and just such a locality as would be usually chosen by the Indians for attacking a party of the strength of Kidder's. The Indians could here ride unobstructed and encircle their victims with a continuous line of armed and painted warriors, while the beleaguered party, from the even character of the surface of the plain, would be unable to find any break or depression from behind which they might make a successful defence. It was probably this relative condition of affairs that had induced Kidder and his doomed comrades to endeavor to push on in the hope of finding ground favorable to their making a stand against their barbarous foes.

The main trail no longer showed the footprints of Kidder's party, but instead Comstock discovered the tracks of shod horses on the grass, with here and there numerous tracks of ponies, all by their appearance proving that both horses and ponies had been moving at full speed. Kidder's party must have trusted their lives temporarily to the speed of their horses—a dangerous venture when contending with Indians. However, this fearful race for life must have been most gallantly contested, because we continued our march several miles further without discovering any evidence of the savages having gained any advantage.

How painfully, almost despairingly exciting must have been this ride for life! A mere handful of brave men struggling to escape the bloody clutches of the hundreds of red-visaged demons, who, mounted on their well-trained war ponies, were straining every nerve and muscle to reek their hands in the life-blood of their victims. It was not death alone that threatened this little band. They were not riding simply to preserve life. They rode, and doubtless prayed as they rode, that they might escape the savage tortures, the worse than death which threatened them. Would that their prayer had been granted!

We began leaving the high plateau and to descend into a valley, through which, at the distance of nearly two miles, meandered a small prairie stream known as Beaver Creek. The valley near the banks of this stream was covered with a dense growth of tall wild grass intermingled with clumps of osiers. At the point where the trail crossed the stream, we hoped to obtain more definite information regarding Kidder's party and their pursuers, but we were not required to wait so long. Within a mile of the stream, I observed several large buz-zards floating lazily in circles through the air, but a short distance to the left of our trail. This, of itself, might not have attracted my attention seriously but for the rank stench which pervaded the atmosphere, reminding one of the horrible sensations experienced upon a battlefield when passing among the decaying bodies of the dead.

As if impelled by one thought, Comstock, the Delawares, and half-a-dozen officers, detached themselves from the column and, separating into squads of one or two, instituted a search for the cause of our hor-rible suspicions. After riding in all directions through the rushes and willows, and when about to relinquish the search as fruitless, one of the Delawares uttered a shout that attracted the attention of the entire command; at the same time he was seen to leap from his horse and assume a stooping posture, as if critically examining some object of interest. Hastening, in common with many others of the party, to his side, a sight met our gaze which even at this remote day makes my very blood curdle. Lying in irregular order, and within a very limited circle, were the mangled bodies of poor Kidder and his party, yet so brutally hacked and disfigured as to be beyond recognition save as human beings.

Every individual of the party had been scalped and his skull broken—the latter done by some weapon, probably a tomahawk—except the Sioux chief Red Bead, whose scalp had simply been removed from his head and then thrown down by his side. This, Comstock informed us, was in accordance with a custom which prohibits an Indian from bearing off the scalp of one of his own tribe. This circumstance, then, told us who the perpetrators of this deed were. They could be none other than the Sioux, led in all probability by Pawnee Killer.

Red Bead, being less disfigured and mutilated than the others, was the only individual capable of being recognized. Even the clothes of all the party has been carried away; some of the bodies were lying in beds of ashes, with partly burned fragments of wood near them, showing that the savages had put some of them to death by the terrible tortures of fire. The sinews of the arms and legs had been cut away, the nose of every man hacked off, and the features otherwise defaced so that it would have been scarcely possible for even a relative to recognize a single one of the unfortunate victims. We could not even distinguish the officer from his men. Each body was pierced by twenty to fifty arrows, and the arrows were found as the savage demons had left them, bristling in the bodies. While the details of that fearful struggle will probably never be known, telling how long and gallantly this ill-fated little band contended for their lives, yet the surrounding circumstances of ground, empty cartridge shells, and distance from where the attack began, satisfied us that Kidder and his men fought as only brave men fight when the watchword is victory or death.

As the officer, his men, and his no less faithful Indian guide had shared their final dangers together and had met the same dreadful fate at the hands of the same merciless foe, it was but fitting that their remains should be consigned to one common grave. This was accordingly done. A single trench was dug near the spot where they had rendered up their lives upon the altar of duty. Silently, mournfully, their comrades of a brother regiment consigned their mangled remains to mother earth, there to rest undisturbed, as we supposed, until the great day of final review. But this was not to be so; while the closest scrutiny on our part had been insufficient to enable us to detect the slightest evidence that would aid us or others in identifying the body of Lieutenant Kidder or any of his men, it will be seen hereafter how the marks of a mother's thoughtful affection were to be the means of identifying the remains of her murdered son, even though months had elapsed after his untimely death.

On the evening of the day following that upon which we had consigned the remains of Lieutenant Kidder and his party to their humble resting place, the command reached Fort Wallace on the Smoky Hill route. From the occupants of the fort we learned much that was interesting regarding events that had transpired during our isolation from all points of communication. The Indians had attacked the fort twice within the past few days, in both of which engagements men were killed on each side. The fighting on our side was principally under the command of Colonel Barnitz, whose forces were composed of detachments of the Seventh Cavalry. The fighting occurred on the level plain near the fort, where, owing to the favorable character of the ground, the Indians had ample opportunity to display their powers both as warriors and horsemen. One incident of the fight was related, which, its correctness being vouched for, is worthy of being here repeated. Both parties were mounted, and the fighting consisted principally of charges and countercharges, the combatants of both sides becoming at times mingled with each other. During one of these attacks a bugler boy belonging to the cavalry was shot from his horse; before any of his comrades could reach him, a powerfully built warrior, superbly mounted on a war pony, was seen to dash at full speed toward the spot where the dying bugler lay. Scarcely checking the speed of his pony, who seemed to divine his rider's wishes, the warrior grasped the pony's mane with one hand and, stooping low as he neared the bugler, seized the latter with the other hand and lifted him from the earth, placing him across his pony in front of him. Still maintaining the full speed of his pony, he was seen to retain the body of the bugler but a moment, then cast it to earth. The Indians being routed soon after and driven from the field, our troops, many of whom had witnessed the strange and daring action of the warrior, recovered possession of the dead, when the mystery became solved. The bugler had been scalped.

Our arrival at Fort Wallace was most welcome as well as opportune. The Indians had become so active and numerous that all travel over the Smoky Hill route had ceased; stages had been taken off the route, and many of the stage stations had been abandoned by the employees, the latter fearing a repetition of the Lookout Station massacre. No despatches or mail had been received at the fort for a considerable period, so that the occupants might well have been considered as undergoing a state of siege. Added to these embarrassments, which were partly unavoidable, an additional and, under the circumstances, a more frightful danger stared the troops in the face. The officer commanding the troops in my absence reported officially to headquarters that the bulk of the provisions issued to his men consisted of "rotten bacon" and "hard bread" that was "no better." Cholera made its appearance among the men, and deaths occurred daily. "I believe that unless we can obtain a more abundant and better supply of rations than we have had, it will be impossible to check this fearful epidemic," the officer said.

I decided to select upward of a hundred of the best mounted men in my command, and with this force open a way through to Fort Harker, a distance of two hundred miles, where I expected to obtain abundant supplies; from which point the latter could be conducted, well protected against Indians by my detachment, back to Fort Wallace. Owing to the severe marching of the past few weeks, the horses of the command were generally in an unfit condition for further service without rest. So that after selecting upward of a hundred of the best, the remainder might for the time be regarded as unserviceable; such they were in fact. Regarding the duties to be performed by the picked detachment as being by far the most important, I chose to accompany it.

The immediate command of the detachment was given to Captain Hamilton of whom mention has been previously made. He was assisted by two other officers. My intention was to push through from Fort Wallace to Fort Hays, a distance of about 150 miles, as rapidly as was practicable; then, being beyond the most dangerous portion of the route, to make the remainder of the march to Fort Harker with half a dozen troopers, while Caption Hamilton with his command should follow leisurely. Under this arrangement I hoped to have a train loaded with supplies at Harker, and in readiness to start for Fort Wallace, by the time Captain Hamilton should arrive.

Leaving Fort Wallace about sunset on the evening of the 15th of July, we began our ride eastward, following the line of the overland stage route. At that date the Kansas Pacific Railway was only completed as far westward as Fort Harker. Between Forts Wallace and Harker we expected to find the stations of the overland stage company, at intervals of ten to fifteen miles. In time of peace these stations are generally occupied by half a dozen employees of the route, embracing the stablemen and relays of drivers. They were well supplied with firearms and ammunition and every facility for defending themselves against Indians. The stables were also the quarters for the men. They were usually built of stone, and one would naturally think that against Indians no better defensive work would be required. Yet such was not the case. The hay and other combustible material usually contained in them enabled the savages, by shooting prepared arrows, to easily set them on fire, and thus drive the occupants out to the open plain, where their fate would soon be settled. To guard against such an emergency, each station was ordinarily provided with what on the Plains is termed a "dug-out." The name implies the character and description of the work. The dug-out was commonly located but a few yards from one of the corners of the stable, and was prepared by excavating the earth so as to form an opening not unlike a cellar, which was usually about four feet in depth, and sufficiently roomy to accommodate at close quarters half a dozen persons. This opening was then covered with earth and loopholed on all sides at a height of a few inches above the original level of the ground. The earth was thrown on top until the dug-out resembled an ordinary mound of earth, some four or five feet in height. To the outside observer, no means apparently were provided for egress or ingress; yet such was not the case. If the entrance had been made above ground, rendering it necessary for the defenders to pass from the stable unprotected to their citadel, the Indians would have posted themselves accordingly, and picked them off one by one as they should emerge from the stable. To provide against this danger, an underground passage was constructed for each case, leading from the dug-out to the interior of the stable. With these arrangements for defence a few determined men could withstand the attacks of an entire tribe of savages. The recent depredations of the Indians had so demoralized the men at the various stations that many of the latter were found deserted, their former occupants having joined their forces with those of other stations. The Indians generally burned the deserted stations.

Marching by night was found to be attended with some disadvantages. The men located at the stations that were still occupied, having no notice of our coming, and having seen no human beings for several days except the war parties of savages who had attacked them from time to time, were in a chronic state of alarm, and held themselves in readiness for defence at a moment's notice. The consequence was that, as we pursued our way in the stillness of the night, and were not familiar with the location of the various stations, we generally rode into close proximity before discovering them. The station men however, were generally on the alert, and, as they did not wait to challenge us or be challenged, but took it for granted that we were Indians, our first greeting would be a bullet whistling over our heads, sometimes followed by a perfect volley from the dug-out. In such a case nothing was left for us to do but to withdraw the column to a place of security, and then for one of our number to creep up stealthily in the darkness to a point within hailing distance. Even this was an undertaking attended by no little danger, as by this time the little garrison of the dug-out would be thoroughly awake and every man at his post, his finger on the trigger of his trusty rifle, and straining both eye and ear to discover the approach of the hateful redskins, who alone were believed to be the cause of all this ill-timed disturbance of their slumbers. Huddled together, as they necessarily would be, in the contracted limits of their subterranean citadel, and all sounds from without being deadened and rendered indistinct by the heavy roof of earth and the few apertures leading to the inside, it is not strange that under the circumstances it would be difficult for the occupant to distinguish between the voice of an Indian and that of a white man. Such was in fact the case, and no sooner would the officer sent forward for that purpose hail the little garrison and endeavor to explain who we were, than, guided by the first sound of his voice, they would respond promptly with their rifles. In some instances we were in this manner put to considerable delay, and although this was at times most provoking, it was not a little amusing to hear the description given by the party sent forward of how closely he hugged the ground when endeavoring to establish friendly relations with the stage people. Finally, when successful, and in conversation with the latter, we inquired why they did not recognize us from the fact that we hailed them in unbroken English. They replied that the Indians resorted to so many tricks that they had determined not to be caught even by that one. Almost at every station we received intelligence of Indians having been seen in the vicinity within a few days of our arrival.

We felt satisfied they were watching our movements, although we saw no fresh signs of Indians until we arrived near Downer's station. Here, while stopping to rest our horses for a few minutes, a small party of our men, who had without authority halted some distance behind, came dashing into our midst and reported that twenty-five or thirty Indians had attacked them some five or six miles in rear and had killed two of their number. As there was a detachment of infantry guarding the station, and time being important, we pushed on toward our destination. The two men reported killed were left to be buried by the troops on duty at the station. Frequent halts and brief rests were made along our line of march; occasionally we would halt long enough to indulge in a few hours' sleep. About three o'clock on the morning of the 18th we reached Fort Hays, having marched about 150 miles in fifty-five hours, including all halts. Some may regard this as a rapid rate of marching; in fact, a few officers of the army who themselves have made many and long marches (principally in ambulances and railroad cars) are of the same opinion. It was far above the usual rate of a leisurely made march, but during the same season and with a larger command I marched sixty miles in fifteen hours. This was officially reported, but occasioned no remark. During the war, and at the time the enemy's cavalry under General J. E. B. Stuart made its famous raid around the Army of the Potomac in Maryland, a portion of our cavalry, accompanied by horse artillery, in attempting to overtake them, marched over ninety miles in twenty-four hours. A year subsequent to the events narrated in this chapter, I marched a small detachment eighty miles in seventeen hours, every horse accompanying the detachment completing the march in as fresh condition apparently as when the march began.

Leaving Hamilton and his command to rest one day at Hays and then to follow on leisurely to Fort Harker, I continued my ride to the latter post, accompanied by Colonels Cook and Custer and two troopers. We reached Fort Harker at two o'clock that night, having made the ride of sixty miles without change of animals in less than twelve hours. As this was the first telegraph station, I immediately sent telegrams to headquarters and to Fort Sedgwick, announcing the fate of Kidder and his party. General A. J. Smith, who was in command of this military district, had his headquarters at Harker. I at once reported to him in person, and acquainted him with every incident worthy of mention that had occurred in connection with my command since leaving him weeks before. Arrangements were made for the arrival of Hamilton's party and for a train containing supplies to be sent back under their escort. Having made my report to General Smith as my next superior officer, and there being no occasion for my presence until the train and escort should be in readiness to return, I applied for and received authority to visit Fort Riley, about ninety miles east of Harker by rail, where my family was then located.

The winter of 1867–68 found me comfortably quartered at Fort Leavenworth, Kansas, on the banks of the Missouri. A considerable portion of my regiment had been ordered to locate at that post in the fall and make that their winter quarters. General Sheridan, then commanding that military department, had also established his headquarters there, so that the post became more than ever the favorite military station in the West. I had not been on duty with my regiment since my rapid ride from Fort Wallace to Fort Harker in July, nor was I destined to serve with it in the field for some time to come. This, at the time, seemed a great deprivation to me, but subsequent events proved most conclusively that it was all for the best, and the result could not have been to me more satisfactory than it was, showing as it did that the best laid plans of mice and men, etc. But I am anticipating.

Those who have read the tabulated list of depredations committed by the Indians may have noticed the name of William Comstock in the column of killed. Comstock was the favorite and best known scout on the central plains. Frequent reference has been made to him in preceding numbers, particularly in the description of the attack of the Indians on the detachment commanded by Robbins and Cook. Strange as it may seem, when his thorough knowledge of the Indian character is considered, he fell a victim to their treachery and barbarity. The Indians were encamped with their village not far from Big Spring station, in western Kansas, and were professedly at peace. Still, no one familiar with the deceit and bad faith invariably practised by the Indians when free to follow the bent of their inclinations ought to have thought of trusting themselves in their power. Yet Comstock, with all his previous knowledge and experience, did that which he would certainly have disapproved in others. He left the camp of the troops, which was but a few miles from the Indian village, and with but a single companion rode to the latter, and spent several hours in friendly conversation with the chiefs. Nothing occurred during their visit to excite suspicion. The Indians assumed a most peaceable bearing toward them and were profuse in their demonstrations of friendship. When the time came for Comstock and his comrade to take their departure, they were urged by the Indians to remain and spend the night in the village.

The invitation was declined, and after the usual salutations the two white men mounted their horses and set out to return to their camp. Comstock always carried in his belt a beautiful white-handled revolver, and wore it on this occasion. This had often attracted the covetous eyes of the savages, and while in the village propositions to barter for it had been made by more than one of the warriors. Comstock invariably refused all offers to exchange it, no matter how tempting. Months before, when riding together at the head of the column, in pursuit of Indians, Comstock, who had observed that I carried a revolver closely resembling his, remarked that I ought to have the pair, and then laughingly added that he would carry his until we found the Indians, and after giving them a sound whipping he would present me the revolver. Frequently during the campaign, when on the march and while sitting around the evening campfire, Comstock would refer to his promise concerning the revolver. After hunting Indians all summer, but never finding them just when we desired them, Comstock not unfrequently joked upon the conditions under which he was to part with his revolver, and fears were expressed that if he carried it until we caught and whipped the Indians, he might be forced to go armed for a long time. None of us imagined then that the revolver which was so often the subject of jest, and of which Comstock was so proud, would be the pretext for his massacre.

Comstock and his companion rode out of the village in the direction of their own camp, totally unconscious of coming danger, and least of all from those whose guests they had just been. They had

Death of Comstock

proceeded about a mile from the village when they observed about a dozen of the young warriors galloping after them. Still suspecting no unfriendly design, they continued their ride until joined by the young warriors. The entire party then rode in company until, as was afterward apparent, the Indians succeeded in separating the two white men, the one riding in front, the other, Comstock, following in rear, each with Indians riding on either side of them. At a preconcerted signal, a combined attack was made by the savages upon the two white men. Both the latter attempted to defend themselves, but the odds and the suddenness of the attack deprived them of all hope of saving their lives. Comstock was fatally wounded at the first onslaught, and soon after was shot from his horse. His companion, being finely mounted, wisely intrusted his life to the speed of his horse, and soon outstripped his pursuers and reached camp with but a few slight wounds. The Indians did not seem disposed to press him as closely as is their usual custom, but seemed only anxious to secure Comstock. He, after falling to the ground severely wounded, was completely riddled by steel-pointed arrows, and his scalp taken. The principal trophy, however, in the opinion of the savages, was the beautifully finished revolver with its white ivory handle, and, as they afterward confessed when peace was proclaimed with their tribe, it was to obtain this revolver that the party of young warriors left the village and followed Comstock to his death. Thoroughly reliable in his reports, brave, modest, and persevering in character, with a remarkable knowledge of the country and the savage tribes infesting it, he was the superior of all men who were scouts by profession with whom I have had any experience.

While sitting in my quarters one day at Fort Leavenworth, late in the fall of 1867, a gentleman was announced whose name recalled a sad and harrowing sight. It proved to be the father of Lieutenant Kidder, whose massacre, with that of his entire party of eleven men, was described in preceding pages. It will be remembered that the savages had hacked, mangled, and burned the bodies of Kidder and his men to such an extent that it was impossible to recognize the body of a single one of the party; even the clothing had been removed, so that we could not distinguish the officer from his men, or the men from each other, by any fragment of their uniform or insignia of their grade. Mr. Kidder, after introducing himself, announced the object of his visit; it was to ascertain the spot where the remains of his son lay buried, and, after procuring suitable military escort to proceed to the grave and disinter his son's remains preparatory to transferring them to a resting place in Dakota, of which territory he was at that time one of the judiciary. It was a painful task I had to perform when I communicated to the father the details of the killing of his son and followers. And equally harassing to the feelings was it to have to inform him that there was no possible chance of his being able to recognize his son's remains. "Was there not the faintest mark or fragment of his uniform by which he might be known?" inquired the anxious parent. "Not one," was the reluctant reply. "And yet, since I now recall the appearance of the mangled and disfigured remains, there was a mere trifle which attracted my attention, but it could not have been your son who wore it." "What was it?" eagerly inquired the father. "It was simply the collar-band of one of those ordinary check overshirts so commonly worn on the plains, the color being black and white; the remainder of the garment, as well as all other articles of dress, having been torn or burned from the body." Mr. Kidder then requested me to repeat the description of the collar and material of which it was made; happily I had some cloth of very similar appearance, and upon exhibiting this to Mr. Kidder, to show the kind I meant, he declared that the body I referred to could be no other than that of his murdered son. He went on to tell how his son had received his appointment in the army but a few weeks before his lamentable death, he only having reported for duty with his company a few days before being sent on the scout which terminated his life; and how, before leaving his home to engage in the military service, his mother, with that thoughtful care and tenderness which only a mother can feel, prepared some articles of wearing apparel, among others a few shirts made from the checked material already described. Mr. Kidder had been to Fort Sedgwick on the Platte, from which post his son had last departed, and there learned that on leaving the post he wore one of the checked shirts and put an extra one in his saddle pockets. Upon this trifling link of evidence Mr. Kidder proceeded four hundred miles west to Fort Wallace, and there being furnished with military escort visited the grave containing the bodies of the twelve massacred men. Upon disinterring the remains a body was found as I had described it, bearing the simple checked collar-band; the father recognized the remains of his son, and thus, as was stated at the close of a preceding chapter, was the evidence of a mother's love made the means by which her son's body was recognized and reclaimed, when all other had failed.

The winter and spring of 1868 were uneventful, so far as Indian hostilities or the movements of troops were concerned. To be on the ground when its services could be made available in case the Indians became troublesome, the Seventh Cavalry left its winter quarters at Fort Leavenworth in April, and marched 290 miles west to a point near the present site of Fort Hays, where the troops established their summer rendezvous in camp. It not being my privilege to serve with the regiment at that time, I remained at Fort Leavenworth some time longer, and later in the summer repaired to my home in Michigan, there amid the society of friends to enjoy the cool breezes of Erie until the time came which would require me to go west.

California Joe

Recalled to Active Duty—My New Command—
California Joe—The Indian Manner of War

Comrades, leave me here a little, while as yet tis early morn;
Leave me here, and when you want me, sound upon the bugle horn.

In this instance, however, the bugle whose summoning notes I was supposed to be listening for was one of peculiar structure, and its tones could only be rendered effective when prompted by the will of the director at Washington. In other words, I was living in involuntary but unregretful retirement from active service. I had spent the winter of 1867–68 most agreeably with many of my comrades at Fort Leavenworth, but in the spring was forced to see them set out for their summer rendezvous for operations against the Indians, and myself compelled by superior authority, or rather by "circumstances over which I had no control," to remain in the rear, a non-combatant in every sense of the word. It is a happy disposition that can content itself in all phases of fortune by the saying that "that which cannot be cured must be endured." I had frequent recourse to this and similar consoling expressions, in the endeavor to reconcile myself to the separation from my command. For fear some of my readers may not comprehend my situation at the time, I will briefly remark in parenthesis, and by way of note of explanation, that for precisely what I have described in some of the preceding chapters, the exact details of which would be out of place here, it had apparently been deemed necessary that my connection with certain events and transactions, every one of which has been fully referred to heretofore, should be submitted to an official examination in order to determine if each and every one of my acts had been performed with a due regard to the customs of war in like cases. To enter into a review of the proceedings which followed, would be to introduce into these pages matters of too personal a character to interest the general reader. It will suffice to say that I was placed in temporary retirement from active duty, and this result seemed satisfactory to those parties most intimately concerned in the matter. When, in the spring of 1868, the time arrived for the troops to leave their winter quarters, and march westward to the Plains, the command with which I had been associated during the preceding year left its station at Fort Leavenworth, Kansas, and marched westward about three hundred miles, to engage in operations against the Indians. While they, under command of General Sully, were attempting to kill Indians, I was studying the problem of how to kill time in the most agreeable manner. My campaign was a decided success. I established my base of operations in a most beautiful little town on the western shores of Lake Erie, from which I projected various hunting, fishing, and boating expeditions. With abundance of friends and companions,

and ample success, time passed pleasantly enough; yet withal there
was a constant longing to be with my comrades in arms in the far
West. I had no reason to believe that I would be permitted to rejoin
them until the following winter. It was on the evening of the 24th of
September, and when about to "break bread" at the house of a friend
in the little town referred to, that I received the following telegram:

HEADQUARTERS DEPARTMENT OF THE MISSOURI,
IN THE FIELD, FORT HAYS, KANSAS, September 24, 1868.

General G. A. CUSTER, Monroe, Michigan:
Generals Sherman, Sully, and myself, and nearly all the officers of your
regiment, have asked for you, and I hope the application will be successful. Can
you come at once? Eleven companies of your regiment will move about the 1st
of October against the hostile Indians, from Medicine Lodge Creek toward the
Wichita Mountains.
(Signed)   P. H. SHERIDAN, Major-General Commanding.

The reception of this despatch was a source of unbounded gratification to me, not only because I saw the opportunity of being actively
and usefully employed opened before me, but there were personal
considerations inseparable from the proposed manner of my return,
which in themselves were in the highest degree agreeable; so much so
that I felt quite forbearing toward each and every one who, whether
intentionally or not, had been a party to my retirement, and was almost disposed to favor them with a copy of the preceding dispatch,
accompanied by an expression of my hearty thanks for the uninten-
tional favor they had thrown in my way.

Knowing that the application of Generals Sherman and Sheridan
and the other officers referred to would meet with a favorable reply
from the authorities at Washington, I at once telegraphed to General
Sheridan that I would start to join him by the next train, not intending
to wait the official order which I knew would be issued by the War
Department. The following day found me on a railway train hastening
to the plains as fast as the iron horse could carry me. The expected
order from Washington overtook me that day in the shape of an official telegram from the Adjutant-General of the Army, directing me
to proceed at once and report for duty to General Sheridan.

At Fort Leavenworth I halted in my journey long enough to cause
my horses to be shipped by rail to Fort Hays. Nor must I omit two

other faithful companions of my subsequent marches and campaigns, named Blucher and Maida, two splendid specimens of the Scotch staghound, who were destined to share the dangers of an Indian campaign and finally meet death in a tragic manner—the one by the hand of the savage, the other by an ill-directed bullet from a friendly carbine. Arriving at Fort Hays on the morning of the 30th, I found General Sheridan, who had transferred his headquarters temporarily from Fort Leavenworth to that point in order to be nearer the field of operations, and better able to give his personal attention to the conduct of the coming campaign. My regiment was at that time on or near the Arkansas River in the vicinity of Fort Dodge, and about three easy marches from Fort Hays. After remaining at General Sheridan's headquarters one day and receiving his instructions, I set out with a small escort across the country to Fort Dodge to resume command of my regiment. Arriving at Fort Dodge without incident, I found General Sully, who at that time was in command of the district in which my regiment was serving. With the exception of a few detachments, the main body of the regiment was encamped on Bluff Creek, a small tributary of the Arkansas, the camp being some thirty miles southeast from Fort Dodge. I had scarcely assumed command when a band of Indians dashed close up to our camp and fired upon us. This was getting into active service quite rapidly. I was in the act of taking my seat for dinner, my ride having given me a splendid relish for the repast, when the shouts and firing of the savages informed me that more serious duties were at hand. Every man flew to arms and almost without command rushed to oppose the enemy. Officers and men provided themselves with rifles or carbines, and soon began delivering a deliberate but ineffective fire against the Indians. The latter, as usual, were merely practising their ordinary *ruse de guerre*, which was to display a very small venturesome force in the expectation of tempting pursuit by an equal or slightly superior force, and, after having led the pursuing force well away from the main body, to surround and destroy it by the aid of overwhelming numbers, previously concealed in a ravine or ambush until the proper moment. On this occasion the stratagem did not succeed. The Indians, being mounted on their fleetest ponies, would charge in single file past our camp, often riding within easy carbine range of our men, displaying great boldness and unsurpassable horsemanship. The soldiers, unaccustomed to firing at such rapidly moving objects, were rarely able to inflict serious damage upon their enemies. Occasionally a pony would be struck and brought to the ground, but the rider always succeeded in being carried away upon the pony of a comrade. It was interesting to witness their marvellous abilities as horsemen; at the same time one could not but admire the courage they displayed. The ground was level, open, and unobstructed; the troops were formed in an irregular line of skirmishers dismounted, the line extending a distance of perhaps two hundred yards. The Indians had a rendezvous behind a hillock on the right, which prevented them from being seen or disturbed by the soldiers. Starting out singly, or by twos and threes, the warriors would suddenly leave the cover of the hillock, and with war whoops and taunts dash over the plain in a line parallel to that occupied by the soldiers, and within easy carbine range of the latter. The pony seemed possessed of the designs and wishes of his dusky rider, as he seemed to fly unguided by bridle, rein, or spur. The warrior would fire and load and fire again as often as he was able to do, while dashing along through the shower of leaden bullets fired above, beneath, in front, and behind him by the excited troopers, until finally, when the aim of the latter improved and the leaden messengers whistled uncomfortably close, the warrior would be seen to cast himself over on the opposite side of his pony, until his foot on the back and his face under the neck of the pony were all that could be seen, the rest of his person being completely covered by the body of the pony. These maneuvers would frequently deceive the recruits among the soldiers; having fired probably about the time the warrior was seen to disappear, the recruit would shout exultingly and call the attention of his comrades to his lucky shot. The old soldiers, however, were not so easily deceived and afterwards would remind their less experienced companion of the terrible fatality of his shots.

Another affair occurred about the same time, but in a different direction from camp. One of the officers, who was commanding a troop, concluded one day that it would be safe to grant permission to a part of his command to leave camp for the purpose of hunting buffalo and obtaining fresh meat for the men. The hunting party, being strong enough to protect itself against almost any ordinary war party of Indians that might present itself, left camp at an early hour in the morning and set out in the direction in which the buffalo were reported to be. The forenoon passed away, noon came, and still no signs of

Killing buffalo for pleasure

the return of the hunters. The small hours of the afternoon began to come and go, and still no tidings from the hunters, who were expected to return to camp after an absence of two or three hours. The officer to whose troop they belonged, and who was of an exceedingly nervous temperament, began to regret having accorded them permission to leave camp, knowing that Indians had been seen in the vicinity. The hunting party had gone by a route across the open country that carried them up a long but very gradual ascent of perhaps two miles, beyond which, on the level plain, the buffalo were supposed to be herding in large numbers. Anxious to learn something concerning the whereabouts of his men, and believing he could obtain a view of the country beyond which might prove satisfactory, the officer, whose suspense was constantly increasing, determined to mount his horse and ride to the summit of the ridge beyond which his men had disappeared in the morning. Taking no escort with him, he leisurely rode off, guided by the trail made by the hunters. The distance to the crest proved much further than it had seemed to the eye before starting. A ride of over two miles had to be made before the highest point was reached, but once there the officer felt well repaid for his exertion, for in the dim deceptions of a beautiful mirage he saw what to him was his hunting party leisurely returning toward camp. Thinking they were still a long distance from him and would not reach him for a considerable time, he did what every prudent cavalryman would have done under similar circumstances—dismounted to allow his horse an opportunity to rest. At the same time he began studying the extended scenery. The camp, seen nestling along the banks of the creek at the base of the ridge, appeared as a pleasant relief to the monotony of the view, which otherwise was undisturbed. Having scanned the horizon in all directions, he turned to watch the approach of his men; when, behold! Instead of his own trusty troopers returning laden with the fruits of the chase, the mirage had disappeared, and he saw a dozen well-mounted warriors riding directly toward him at full speed. They were still far enough away to enable him to mount his horse and have more than an even chance to outstrip them in the race to camp. But no time was to be thrown away; the beauties of natural scenery had, for the time at least, lost their attraction. Camp never seemed so inviting before. Heading his horse toward camp and gathering the reins in one hand and holding his revolver in the other, the officer set out to make his escape. Judgment had to be employed in riding this race, for the distance being fully two miles before a place of safety could be reached, his horse, not being high-bred and accustomed to going such a distance at full speed, might, if forced too rapidly at first, fail before reaching camp. Acting upon this idea, a tight rein was held and as much speed kept in reserve as safety would permit. This enabled the Indians to gain on the officer, but at no time did he feel that he could not elude his pursuers. His principal anxiety was confined to the character of the ground, care being taken to avoid the rough and broken places. A single misstep or a stumble on the part of his horse, and his pursuers would be upon him before he could rise. The sensations he experienced during that flying ride could not have been enviable. Soon the men in camp discerned his situation and, seizing their carbines hastened out to his assistance. The Indians were soon driven away and the officer again found himself among his friends. The hunters also made their appearance shortly after, well supplied with game. They had not found the buffalo as near camp as they had expected, and after finding them were carried by a long pursuit in a different direction from that taken by them in the morning. Hence their delay in returning to camp.

This and similar occurrences, added to the attack made by the Indians on the camp the afternoon I joined, proved that unless we were to consider ourselves as actually besieged and were willing to accept the situation, some decisive course must be adopted to punish the Indians for their temerity. No offensive measures had been attempted since the infantry and cavalry forces of General Sully had marched up the hill and then, like the forces of the king of France, had marched down again. The effect of this movement, in which the Indians gained a decided advantage, was to encourage them in their attempts to annoy and disturb the troops, not only by prowling about camp in considerable numbers and rendering it unsafe, as has been seen, to venture beyond the chain of sentinels, but by waylaying and intercepting all parties passing between camp and the base of supplies at Fort Dodge. Knowing, from my recent interview with General Sheridan, that activity was to characterize the future operations of the troops, particularly those of the cavalry, and that the sooner a little activity was exhibited on our part the sooner perhaps might we be freed from the aggressions of the Indians, I returned from the afternoon skirmish to my tent and decided to begin offensive movements that same night, as soon as darkness should conceal the march of the troops. It was deemed most prudent, and to promise greatest chance of success, to make these movements at night, as during the hours of daylight the Indians no doubt kept close watch over everything transpiring in the vicinity of camp, and no scouting party could have taken its departure in daylight unobserved by the watchful eyes of the savages. Four separate detachments were at once ordered to be in readiness to move immediately after dark. Each detachment numbered about one hundred cavalry well mounted and well armed. Guides who knew the country well were assigned to each, and each party was commanded and accompanied by zealous and efficient officers. The country was divided into four sections, and to each detachment was assigned one of the sections, with orders to thoroughly scout the streams running through it. It was hoped that some of these parties might, if in no other way, stumble upon a campfire or other indication of the rendezvous of the Indians; but subsequent experience only confirmed in the opinion that Indians seldom, if ever, permit hostile parties to stumble upon them unless the stumblers are the weaker party. Before proceeding further in my narrative I will introduce to the reader a personage who is destined to appear at different intervals, and upon interesting occasions, as the campaign proceeds. It is usual on the plains, and particularly during time of active hostilities, for every detachment of troops to be accompanied by one or more professional scouts or guides. These guides are employed by the government at a rate of compensation far in excess of that paid to the soldiers, some of the most experienced receiving pay about equal to that of a subaltern in the line. They constitute a most interesting as well as useful and necessary portion of our frontier population. Who they are, whence they come or whither they go, their names even, except such as they choose to adopt or which may be given them, are all questions which none but themselves can answer. As their usefulness to the service depends not upon the unravelling of either of these mysteries, but little thought is bestowed upon them. "Do you know the country thoroughly?" and "Can you speak any of the Indian languages?" constitute the only examination which civil or uncivil service reform demands on the plains. If the evidence on these two important points is satisfactory, the applicant for a vacancy in the corps of scouts may consider his position as secured, and the door to congenial employment, most often leading to a terrible death, opens before him. They are almost invariably men of very superior judgment or common sense, with education generally better than that of the average frontiersman. Their most striking characteristics are love of adventure; a natural and cultivated knowledge of the country without recourse to maps; deep hatred of the Indian; an intimate acquaintance with all the habits and customs of the latter, whether pertaining to peace or war; and last but most necessary to their calling, skill in the use of firearms and in the management of a horse. The possessor of these qualifications, and more than the ordinary amount of courage, may feel equal to discharge the dangerous and trying duties of a scout. In concentrating the calvary, which had hitherto been operating in small bodies, it was found that each detachment brought with it the scouts who had been serving with them. When I joined the command I found quite a number of these scouts attached to various parts of the command, but for the purposes of organization it was deemed best to unite them into a separate detachment under command of one of their own number. Being unacquainted personally with the merits or demerits of any of them, the selection of a chief had necessarily to be made somewhat at random. There was one among their number whose appearance would have attracted the notice of any casual observer. He was a man about forty years of age, perhaps older, over six feet in height, and possessing a well-proportioned frame. His head was covered with a luxuriant crop of long, almost black hair, strongly inclined to curl, and so long as to fall carelessly over his shoulders. His face, at least so much of it as was not concealed by the long, waving brown beard and moustache, was full of intelligence and pleasant to look upon. His eye was undoubtedly handsome, black and lustrous, with an expression of kindness and mildness combined. On his head was generally to be seen, whether asleep or awake, a huge sombrero or black slouch hat. A soldier's overcoat with its large circular cape, a pair of trousers with the legs tucked in the top of his long boots, usually constituted the outside make-up of the man whom I selected as chief scout. He was known by the euphonious title of "California Joe," no other name seemed ever to have been given him, and no other name ever seemed necessary. His military armament consisted of a long breech-loading Springfield musket, from which he was inseparable, and a revolver and hunting-knife, both the latter being carried in his waist-belt. His mount completed his equipment for the field, being instead of a horse a finely-formed mule, in whose speed and endurance he had every confidence. Scouts usually prefer a good mule to a horse, and wisely too, for the reason that in making their perilous journeys, either singly or by twos or threes, celerity is one principal condition to success. The object with the scout is not to outrun or overwhelm the Indians, but to avoid both by secrecy and caution in his movements. On the plains at most seasons of the year the horse is incapable of performing long or rapid journeys without being supplied with forage on the route. This must be transported, and in the case of scouts would necessarily be transported on the back of the horse, thereby adding materially to the weight that must be carried. The mule will perform a rapid and continuous march without forage, being able to subsist on the grazing to be obtained in nearly all the valleys on the plains during the greater portion of the year. California Joe was an inveterate smoker, and was rarely seen without his stubby, dingy-looking brierwood pipe in full blast. The endurance of his smoking powers was only surpassed by his loquacity. His pipe frequently became exhausted and required refilling, but California Joe seemed never to lack for material or disposition to carry on a conversation, principally composed of personal adventures among the Indians, episodes in mining life, or experience in overland journeying before the days of steam engines and palace cars rendered a trip across the plains a comparatively uneventful one. It was evident from the scraps of information volunteered from time to time that there was but little of the Western country from the Pacific to the Missouri River with which

California Joe was not intimately acquainted. He had lived in Oregon years before, and had become acquainted from time to time with most of the officers who had served on the plains or on the Pacific Coast.

As the four detachments already referred to were to move as soon as it was dark, it was desirable that the scouts should be at once organized and assigned. So, sending for California Joe, I informed him of his promotion and what was expected of him and his men. After this official portion of the interview had been completed, it seemed proper to Joe's mind that a more intimate acquaintance between us should be cultivated, as we had never met before. His first interrogatory, addressed to me in furtherance of this idea, was frankly put as follows: "See hyar, Gineral, in order that we hev no misonderstandin', I'd jest like to ask ye a few questions." Seeing that I had somewhat of a character to deal with, I signified my perfect willingness to be interviewed by him. "Are you an ambulance man ur a hoss man?" Pretending not to discover his meaning, I requested him to explain. "I mean do you b'leve in catchin' Injuns in ambulances or on hossback?" Still assuming ignorance, I replied, "Well, Joe, I believe in catching Indians wherever we can find them, whether they are found in ambulances or on horseback." This did not satisfy him. "That ain't what I'm drivin' at. S'pose you're after Injuns and really want to hev a tussle with 'em, would ye start after 'em on hossback, or would ye climb into an ambulance and be haulded after 'em? That's the pint I'm headin' fur." I answered, "I would prefer the method on horseback provided I really desired to catch the Indians; but if I wished them to catch me, I would adopt the ambulance system of attack." This reply seemed to give him complete satisfaction. "You've hit the nail squar on the hed. I've bin with 'em on the plains whar they started out after the Injuns on wheels, jist as ef they war goin' to a town funeral in the States, an' they stood 'bout as many chances uv catchin' Injuns az a six-mule team wud uv catchin' a pack of thievin' Ki-o-tees, jist as much. Why that sort uv work is only fun fur the Injuns; they don't want anything better. Ye ort to've seen how they peppered it to us, an' we a doin' nuthin' a' the time. Sum uv 'em wuz 'fraid the mules war goin' to stampede and run off with the train an' all our forage and grub, but that wuz impossible; fur besides the big loads uv corn an' bacon an' baggage the wagons hed in them, thar war from eight to a dozen infantry men piled into them besides. Ye ort to hev heard the quartermaster in charge uv the train tryin' to drive the infantry men out of the wagons and git them into the fight. I 'spect he wuz an Irishman by his talk, fur he sed to them, 'Git out uv thim wagons, git out uv thim wagons; yez 'll hev me tried fur disobadience uv ordhers fur marchin' tin min in a wagon whin I've ordhers but fur ait!'"

How long I might have been detained listening to California Joe's recital of incidents of first campaigns, sandwiched here and there by his peculiar but generally correct ideas of how to conduct an Indian campaign properly, I do not know; time was limited, and I had to remind him of the fact to induce him to shorten the conversation. It was only deferred, however, as on every occasion thereafter California Joe would take his place at the head of the column on the march, and his nearest companion was made the receptacle of a fresh installment of Joe's facts and opinions.

What were the chances of success to the four detachments that had departed on this all night's ride? Next to nothing. Still, even if no Indians could be found, the expeditions would accomplish this much: They would leave their fresh trails all over the country within a circuit of twenty miles of our camp, trails which the practised eyes of the Indians would be certain to fall upon in daylight, and inform them for the first time that an effort was being made to disturb them if nothing more.

Three of the scouting columns can be disposed of now by the simple statement that they discovered no Indians, nor the remains of any camps or lodging places indicating the recent presence of a war party on any of the streams visited by them. The fourth detachment was the one that California Joe had accompanied as scout. What a feather it would be in his cap if, after the failure of the scouts accompanying the other columns to discover Indians, the party guided by him should pounce upon the savages, and by a handsome fight settle a few of the old scores charged against them!

The night was passing away uninterrupted by any such event, and but a few hours more intervened before daylight would make its appearance. The troops had been marching constantly since leaving camp; some were almost asleep in their saddles when the column was halted, and word was passed along from man to man that the advance guard had discovered signs indicating the existence of Indians near at hand. Nothing more was necessary to dispel all sensations of sleep and to place every member of the command on the alert.

It was difficult to ascertain from the advance guard, consisting of a non-commissioned officer and a few privates, precisely what they had seen. It seemed that in the valley beyond, into which the command was about to descend, and which could be overlooked from the position the troops then held, something unusual had been seen by the leading troopers just as they had reached the crest. What this mysterious something was, or how produced, no one could tell; it appeared simply for a moment, and then only as a bright flash of light of varied colors; how far away it was impossible to determine in the heavy darkness of the night. A hasty consultation of the officers took place at the head of the column, when it was decided that in the darkness which then reigned, it would be unwise to move to the attack of an enemy until something more was known of the numbers and position of the foe. As the moon would soon rise and dispel one of the obstacles to conducting a careful attack, it was determined to hold the troops in readiness to act upon a moment's notice, and at the same time send a picked party of men, under guidance of California Joe, to crawl as close to the supposed position of the Indians as possible, and gather all the information available. But where was California Joe all this time? Why was he not at the front where his services would be most likely in demand? Search was quietly made for him all along both flanks of the column, but on careful inquiry it seemed that he had not been seen for some hours, and then at a point many miles from that at which the halt had been ordered. This was somewhat remarkable, and admitted of no explanation—unless, perhaps, California Joe had fallen asleep during the march and been carried away from the column; but this theory gained no supporters. His absence at this particular time, when his advice and services might prove so invaluable, was regarded as most unfortunate. However, the party to approach the Indian camp was being selected when a rifle shot broke upon the stillness of the scene, sounding in the direction of the mysterious appearance which had first attracted the attention of the advanced troopers. Another moment, and the most powerful yells and screams rose in the same direction, as if a terrible conflict was taking place. Every carbine was advanced ready for action, each trigger was carefully sought, no one as yet being able to divine the cause of this sudden outcry, when in a moment who should come charging wildly up to the column, now dimly visible by the first rays of the moon, but California Joe, shouting and striking wildly to the right and left as if beset by a whole tribe of warriors. Here, then, was the solution of the mystery. Not then, but in a few hours, everything was rendered clear. Among the other traits or peculiarities of his character, California Joe numbered an uncontrollable fondness for strong drink; it was his one great weakness—a weakness to which he could only be kept from yielding by keeping all intoxicating drink beyond his reach. It seemed, from an after development of the affair, that the sudden elevation of California Joe, unsought and unexpected as it was, to the position of chief scout was rather too much good fortune to be borne by him in a quiet or undemonstrative manner. Such a profusion of greatness had not been thrust upon him so often as to render him secure from being affected by his preferment. At any rate he deemed the event deserving of celebration—professional duties to the contrary notwithstanding—and before proceeding on the night expedition had filled his canteen with a bountiful supply of the worst brand of whiskey, such as is only attainable on the frontier. He, perhaps, did not intend to indulge to that extent which might disable him from properly performing his duties; but in this, like many other good men whose appetites are stronger than their resolutions, he failed in his reckoning. As the liquor which he imbibed from time to time after leaving camp began to produce the natural or unnatural effect, Joe's independence greatly increased until the only part of the expedition which he recognized as at all important was California Joe. His mule, no longer restrained by his hand, gradually carried him away from the troops, until the latter were left far in the rear. This was the relative position when the halt was ordered. California Joe, having indulged in drink sufficiently for the time being, concluded that the next best thing would be a smoke; nothing would be better to cheer him on his lonely night ride. Filling his ever present brierwood with tobacco, he next proceeded to strike a light, employing for this purpose a storm or tempest match; it was the bright and flashing colors of this which had so suddenly attracted the attention of the advance guard. No sooner was his pipe lighted than the measure of his happiness was complete, his imagination picturing him to himself, perhaps, as leading in a grand Indian fight. His mule by this time had turned toward the troops, and when California Joe set up his unearthly howls, and began his imaginary charge into an Indian village, he was carried at full speed straight to the column where his good fortune alone prevented him from receiving a volley. His blood was up, and all efforts to quiet or suppress him proved unavailing, until finally the officer in command was forced to bind him hand and foot, and in this condition secured him on the back of his faithful mule. In this sorry plight the chief scout continued until the return of the troops to camp, when he was transferred to the tender mercies of the guard as a prisoner for misconduct. Thus ended California Joe's career as chief scout. Another was appointed in his stead, but we must not banish him from our good opinion yet. As a scout, responsible only for himself, he will reappear in these pages with a record that redounds to his credit.

Nothing was accomplished by the four scouting parties except, perhaps, to inspire the troops with the idea that they were no longer to be kept acting merely on the defensive, while the Indians, no doubt, learned the same fact, and at the same time. The cavalry had been lying idle, except when attacked by the Indians, for upward of a month. It was reported that the war parties, which had been so troublesome for some time, came from the direction of Medicine Lodge Creek, a stream running in the same general direction as Bluff Creek, and about two marches from the latter in a northeasterly direction. It was on this stream—Medicine Lodge Creek—that the great peace council had been held with all the southern tribes with whom we had been and were then at war, the government being represented at the council Senators and other members of Congress, officers high in rank in the army, and prominent gentlemen selected from the walks of civil life. The next move, after the unsuccessful attempt in which California Joe created the leading sensation, was to transfer the troops across from Bluff Creek to Medicine Lodge Creek, and to send scouting parties up and down the latter in search of our enemies. This movement was made soon after the return of the four scouting expeditions sent out from Bluff Creek. As our first day's march was to be a short one, we did not break camp on Bluff Creek until a late hour in the morning. Soon everything was in readiness for the march, and like a travelling village of Bedouins, the troopers and their train of supplies stretched out into a column. First came the cavalry, moving in a column of fours; Next came the immense wagon train, containing the tents, forage, rations, and extra ammunition of the command, a very necessary but unwieldy portion of a mounted military force. Last of all came the rear guard, usually consisting of about one company. On this occasion it was the company commanded by the officer whose narrow escape from the Indians while in search of a party of his men

The Indian manner of war.

who had gone buffalo hunting has been already described in this chapter. The conduct of the Indians on this occasion proved that they had been keeping an unseen but constant watch on everything transpiring in or about camp. The column had scarcely straightened itself out in commencing the march, and the rear guard had barely crossed the limits of the deserted camp, when out from a ravine near by dashed a war party of fully fifty well-mounted, well-armed warriors. Their first onslaught was directed against the rear guard, and a determined effort was made to drive them from the train, and thus place the latter at their mercy, to be plundered of its contents. After disposing of flankers, for the purpose of resisting any efforts that might be made to attack the train from either flank, I rode back to where the rear guard were engaged to ascertain if they required reinforcements. At the same time orders were given for the column of troops and train to continue the match, as it was not intended that so small a party as that attacking us should delay our march by any vain effort on our part to ride them down, or overhaul them, when we knew they could outstrip us if the contest was to be decided by a race. Joining the rear guard, I had an opportunity to witness the Indian mode of fighting in all its perfection. Surely no race of men, not even the famous Cossacks, could display more wonderful skill in feats of horsemanship than the Indian warrior on his native plains, mounted on his well-trained war pony, voluntarily running the gauntlet of his foes, drawing and receiving the fire of hundreds of rifles, and in return sending back perfect shower of arrows, or, more likely still, well-directed shots from some souvenir of a peace commission in the shape of an improved breech-loader. The Indian warrior is capable of assuming positions on his pony, the latter at full speed, which no one but an Indian could maintain for a single moment without being thrown to the ground. The pony, of course, is perfectly trained, and seems possessed of the spirit of his rider. An Indian's wealth is most generally expressed by the number of his ponies. No warrior or chief is of any importance or distinction who is not the owner of a herd of ponies numbering from twenty to many hundreds. He has for each special purpose a certain number of ponies, those that are kept as pack animals being the most inferior in quality and value; then the ordinary riding ponies used on the march or about camp, or when visiting neighboring villages; next in consideration is the "buffalo pony," trained to the hunt, and only employed when dashing into the midst of the huge buffalo herds, when the object is either food from the flesh or clothing and shelter for the lodges to be made from the buffalo hide; last, or rather first, considering its value and importance, is the "war pony," the favorite of the herd, fleet of foot, quick in intelligence, and full of courage. It may be safely asserted that the first place in the heart of the warrior is held by his faithful and obedient war pony.

Indians are extremely fond of bartering, and are not behindhand in catching the points of a good bargain. They will sign treaties relinquishing their lands, and agree to forsake the burial ground of their forefathers; they will part, for due consideration, with their bow and arrows, and their accompanying quiver, handsomely wrought in dressed furs; their lodges even may be purchased at not an unfair valuation, and it is not an unusual thing for a chief or warrior to offer to exchange his wife or daughter for some article that may have taken his fancy. This is no exaggeration; but no Indian of the plains has ever been known to trade, sell, or barter away his favorite war pony. To the warrior, his battle horse is as the apple of his eye. Neither love nor money can induce him to part with it.

The officer in command of the rear guard expressed the opinion that he could resist successfully the attacks of the savages until a little later, when it was seen that the latter were receiving accessions to their strength and were becoming correspondingly bolder and more difficult to repulse, when a second troop of cavalry was brought from the column, as a support to the rear guard. These last were ordered to fight on foot, their horses, in charge of every fourth trooper, being led near the train. The men, being able to fire so much more accurately when on foot, compelled the Indians to observe greater caution in their manner of attack. Once a warrior was seen to dash out from the rest in the peculiar act of "circling," which was simply to dash along in front of the line of troopers, receiving their fire and firing in return. Suddenly his pony, while at full speed, was seen to fall to the ground, showing that the aim of at least one of the soldiers had been effective. The warrior was thrown over and beyond the pony's head, and his capture by the cavalry seemed a sure and easy matter to be accomplished. I saw him fall, and called to the officer commanding the troop that had remained mounted to gallop forward and secure the Indian. The troop advanced rapidly, but the comrades of the fallen Indian had also witnessed his mishap and were rushing to his rescue. He was on his feet in a moment, and the next moment another warrior, mounted on the fleetest of ponies, was at his side, and with one leap the dismounted warrior placed himself astride the pony of his companion; and thus doubly burdened, the gallant little steed, with his no less gallant riders, galloped lightly away, with about eighty cavalrymen, mounted on strong domestic horses, in full cry after them.

The combined strength and resistance of two full troops of cavalry were required to defend the train from the vigorous and dashing attacks of the Indians, but our march was not delayed. At last, finding that the command was not to be diverted from its purpose, or hindered in completing its regular march, the Indians withdrew, leaving us to proceed unmolested. These contests with the Indians, while apparently yielding the troops no decided advantage, were of the greatest value in view of future and more extensive operations against the savages. Many of the men and horses were far from being familiar with actual warfare, particularly of this irregular character. Some of the troopers were quite inexperienced as horsemen, and still more inexpert in the use of their weapons, as their inaccuracy of fire when attempting to bring down an Indian within easy range clearly proved. Their experience, resulting from these daily contests with the red men, was to prove of incalculable benefit and fit them for the duties of the coming campaign. Our march was completed to Medicine Lodge Creek, where a temporary camp was established, while scouting parties were sent both up and down the stream as far as there was the least probability of finding Indians. The party, consisting of three troops, which scouted down the valley of Medicine Lodge Creek, proceeded down to the point where was located and then standing the famous "medicine lodge," an immense structure erected by the Indians, and used by them as a council house, where once in each year the various tribes of the southern plains were wont to assemble in mysterious conclave to consult the Great Spirit as to the future, and to offer up rude sacrifices and engage in imposing ceremonies, such as were believed to be appeasing and satisfactory to the Indian Deity. In the conduct of these strange and interesting incantations, the presiding or directing personages are known among the Indians as "medicine men." They are the high priests of the red man's religion, and in their peculiar sphere are superior in influence and authority to all others in the tribe, not excepting the head chief. No important step is proposed or put in execution, whether relating to war or peace, even the probable success of a contemplated hunt, but is first submitted to the powers of divination confidently believed to be possessed by the medicine man of the tribe. He, after a series of enchantments, returns the answer supposed to be prompted by the Great Spirit, as to whether the proposed step is well advised and promises success or not. The decisions given by the medicine men are supreme and admit of no appeal. The medicine lodge just referred to had been used as the place of assembly of the grand council held between the warlike tribes and the representatives of the government. The medicine lodge was found in a deserted but well-preserved condition. Here and there, hanging overhead, were collected various kinds of herbs and plants, vegetable offerings no doubt to the Great Spirit; while, in strange contrast to these peaceful specimens of the fruits of the earth, were trophies of the war path and the chase, the latter being represented by the horns and dressed skins of animals killed in the hunt, some of the skins being beautifully ornamented in the most fantastic of styles peculiar to the Indian idea of art. Of the trophies relating to war, the most prominent were human scalps, representing all ages and sexes of the white race. These scalps, according to the barbarous custom, were not composed of the entire covering of the head, but of a small surface surrounding the crown, and usually from three to four inches in diameter, constituting what is termed the scalp lock. To preserve the scalp from decay, a small hoop of about double the diameter of the scalp is prepared from a small withe, which grows on the banks of some of the streams in the West. The scalp is placed inside the hoop, and properly stretched by a network of thread connecting the edges of the scalp with the circumference of the hoop. After being properly cured, the dried fleshy portion of the scalp is ornamented in bright colors, according to the taste of the captor, sometimes the addition of beads of bright and varied colors being made to heighten the effect. In other instances the hair is dyed, either to a beautiful yellow or golden, or to crimson. Several of these horrible evidences of past depredations upon the defenceless inhabitants of the frontier, or overland emigrants, were brought back by the troopers on their return from their scout. Old trails of small parties of Indians were discovered, but none indicating the recent presence of war parties in that valley were observable. The command was then marched back to near its former camp on Bluff Creek, from whence, after a sojourn of three or four days, it marched to a point on the north bank of the Arkansas River, about ten miles below Fort Dodge, there to engage in earnest preparation and reorganization for the winter campaign, which was soon to be inaugurated, and in which the Seventh Cavalry was to bear so prominent a part. We pitched our tents on the banks of the Arkansas on the 21st of October, 1868, there to remain usefully employed until the 12th of the following month, when we mounted our horses, bade adieu to the luxuries of civilization, and turned our faces toward the Wichita Mountains in the endeavor to drive from their winter hiding places the savages who had during the past summer waged such ruthless and cruel war upon our exposed settlers on the border.

Expedition in the snow

Lessons Learned—Seventh Cavalry Re-Organized— Expedition in the Snow—Battle of the Washita

In concluding to go into camp for a brief period on the banks of the Arkansas, two important objects were in view: First, to devote the time to refitting, reorganizing, and renovating generally that portion of the command which was destined to continue active operations during the inclement winter season; second, to defer our movement against the hostile tribes until the last traces of the fall season had disappeared and winter in all its bitter force should be upon us. We had crossed weapons with the Indians time and again during the mild summer months, when the rich verdure of the valleys served as bountiful and inexhaustible granaries in supplying forage to their ponies, and the immense herds of buffalo and other varieties of game roaming undisturbed over the Plains supplied all the food that was necessary to subsist the war parties, and at the same time allow their villages to move freely from point to point; and the experience of both officers and men went to prove that in attempting to fight Indians in the summer season we were yielding to them the advantages of climate and supplies—we were meeting them on ground of their own selection, and at a time when every natural circumstance controlling the result of a campaign was wholly in their favor; and as a just consequence the troops, in nearly all these contests with the red men, had come off second best. During the grass season nearly all Indian villages are migratory, seldom remaining longer than a few weeks at most in any one locality, depending entirely upon the supply of grass; when this becomes exhausted the lodges are taken down, and the entire tribe or band moves to some other point, chosen with reference to the supply of grass, water, wood, and game. The distance to the new location is usually but a few miles. During the fall, when the buffaloes are in the best condition to furnish food, and the hides are suitable to be dressed as robes, or to furnish covering for the lodges, the grand annual hunts of the tribes take place, by which the supply of meat for the winter is procured. This being done, the chiefs determine upon the points at which the village shall be located; if the tribe is a large one, the village is often subdivided, one portion or band remaining at one point, other portions choosing localities within a circuit of thirty or forty miles. Except during seasons of the most perfect peace, and when it is the firm intention of the chiefs to remain on friendly terms with the whites at least during the winter and early spring months, the localities selected for their winter resorts are remote from the military posts and frontier settlements, and the knowledge that might lead to them carefully withheld from every white man. Even during a moderate winter season, it is barely possible for the Indians to obtain sufficient food for their ponies to keep the latter in anything above a starving condition. Many of the ponies actually die from want of forage, while the remaining ones become so weak and attenuated that it requires several weeks of good grazing in the spring to fit them for service—particularly such service as is required from the war ponies. Guided by these facts, it was evident that if we chose to avail ourselves of the assistance of so exacting and terrible an ally as the frosts of winter—an ally who would be almost as uninviting to friends as to foes—we might deprive our enemy of his points of advantage, and force him to engage in a combat in which we should do for him what he had hitherto done for us; compel him to fight upon ground and under circumstances of our own selection. To decide upon making a winter campaign against the Indians was certainly in accordance with that maxim in the art of war which directs one to do that which the enemy neither expects nor desires to be done. At the same time it would dispel the old-fogy idea, which was not without supporters in the army, and which was confidently relied on by the Indians themselves, that the winter season was an insurmountable barrier to the prosecution of a successful campaign. But aside from the delay which was necessary to be submitted to before the forces of winter should produce their natural but desired effect upon our enemies, there was much to be done on our part before we could be ready to cooperate in an offensive movement.

The Seventh Cavalry, which was to operate in one body during the coming campaign, was a comparatively new regiment, dating its existence as an organization from July 1866. The officers and companies had not served together before with much over half their full force. A large number of fresh horses were required and obtained; these had to be drilled. All the horses in the command were to be newly shod, and an extra fore and hind shoe fitted to each horse; these, with the necessary nails, were to be carried by each trooper in the saddle pocket. It has been seen that the men lacked accuracy in the use of their carbines. To correct this, two drills in target practice were ordered each day. The companies were marched separately to the ground where the targets had been erected, and, under the supervision of the troop officers, were practised daily in firing at targets placed one hundred, two hundred, and three hundred yards distant. The men had been previously informed that out of the eight hundred men composing the command, a picked corps of sharpshooters would be selected, numbering forty men, and made up of the forty best marksmen in the regiment. As an incentive to induce every enlisted man, whether non-commissioned officer or private, to strive for appointment in the sharpshooters, it was given out from headquarters that the men so chosen would be regarded, as they really would deserve to be, as the *élite* of the command; not only regarded as such, but treated with corresponding consideration. For example, they were to be marched as a separate organization, independently of the column, a matter which in itself is not so trifling as it may seem to those who have never participated in a long and wearisome march. Then again no guard or picket duty was to be required of the sharpshooters, which alone was enough to encourage every trooper to excel as a marksman. Besides these considerations, it was known that, should we encounter the enemy, the sharpshooters would be most likely to be assigned a post of honor, and would have superior opportunities for acquiring distinction and rendering good service. The most generous as well as earnest rivalry at once sprung up, not only between the various companies, as to which should secure the largest representation among the sharpshooters, but the rivalry extended to individuals of the same company, each of whom seemed desirous of the honor of being considered "one of the best shots."

At end of the period named, by taking the record of each trooper's target practice, I was enabled to select forty marksmen in whose ability to bring down any warrior, whether mounted or not, who might challenge us, as we had often been challenged before, I felt every confidence. They were a superb body of men, and felt the greatest pride in their distinction. A sufficient number of non-commissioned officers, who had proven their skill as marksmen, were included in the organization—among them, fortunately, a first sergeant, whose expertness in the use of any firearm was well established throughout the command. I remember having seen him, while riding at full speed, bring down four buffaloes by four consecutive shots from his revolver. When it is remembered that even experienced hunters are usually compelled to fire half a dozen shots or more to secure a single buffalo, this statement will appear the more remarkable. The forty sharpshooters being supplied with their complement of sergeants and corporals, and thus constituting an organization by themselves, only lacked one important element, a suitable commander—a leader who, aside from being a thorough soldier, should possess traits of character that would not only enable him to employ skilfully the superior abilities of those who were to constitute his command, but at the same time feel that *esprit de corps* (the spirit of the group) that is so necessary to both officers and soldiers when success is to be achieved. Fortunately, in my command were a considerable number of young officers, nearly all of whom were full of soldierly ambition, and eager to grasp any opportunity that opened the way to honorable preferment. The difficulty was not in finding an officer properly qualified in every way to command the sharpshooters, but, among so many who I felt confident would render a good account of themselves if assigned to that position, to designate a leader *par excellence.* The choice fell upon Colonel Cook, a young officer whose acquaintance the reader will remember to have made in connection with the plucky fight he had with the Indians near Fort Wallace the preceding summer. Colonel Cook, at the breaking out of the rebellion, although then but a lad of sixteen years, entered one of the New York cavalry regiments, commencing at the foot of the ladder. He served in the cavalry arm of the service throughout the war, participating in Sheridan's closing battles near Richmond, his services and gallantry resulting in his promotion to the rank of lieutenant-colonel. While there were many of the young officers who would have been pleased if they instead of another had been chosen, there was no one in the command, perhaps, who did not regard the selection as a most judicious one. Future events only confirmed this judgment.

After everything in the way of reorganization and refitting that might be considered actually necessary had been ordered, another step—bordering on the ornamental perhaps, although in itself useful—was taken. This was what is termed in the cavalry "coloring the horses," which does not imply, as might be inferred from the expression, that we actually changed the color of our horses, but merely classified or arranged them throughout the different squadrons and troops according to the color. Hitherto the horses had been distributed to the various companies of the regiment indiscriminately, regardless of color, so that in each company and squadron horses were found of every color. For uniformity of appearance it was decided to devote one afternoon to a general exchange of horses. The troop commanders were assembled at headquarters and allowed, in the order of their rank, to select the color they preferred. This being done, every public horse in the command was led out and placed in line: the grays collected at one point, the bays—of which there was a great preponderance in numbers—at another, the blacks at another, the sorrels by themselves; then the chestnuts, the blacks, the browns; and last of all came what were jocularly designated the "brindles," being the odds and ends so far as colors were concerned—roans and other mixed colors—the junior troop commander of course becoming the reluctant recipient of these last, valuable enough except as to color. The exchanges having been completed, the men of each troop led away to their respective picket or stable lines their newly-acquired chargers. It was surprising to witness what a great improvement in the handsome appearance of the command was effected by this measure. The change when first proposed had not been greeted with much favor by many of the troopers who by long service and association in times of danger had become warmly attached to their horses; but the same reasons that had endeared the steed to the soldier in the one instance, soon operate in the same manner to render the new acquaintances fast friends.

Among the other measures adopted for carrying the war to our enemy's doors, and in a manner "fight the devil with fire," was the employment of Indian allies. These were to be procured from the "reservation Indians," tribes who, from engaging in long and devastating wars with the whites and with other hostile bands, had become so reduced in power as to be glad to avail themselves of the protection and means of subsistence offered by the reservation plan. These tribes were most generally the objects of hatred in the eyes of their more powerful and independent neighbors of the Plains, and the latter, when making their raids and bloody incursions upon the white settlements of the frontiers, did not hesitate to visit their wrath equally upon whites and reservation Indians. To these smaller tribes it was a welcome opportunity to be permitted to ally themselves to the forces of the government, and endeavor to obtain that satisfaction which acting alone they were powerless to secure. The tribes against which we proposed to operate during the approaching campaign had been particularly cruel and relentless in their wanton attacks upon the Osages and Kaws, two tribes living peaceably and contentedly on well-chosen reservations in southwestern Kansas and the northern portion of the Indian Territory. No assistance in fighting the hostile tribes was desired, but it was believed, and correctly too, that in finding the enemy and in discovering the location of his winter hiding places, the experience and natural tact and cunning of the Indians would be a powerful auxiliary if we could enlist them in our cause. In addition to the monthly rate of compensation which the government agreed to give them, they were also to be armed, clothed, and mounted at government expense.

Advices from General Sheridan's headquarters, then at Fort Hays, Kansas, were received early in November, informing us that the time for resuming active operations was near at hand, and urging the early completion of all preliminaries looking to that end. To use Fort

Dodge as our base of supplies, and keep open to that point our long line of communications, would have been, considering the character of the country and that of the enemy to be encountered, an impracticable matter with our force. To remedy this a temporary base was decided upon, to be established about one hundred miles south of Fort Dodge, at some point yet to be determined, from which we could obtain our supplies during the winter. With this object in view, an immense train, consisting of about four hundred army wagons, was loaded with forage, rations, and clothing, for the supply of the troops composing the expedition. A guard composed of a few companies of infantry was detailed to accompany the trains and to garrison the point that was to be selected as the new base of supplies. Everything being in readiness, the cavalry moved from its camp on the north bank of the Arkansas on the morning of the 12th of November, and after fording the river began its march toward the Indian Territory. That night we encamped on Mulberry Creek, where we were joined by the infantry and the supply train. General Sully, commanding the district, here took active command of the combined forces. Much anxiety existed in the minds of some of the officers, lest the Indians should attack us while on the march, when, hampered as we should be in the protection of so large a train of wagons, we might fare badly. The country over which we were to march was favorable to us, as we were able to move our trains in four parallel columns formed close together. This arrangement shortened our flanks and rendered them less exposed to attack.

Nothing occurred giving us any clue as to the whereabouts of Indians until we had been marching several days and were moving down the valley of Beaver Creek, when our Indian guides discovered the trail of in Indian war party, numbering, according to their estimate, from 100 to 150 warriors, mounted and moving in a northeasterly direction. The trail was not over twenty-four hours old, and by following it to the point where it crossed Beaver Creek, almost the exact numbers and character of the party could be determined from the fresh signs at the crossing. Everything indicated that it was a war party sent from the very tribes we were in search of, and the object, judging from the direction they had been moving, and other circumstances, was to make a raid on the settlements in Western Kansas. As soon as we had reached camp for the night, I requested that I might be permitted to take the cavalry belonging to the expedition, leaving the trains to be guarded by the infantry, whose numbers were ample for this purpose, and with the Indian scouts as trailers set out early the next morning, following the trail of the war party, not in the direction taken by them, as this would be an idle attempt, but in the direction from which they came, expressing the conviction that such a course would in all probability lead us direct to the villages of the marauders, which was the ultimate object of the movement we were thus engaged in. By doing so, we might be able to strike a prompt blow against our enemies and visit swift punishment upon the war party, whose hostile purposes were but too evident. In these views I was sustained by the opinions of our Indian allies, who expressed confidence in their ability to take the trail and follow it back to the villages. The officer to whom my application was submitted, and whose sanction was necessary before I could be authorized to execute my proposed plan, returned an elaborate argument attempting to prove that no successful results could possibly attend the undertaking I had suggested, and ended with the remark that it was absurd to suppose for one moment that a large military force such as ours and accompanied by such an immense train of wagons, could move into the heart of the Indian country and their presence remain undiscovered by the watchful savages for even a single day. This specious reasoning sounded well—read well—but it gave no satisfaction to the men and officers of the cavalry, all of whom thought they saw a fine opportunity neglected. However, we shall strike this trail again, but on different ground and under different circumstances. Great as was our temporary disappointment at being restrained, the result satisfied all of us that, for very different reasons from those adduced to withhold us from making the proposed movement, all, as the sequel proved, was for the best. On the sixth day after leaving our camp on the north bank of the Arkansas, the expedition arrived at the point that was chosen as our future base, where the infantry were to remain and erect quarters for themselves and storehouses for the military supplies. The point selected—which was then given the name it now bears, Camp Supply—was in the angle formed by Wolf and Beaver Creeks, about one mile above the junction of these two streams.

Within two or three days of our arrival the hearts of the entire command were gladdened by the sudden appearance in our midst of strong reinforcements. These reinforcements consisted of General Sheridan and staff. Hearing of his near approach, I mounted my horse and was soon galloping beyond the limits of camp to meet him. If there were any persons in the command who hitherto had been in doubt as to whether the proposed winter campaign was to be a reality or otherwise, such persons soon had cause to dispel all mistrust on this point. Selecting from the train a sufficient number of the best teams and wagons to transport our supplies of rations and forage, enough to subsist the command for a period of thirty days, our arrangements were soon completed by which the cavalry, consisting of eleven companies and numbering between eight and nine hundred men, were ready to resume the march. In addition we were to be accompanied by a detachment of scouts, among the number being California Joe. Our Indian allies from the Osage tribe, headed by Little Beaver and Hard Rope, also joined us.

After remaining at Camp Supply six days, nothing was required but the formal order directing the movement to commence. This came in the shape of a brief letter of instructions from Department headquarters. Of course, as nothing was known positively as to the exact whereabouts of the Indian villages, the instructions had to be general in terms. In substance, I was to march my command in search of the winter hiding places of the hostile Indians, and wherever found to administer such punishment for past depredations as my force was able to. On the evening of November 22nd, orders were issued to be in readiness to move promptly at daylight the following morning.

Alas! some of our number were destined never to return. It began snowing the evening of the 22nd, and continued all night, so that when the shrill notes of the bugle broke the stillness of the morning air at reveille on the 23rd, we awoke at four o'clock to find the ground covered with snow to a depth of over one foot, and the storm still raging in full force. Surely this was anything but an inviting prospect as we stepped from our frail canvas shelters and found ourselves standing in the constantly and rapidly increasing depth of snow which appeared in every direction. "How will this do for a winter campaign?" was the half sarcastic query of the adjutant, as he came trudging back to the tent through a field of snow extending almost to the top of his tall troop boots, after having received the reports of the different companies at reveille. "Just what we want," was the reply.

It still lacked some minutes of daylight when the various commanders reported their commands in readiness to move, save the final act of saddling the horses, which only arrested the signal sounds of the chief bugler at headquarters. "Boots and saddles" rang forth, and each trooper grasped his saddle, and the next moment was busily engaged arranging and disposing of the few buckles and straps upon which the safety of his seat and the comfort of his horse depended. While they were thus employed, my horse being already saddled and held near by, by the orderly, I improved the time to gallop through the darkness across the narrow plain to the tents of General Sheridan, and say good-by. I found the headquarter tents wrapped in silence, and at first imagined that no one was yet stirring except the sentinel in front of the General's tent, who kept up his lonely tread, apparently indifferent to the beating storm. But I had no sooner given the bridlerein to my orderly than the familiar tones of the General called out, letting me know that he was awake, and had been an attentive listener to our notes of preparation. His first greeting was to ask what I thought about the snow and the storm. To which I replied that nothing could be more to our purpose. We could move and the Indian villages could not. If the snow only remained on the ground one week, I promised to bring the General satisfactory evidences that my command had met the Indians. With an earnest injunction from my chief to keep him informed, if possible, should anything important occur, and many hearty wishes for a successful issue to the campaign, I bade him adieu. The band took its place at the head of the column, preceded by the guides and scouts, and when the march began it was to the familiar notes of that famous old marching tune, "The Girl I Left Behind Me."

The snow continued to descend in almost blinding clouds. Even the appearance of daylight aided us but little in determining the direction of our march. So dense and heavy were the falling lines of snow that all view of the surface of the surrounding country, upon which the guides depended to enable them to run their course, was cut off. None of the command except the Indian guides had ever visited the route we desired to follow, and they were forced to confess that until the storm abated sufficiently to permit them to catch glimpses of the landmarks of the country, they could not undertake to guide the troops to the point where we desired to camp that night. Here was a serious obstacle encountered quite early in the campaign.

The point at which we proposed to encamp for the night was on Wolf Creek, only some twelve or fifteen miles from Camp Supply, it not being intended that our first day's progress should be very great.

There was but one course to pursue now that the guides could no longer conduct us with certainty and that was to be guided—like the mariner in mid-ocean—by the never-failing compass. There are few cavalry officers but what carry a compass in some more or less simple form. Mine was soon in my hand, and having determined as accurately as practicable, from my knowledge of the map of the country, the direction in which we ought to move in order to strike Wolf Creek at the desired camping ground, I became for the time guide to the column. And after marching until about 2 PM, we reached the valley of Wolf Creek, where a resting place for the night was soon determined. There was still no sign of abatement on the part of the weather. Timber was found along the banks of the creek in ample quantity to furnish us with fuel, but so imbedded in snow as to render the prospect of a campfire very remote and uncertain. Our march of fifteen miles through the deep snow and blinding storm had been more fatiguing to our horses than an ordinary march of thirty miles would have been. Our wagons were still far in rear. While they were coming up, every man in the command, officers as well as enlisted men, set briskly to work in gathering a good supply of wood, as our personal comfort in camp in such weather would be largely dependent on the quality and quantity of our firewood. Fallen and partly seasoned trees were in great demand, and, when discovered in the huge beds of snow, were soon transformed, under the vigorous blows of a score of axes, into available fuel. It was surprising as well as gratifying to witness the contentment and general good humor everywhere prevailing throughout the command. Fires were soon blazing upon the grounds assigned to the different troops, and upon the arrival of the wagons, which occurred soon after, the company cooks were quickly engaged in preparing the troopers' dinner, while the servants of the officers were employed in a similar manner for the benefit of the latter. While the cooks were so engaged, officers and men were busily occupied in pitching the tents, an operation which under the circumstances was most difficult to perform satisfactorily. So rapidly did the large flakes continue to fall that the most energetic efforts of two persons were insufficient to keep the ground properly clear.

Tents up at last, dinner was not long in being prepared, and even less time employed in disposing of it. A good cup of strong coffee went far toward reconciling us to everything that had but a few moments before appeared somewhat uninviting. By this time a cheerful fire was blazing in the centre of our tent; my comfortable bed of buffalo robes was prepared on a framework of strong boughs, and with my ever-faithful dogs lying near me, I was soon reclining in a state of comparative comfort, watching the smoke as it ascended through the narrow apex of the tent, there to mingle with the descending flakes of snow. In regard to the storm still prevailing outside, and which in itself or its effects we were to encounter the following morning and for an indefinite period thereafter, I consoled myself with the reflection that to us it was as an unpleasant remedy for the removal of a still more unpleasant disease. If the storm seemed terrible to us, I believed it would prove to be even more terrible to our enemies, the Indians. Promptly at the appointed hour, four o'clock the following morning, camp was bustling and active in response to the bugle notes of reveille. The storm had abated, the snow had ceased falling, but that which had fallen during the previous twenty-four hours now covered the ground to a depth of upward of eighteen inches. The sky was clear, however, or, to adopt the expressive language of California Joe, "the travellin' was good overhead."

All of the second day we continued to march up the valley of the stream we had chosen as our first camping ground. The second night we encamped under circumstances very similar to those which attended us the first night, except that the storm no longer disturbed us. The snow did not add to our discomfort particularly, save by increasing the difficulty of obtaining good and sufficient fuel. Our purpose was to strike the Canadian River in the vicinity of "Antelope Hills," which are famous and prominent landmarks in that region, and then be governed in our future course by circumstances. Resuming the march at daylight on the morning of the third day, our route still kept us in the valley of Wolf Creek. Nothing was particularly worthy of notice during our third day's march, except the immense quantities of game to be seen seeking weak shelter from the storm offered by the little strips of timber extending along the valleys of Wolf Creek and its tributaries. Even the buffalo, with their huge, shaggy coats—sufficient, one would imagine, to render the wearer indifferent to the blasts of winter—were frequently found huddled together in the timber, and so drowsy or benumbed from the effects of the cold as to not discover our approach until we were within easy pistol range. Seeing a fine herd of young buffaloes a short distance in the advance, I determined to test the courage of my staghounds Blucher and Maida.

Approaching as near the herd as possible before giving them the alarm, I managed to single out and cut off from the main herd a fine yearling bull. My horse, a trained hunter, was soon alongside, but I was unable to use my pistol to bring the young buffalo down, as both the dogs were running close to either side, resolutely attacking him and endeavoring to pull him down. It was a new experience to them; a stag they could easily have mastered, but a lusty young buffalo bull was an antagonist of different calibre. So determined had the dogs become, their determination strengthened no doubt by the occasional vigorous blows received from the ready hoofs of the buffalo, that I could not call them off; neither could I render them assistance from my pistol, for fear of injuring them. There was nothing left for me to do but to become a silent—although far from disinterested participant in the chase. The immense drifts of snow through which we were struggling at our best pace would soon vanquish one or the other of the party; it became a question of endurance simply, and the buffalo was the first to come to grief. Finding escape by running impossible, he boldly came to bay and faced his pursuers; in a moment both dogs had grappled with him as if he had been a deer. Blucher seized him by the throat, Maida endeavored to secure a firm hold on the shoulders. The result was that Blucher found himself well trampled in snow, and but for the latter would have been crushed to death. Fearing for the safety of my dogs, I leaped, drawing my hunting knife and watching a favorable opportunity, I succeeded in cutting the hamstrings of the buffalo, which had the effect to tumble him over in the snow, where I was enabled to despatch him with my pistol.

If any prowling bands or war parties belonging to either of the tribes with which we were at war were moving across the Canadian in either direction, it was more than probable that their crossing would be made at some point above us, and not more than ten or fifteen miles distant. The season was rather far advanced to expect any of these parties to be absent from the village, but the trail of the war party, discovered by our Indian guides just before the expedition reached Camp Supply, was not forgotten, and the heavy storm of the past few days would be apt to drive them away from the settlements and hasten their return to their village. We had every reason to believe that the latter was located somewhere south of the Canadian. After discussing the matter with Little Beaver and Hard Rope, and listening to the suggestions of California Joe and his confrères, I decided to start a strong force up the valley of the Canadian at daybreak the following morning, to examine the banks and discover, if possible, if Indians had been in the vicinity since the snow had fallen. Three full troops of cavalry under Major Joel H. Elliot, Seventh Cavalry, were ordered to move without wagons or *otro impedimento* (other impediments), each trooper to carry one hundred rounds of ammunition, one day's rations, and forage. Their instructions were to proceed up the north bank of the Canadian a distance of fifteen miles. If any trail of Indians was discovered, pursuit was to be taken up at once, at the same time sending information of the fact back to the main command, indicating the number and character of the Indians as determined by their trail, and particularly the direction in which they were moving, in order that the main body of the troops might endeavor if possible to intercept the Indians. In the mean time I informed Major Elliot that as soon as it was fairly daylight I would commence crossing the main command over the Canadian—an operation which could not be performed hastily, as the banks were almost overflowing, the current being very rapid and the water filled with floating snow and ice. After making the crossing I would, in the absence of any reports from him, march up the bluffs forming Antelope Hills and strike nearly due south, aiming to encamp that night on one of the small streams forming the headwaters of the Washita River, where we would again unite the two portions of the command and continue our march to the south.

Major Elliot was a very zealous officer, and daylight found him and his command on the march in the execution of the duty to which they had been assigned. Those of us who remained behind were soon busily occupied in making preparations to effect a crossing of the Canadian. California Joe had been engaged since early dawn searching for a ford which would be practicable for our wagons; the troopers and horses could cross almost anywhere. A safe fording place barely practicable was soon reported, and the cavalry and wagon train began moving over.

One by one the huge army wagons, with their immense white covers, began the long ascent which was necessary to overcome before attaining the level of the plains. As fast as they reached the high ground the leading wagons were halted and parked to await the arrival of the last to cross the river. In the mean time the cavalry had closed up and dismounted, except the rear guard, which was just then to be seen

approaching from the river, indicating that "everything was closed
up." I was about to direct the chief bugler to sound "To horse," when
far in the distance, on the white surface of the snow, I descried a
horseman approaching us as rapidly as his tired steed could carry him.
The direction was that in which Elliot's command was supposed to be,
and the horseman approaching could be none other than a messenger
from Elliot. "What tidings would he bring?" was my first thought.
Perhaps Elliot could not find a ford by which to cross the Canadian,
and simply desired instructions as to what his course should be. Perhaps he has discovered an Indian trail—a fresh one; but it must be
fresh if one at all, as the snow is scarcely three days old. If a trail has
been discovered, then woe unto the luckless Indians whose footprints
are discoverable in the snow; for so long as that remains and the endurance of men and horses holds out, just so long will we follow that
trail, until the pursuer and pursued are brought face to face, or the one
or the other succumbs to the fatigues and exhaustion of the race. By
means of my field glass I was able to make out the familiar form of
"Corbin," one of the scouts. After due waiting, when minutes seemed
like hours, the scout galloped up to where I was waiting, and in a few
hurried, almost breathless words, informed me that Elliot's command,
after moving up the north bank of the Canadian about twelve miles,
had discovered the trail of an Indian war party numbering upwards of
150 strong; that the trail was not twenty-four hours old, and the party
had crossed the Canadian and taken a course a little east of south.
Elliot had crossed his command, and at once taken up the pursuit as
rapidly as his horses could travel. Here was news, and of a desirable
character. I asked the scout if he could overtake Elliot if furnished
with a fresh horse. He thought he could. A horse was at once supplied
him, and he was told to rejoin Elliot as soon as possible, with instructions to continue the pursuit with all possible vigor, and I would move
with the main command in such direction as to strike his trail about
dark. If the Indians changed their general direction, he was to inform
me of the fact; and if I could not overtake him by eight o'clock that
night, Elliot was to halt his command and await my arrival, when the
combined force would move as circumstances might determine. My
resolution was formed in a moment, and as quickly put in train of execution. The bugle summoned all the officers to report at once. There
was no tardiness on their part, for while they had not heard the report
brought in by the scout, they had witnessed his unexpected arrival and

his equally sudden departure—circumstances which told them plainer than mere words that something unusual was in the air. The moment they were all assembled about me I acquainted them with the intelligence received from Elliot, and at the same time informed them that we would at once set out to join in the pursuit—a pursuit which could and would only end when we overtook our enemies. And in order that we should not be trammelled in our movements, it was my intention then and there to abandon our train of wagons, taking with us only such supplies as we could carry on our persons and strapped to our saddles. The train would be left under the protection of about eighty men detailed from the different troops, and under command of one officer, to whom orders would be given to follow us with the train as rapidly as the character of our route would permit. Each trooper was to carry with him one hundred rounds of ammunition, a small amount of coffee and hard bread, and on his saddle an equally small allowance of forage for his horse. Tents and extra blankets were to be left with the wagons. We were to move in light marching order as far as this was practicable. Then taking out my watch, the officers were notified that in twenty minutes from that time "the advance" would be sounded and the march in pursuit begun—the intervening time to be devoted to carrying out the instructions just given. In a moment every man and officer in the command was vigorously at work preparing to set out for a rough ride, the extent or result of which no one could foresee. Wagons were emptied, mess chests called upon to contribute from their stores, ammunition chests opened and their contents distributed to the troopers. The most inferior of the horses were selected to fill up the detail of eighty cavalry which was to remain and escort the train; an extra amount of clothing was donned by some who realized that when the bitter, freezing hours of night came we would not have the comforts of tents and campfire to sustain us. If we had looked with proper dread upon the discomforts of the past three days, the severity of the storm, the deep snow, and our limited facilities for withstanding the inclemencies of midwinter even when provided with shelter, food, and fire, what was the prospect now opened before us when we proposed to relinquish even the few comforts we had at command, and start out on a mission not only full of danger, but where food would be very limited, and then only of the plainest kind? Shelterless we should be in the midst of the wide, open plains, where the winds blow with greater force, and owing to our proximity to the Indians even fires would be too costly an aid to our comfort to be allowed. Yet these thoughts scarcely found a place in the minds of any members of the command. All felt that a great opportunity was before us, and to improve it only required determination and firmness on our part.

Before proceeding to narrate the incidents of the pursuit which led us to the Battle of the Washita, I will refer to the completion of our hasty preparations to detach ourselves from the encumbrance of our immense wagon train. Where or when it would again join us no one could foretell; in all probability, however, not until the pursuit had terminated and we had met and vanquished our savage foes, or had been defeated by them. Under existing orders, the guard for the protection of our train was each day under the command of the officer of the day, the tour of duty of the latter continuing twenty-four hours, beginning in the morning. On that day the duties of officer of the day fell in regular routine upon Captain Louis McLane Hamilton, Seventh Cavalry, a grandson of Alexander Hamilton. Of course this detail would require him to remain behind with the train while his squadron, one of the finest in the command, would move forward to battle under charge of another. To a soldier of Hamilton's pride and ambition, to be left behind in this inglorious manner was galling in the extreme. He foresaw the situation at once, and the moment that intelligence of the proposed movement reached him he came galloping up from the rear in search of me. I was busily engaged at the time superintending the hurried arrangements for commencing the pursuit. Coming up to me, with a countenance depicting the most earnest anxiety, his first words were to frame an inquiry as to whether I intended him to remain behind. Fully appreciating his anxious desire to share with his comrades the perils of the approaching conflict, and yet unable to substitute, without injustice, another officer for him unless with the consent of the former, I could not give him the encouragement he desired. The moment that the plans for pursuit were being formed, I remembered that the accidents of service were to deprive the pursuing column of the presence and aid of one whose assistance in such an emergency could always be confidently relied upon. Some of his brother officers had bethought themselves of the same, and at once came to me with the remark that "we ought to have Hamilton with us." My only reply was that while my desires were all one way, my duty prescribed that Hamilton should remain with the guard and train, it being his detail, and it also being necessary that some officer should remain upon this important duty. I answered his repeated request, that while I desired him in command of his squadron, particularly then of all times, I was powerless to have it so without being unjust to some other officer. While forced to admit this to be true, he added, "It seems hard that I must remain." Finally I said to him that all I could do would be to allow him to get some other officer to willingly take his place with the train, adding that some officer might be found in the command who, from indisposition or other causes, did not feel able to undertake a rapid and tiresome pursuit such as we would probably have, and under such circumstances I would gladly order the change. He at once departed in search of someone who would assume his duties with the train and leave him free to resume his post at the head of his splendid squadron—that squadron in whose organization and equipment he had displayed such energy and forethought, and whose superior excellency and efficiency long bore the impress of his hand. I am thus minute in detailing these circumstances affecting the transfer of Captain Hamilton from one duty to another, as the sad sequel will show how intimately connected the destiny of one of the parties was with the slight matter of this change. Hamilton had been absent but a few minutes when he returned overflowing with joy, and remarked that an officer had been found who consented to take his place, ending with the question, "Shall I join my squadron?" To this I gladly assented, and he galloped to another part of the field, where his men were, to hasten and superintend their preparations for the coming struggle.

During all this time Elliot with his three companies of cavalry was following hard and fast upon the trail left by the Indians in the deep snow. By being informed, as we were, of the direction in which the trail was leading, and that direction being favorable to our position, the main command by moving due south would strike the trail of the Indians, and of Elliot also, at some point not far in rear perhaps of Elliot's party. Everything being in readiness to set out at the expiration of the allotted twenty minutes, "the advance" was sounded and the pursuit on our part began. Our route carried us across the broad, open plains, the snow over a foot in depth, with surface of course unbroken. This rendered it exceedingly fatiguing to the horses moving in the advance, and changes were frequently rendered necessary. The weather, which during the past few days had been so bitterly cold, moderated on that day sufficiently to melt the upper surface of the snow. After leaving the wagon train, we continued our march rapidly during the remaining hours of the forenoon and until the middle of the afternoon. Still no tidings from Elliot's party nor any sign of a trail. No halt was made during the day either for rest or refreshment. Toward evening we began to feel anxious concerning Elliot's detachment. Could it be that the Indians had discovered that they were pursued, and had broken up into smaller parties or changed the direction of their trail? If so, could Elliot's messengers reach us in time to make the information valuable to us? We had hurried along, our interest increasing with each mile passed over, until the sun was not more than one hour high above the western horizon; and still, strain our eyes as we would, and scan the white surface of the plains in every direction in our front, the snow seemed unbroken and undisturbed as far as the eye could reach. Our scouts and Indian guides were kept far out in front and on the proper flank, to discover, if possible, the trail. At last one of the scouts gave the signal that the trail had been discovered, and in a few moments the command had reached it, and we were now moving with lighter and less anxious hearts. After studying the trail our Osage warriors informed us that the Indians whose trail we were pursuing were undoubtedly a war party, and had certainly passed where we then were during the forenoon. This was encouraging, and a free rein was given to our horses as we hastened along through the snow. The object now was to overtake as soon as practicable the party of Elliot, which from the heavy trail we could see was in advance of us. The almost level and unbroken character of the country enabled us to see for miles in all directions, and in this way we knew that Elliot must be many miles ahead of our party. At the same time I could see that we were gradually descending into a valley, probably of some stream, and far in advance appeared the dim outline of timber, such as usually fringes the banks of many of the Western streams. Selecting a few well-mounted troopers and some of the scouts, I directed them to set out at a moderate gallop to overtake Elliot, with orders to the latter to halt at the first favorable point where wood and water could be obtained, and await our arrival, informing him at the same time that after allowing the men an hour to prepare a cup of coffee and to feed and rest their horses, it was my intention to continue the pursuit during the night—a measure to which I felt urged by the slight thawing of the snow that day, which might result in our failure if we permitted the Indians to elude us until the snow had disappeared. Satisfied now that we were on the right course, our anxiety lessened, but our interest increased. Soon after dark we reached the valley whose timbered surface we had caught faint glimpses of hours before. Down this valley and through this sparse timber the trail led us. Hour after hour we struggled on, hoping to overtake the three troops in advance, for hunger, unappeased since before day-light, began to assert its demands in the strongest terms. Our faithful horses were likewise in great need of both food and water, as well as rest, as neither had been offered them since four o'clock in the morn-ing. So far had Elliot pushed his pursuit that our scouts were a long time in reaching him, and it was nine o'clock at night when the main command arrived at the point where he and his three troops were found halted. A stream of good water with comparatively deep banks ran nearby, while the valley at this point was quite heavily timbered.

To enable the men to prepare a cup of coffee, and at the same time give no evidence of our presence to the Indians, who, for all we knew, might be not far from us, advantage was taken of the deep banks of the creek, and by building small fires down under the edge of the bank, they were prevented from being seen, except at a small distance. At the same time the horses were relieved of their saddles and unbit-ted, and a good feed of oats distributed to each. Officers and men were glad to partake of the same quality of simple fare that night, consisting only of a most welcome and refreshing cup of good strong coffee and a handful of army crackers—"hard tack." By waiting an hour we not only gained by rest and refreshment, but the light of the moon would then probably be sufficient to guide us on our night ride. When the hour had nearly expired, we began our preparations in the most quiet manner to resume the pursuit.

As soon as each troop was in readiness to resume the pursuit, the troop commander reported the fact at headquarters. Ten o'clock came and found us in our saddles. Silently the command stretched out its long length as the troopers filed off four abreast. First came two of our Osage scouts on foot; these were to follow the trail and lead the command; they were our guides, and the panther, creeping upon its prey, could not have advanced more cautiously or quietly than did these friendly Indians, as they seemed to glide rather than walk over the snow-clad surface. To prevent the possibility of the command coming precipitately upon our enemies, the two scouts were directed to keep three or four hundred yards in advance of all others; then

came, in single file, remainder of our Osage guides and the white
scouts—among the rest California Joe. With these I rode, that I might
be as near the advance guard as possible. The cavalry followed in
rear, at the distance of a quarter or half a mile; this precaution was
necessary, from the fact that the snow, which had thawed slightly during the day, was then freezing, forming a crust which, broken by the
tread of so many hundreds of feet, produced a noise capable of being heard at a long distance. Orders were given prohibiting even a
word being uttered above a whisper. No one was permitted to strike
a match or light a pipe—the latter a great deprivation to the soldier.
In this silent manner we rode mile after mile. Occasionally an officer
would ride by my side and whisper some inquiry or suggestion, but
aside from this our march was unbroken by sound or deed. At last we
discovered that our two guides in front had halted and were awaiting
my arrival. Word was quietly sent to halt the column until inquiry in
front could be made. Upon coming up with the two Osages we were
furnished an example of the wonderful and peculiar powers of the
Indian. One of them could speak broken English, and in answer to
my question as to "What is the matter?" he replied, "Me don't know,
but me smell fire." By this time several of the officers had quietly
ridden up, and upon being informed of the Osage's remark, each
endeavored, by sniffing the air, to verify or disprove the report. All
united in saying that our guide was mistaken. Some said he was probably frightened, but we were unable to shake the confidence of the
Osage warrior in his first opinion. I then directed him and his companion to advance even more cautiously than before, and the column,
keeping up the interval, resumed its march. After proceeding about
half a mile, perhaps further, again our guides halted, and upon coming up with them I was greeted with the remark, uttered in a whisper,
"Me told you so;" and sure enough, looking in the direction indicated,
were to be seen the embers of a wasted fire, scarcely a handful, yet
enough to prove that our guide was right, and to cause us to feel the
greater confidence in him. The discovery of these few coals of fire
produced almost breathless excitement. The distance from where we
stood was from seventy-five to a hundred yards, not in the line of our
march, but directly to our left, in the edge of the timber. We knew
at once that none but Indians, and they hostile, had built that fire.
Where were they at that moment? Perhaps sleeping in the vicinity of
the fire.

I called for a few volunteers to quietly approach the fire and discover whether there were Indians in the vicinity; if not, to gather such information as was obtainable as to their numbers and departure. All the Osages and a few of the scouts quickly dismounted, and with rifles in readiness and fingers on the triggers silently made their way to the nearest point of the timber, Little Beaver and Hard Rope leading the way. After they had disappeared in the timber they still had to pass over more than half the distance before reaching the fire. These moments seemed like hours, and those of us who were left sitting on our horses, in the open moonlight, and within easy range from the spot where the fire was located, felt anything but comfortable during this suspense. If Indians, as then seemed highly probable, were sleeping around the fire, our scouts would arouse them and we would be in fair way to be picked off without being in a position to defend ourselves. The matter was soon determined. Our scouts soon arrived at the fire and discovered it to be deserted. Again did the skill and knowledge of our Indian allies come in play. Had they not been with us we should undoubtedly have assumed that the Indians who had occasion to build the fire and those we were pursuing constituted one party. From examining the fire and observing the great number of pony tracks in the snow, the Osages arrived at a different conclusion, and were convinced that we were then on the ground used by the Indians for grazing their herds of ponies. The fire had been kindled by the Indian boys, who attend to the herding, to warm themselves by, and in all probability we were then within two or three miles of the village. I will not endeavor to describe the renewed hope and excitement that sprung up. Again we set out, this time more cautiously if possible than before, the command and scouts moving at a greater distance in rear.

In order to judge of the situation more correctly, I this time accompanied the two Osages. Silently we advanced, I mounted, they on foot, keeping at the head of my horse. Upon nearing the crest of each hill, as is invariably the Indian custom, one of the guides would hasten a few steps in advance and peer cautiously over the hill. Accustomed to this, I was not struck by observing it until once, when the same one who discovered the fire advanced cautiously to the crest and looked carefully into the valley beyond. I saw him place his hand above his eyes as if looking intently at some object, then crouch down and come creeping back to where I waited for him. "What is it?" I inquired as soon as he reached my horse's side. "Heaps Injuns down there," pointing in the direction from which he had just come. Quickly dismounting and giving the reins to the other guide, I accompanied the Osage to the crest, both of us crouching low so as not to be seen in the moonlight against the horizon. Looking in the direction indicated, I could indistinctly recognize the presence of a large body of animals of some kind in the valley below, and at a distance which then seemed not more than half a mile. I looked at them long and anxiously, the guide uttering not a word, but was unable to discover anything in their appearance different from what might be presented by a herd of buffalo under similar circumstances. Turning to the Osage, I inquired in a low tone why he thought there were Indians there. "Me heard dog bark," was the satisfactory reply. Indians are noted for the large number of dogs always found in their villages, but never accompanying their war parties. I waited quietly to be convinced; I was assured, but wanted to be doubly so. I was rewarded in a moment by hearing the barking of a dog in the heavy timber off to the herd, and soon after I heard the tinkling of a small bell; this convinced me that it was really the Indian herd I then saw, the bell being one worn around the neck of some pony who was probably the leader of the herd. I turned to retrace my steps when another sound was borne to my ear through the cold, clear atmosphere of the valley—it was the distant cry of an infant; and savages though they were, and justly outlawed by the number and atrocity of their recent murders and depredations on the helpless settlers of the frontier, I could not but regret that in a war such as we were forced to engage in, the mode and circumstances of battle would possibly prevent discrimination.

Leaving the two Osages to keep a careful lookout, I hastened back until I met the main party of the scouts and Osages. They were halted and a message sent back to halt the cavalry, enjoining complete silence, and directing every officer to ride to the point we then occupied. The hour was then past midnight. Soon they came, and after dismounting and collecting in a little circle, I informed them of what I had seen and heard; and in order that they might individually learn as much as possible of the character of the ground that location of the village, I proposed that all should remove their sabres, that their clanking might make no noise, and proceed gently to the crest and there obtain a view of the valley beyond. This was done; not a word was spoken until we crouched together and cast our eyes in the direction of the herd and village. In whispers I briefly pointed out everything that was to be seen, then motioned all to return to where we had left our sabres; then, standing in a group upon the ground or crust of snow, the plan of the attack was explained to all and each assigned his part. The general plan was to employ the hours between then and daylight to completely surround the village, and, at daybreak, or as soon as it was barely light enough for the purpose, to attack the Indians from all sides. The command, numbering, as has been stated, about eight hundred mounted men, was divided into four nearly equal detachments. Two of them set out at once, as they had each to make a circuitous march of several miles in order to arrive at the points assigned them from which to make their attack. The third detachment moved to its position about an hour before day, and until that time remained with the main or fourth column. This last, whose movements I accompanied, was to make the attack from the point from which we had first discovered the herd and village. Major Elliot commanded the column that moved around from our left to a position almost in rear of the village; while Colonel Thompson commanded the one which moved in a corresponding manner from our right to a position that was to connect with that of Major Elliot. Colonel Myers commanded the third column which was to take position in the valley and timber a little less than a mile to my right. By this disposition it was hoped to prevent the escape of every inmate of the village. That portion of the command which I proposed to accompany consisted of A, C, D, and K troops, Seventh Cavalry, the Osages and scouts, and Colonel Cook with his forty sharpshooters. Captain Hamilton commanded one of the squadrons, Colonel West the other. After the first two columns had departed for their posts—it was still four hours before the hour of attack—the men of the other two columns were permitted to dismount, but much intense suffering was unavoidably sustained. The night grew extremely cold towards morning; no fires of course could be permitted, and the men were even ordered to desist from stamping their feet and walking back and forth to keep warm, as the crushing of the snow beneath produced so much noise that it might give the alarm to our wily enemies.

After being satisfied that all necessary arrangements were made for the attack, I imitated the example of some of my comrades, and gathering the cavalry cape of my greatcoat about my head, lay down and slept soundly for perhaps an hour. At the end of that time I awoke, and on consulting my watch found there remained nearly two hours before we would move to the attack. Walking about among the horses and troopers, I found the latter generally huddled at the feet of the former in squads of three and four, in the endeavor to keep warm. Occasionally I would find a small group engaged in conversation, the muttered tones and voices strangely reminding me of those heard in the death-chamber. The officers had disposed of themselves in similar but various ways; here at one place were several stretched out together upon the snow, the body of one being used by the others as a pillow. Nearly all were silent; conversation had ceased, and those who were prevented by the severe cold from obtaining sleep were no doubt fully occupied in their minds with thoughts upon the morrow and the fate that might be in store for them.

I joined another group nearby, consisting of most of the white scouts. Here were California Joe and several of his companions. One of the latter deserves a passing notice. He was a low, heavy-set Mexican, with features resembling somewhat those of the Ethiopian— thick lips, depressed nose, and low forehead. He was quite a young man, probably not more than twenty-five years of age, but had passed the greater portion of his life with the Indians, had adopted their habits of life and modes of dress, and had married among them. Familiar with the language of the Cheyennes and other neighboring tribes, he was invaluable both as a scout and interpreter. His real name was Romero, but some of the officers of the command, with whom he was a sort of favorite, had dubbed him Romeo, and by this name he was always known, a sobriquet to which he responded as readily as if he had been christened under it.

The scouts, like nearly all the other members of the command, had been interchanging opinions as to the result of the movements of the following day. Addressing the group, I began the conversation with the question as to what they thought of the prospect of our having a fight. "Fight!" responded California Joe; "I havn't nary doubt concernin' that part uv the business; what I've been tryin' to get through my topknot all night is whether we'll run aginst more than we bargain fur." "Then you do not think the Indians will run away, Joe?" "Run away! How in creation can Injuns or anybody else run away when we'll have 'em clean surrounded afore daylight?" "Well, suppose then that we succeed in surrounding the village, do you think we can hold our own against the Indians?" "That's the very pint that's been botherin'

me ever since we planted ourselves down here, and the only conclusion I kin come at is that it's purty apt to be one thing or t'other; if we
pump these Injuns at daylight, we're either goin' to make a spoon or
spile a horn, an' that's my candid judgment, sure. One thing's certain,
ef them Injuns doesn't har anything uv us till we open on 'em at daylight, they'll be the most powerful 'stonished redskins that's been in
these parts lately—they will, sure. An' ef we git the bulge on 'em, and
keep puttin' it to 'em sort a lively like, we'll sweep the platter—thar
won't be nary trick left for 'em. As the deal stands now, we hold the
keerds and are holdin' over 'em; they've got to straddle our blind or
throw up their hands. Howsomever, thar's a mighty sight in the draw."

The night passed in quiet. I anxiously watched the opening signs of
dawn in order to put the column in motion. We were only a few hundred yards from the point from which we were to attack. The moon
disappeared about two hours before dawn, and left us enshrouded in
thick and utter darkness, making the time seem to drag even slower
than before.

At last faint signs of approaching day were visible, and I proceeded
to collect the officers, awakening those who slept. We were standing
in a group near the head of the column, when suddenly our attention
was attracted by a remarkable sight, and for a time we felt that the
Indians had discovered our presence. Directly beyond the crest of
the hill that separated us from the village, and in a line with the supposed location of the latter, we saw rising slowly but perceptibly, as
we thought, up from the village, and appearing in bold relief against
the dark sky as a background, something that we could only compare
to a signal rocket, except that its motion was slow and regular. All
eyes were turned to it in blank astonishment, and but one idea seemed
to be entertained, and that was that one or both of the two attacking column under Elliot or Thompson had encountered a portion
of the village, and this that we saw was the signal to other portions
of the band near at hand. Slowly and majestically it continued to rise
above the crest of the hill, first appearing as a small brilliant flaming
globe of bright golden hue. As it ascended still higher it seemed to
increase in size, to move more slowly, while its colors rapidly changed
from one to the other, exhibiting in turn the most beautiful combinations of prismatic tints. There seemed to be not the shadow of doubt
that we were discovered. The strange apparition in the heavens maintained its steady course upward. One anxious spectator, observing it

apparently at a standstill, exclaimed, "How long it hangs fire! Why don't it explode?" still keeping the idea of a signal rocket in mind. It had risen perhaps to the height of half a degree above the horizon as observed from our position, when, lo! the mystery was dispelled. Rising above the mystifying influences of the atmosphere, that which had appeared so suddenly before us, and excited our greatest apprehensions, developed into the brightest and most beautiful of morning stars. Often since that memorable morning have I heard officers remind each other of the strange appearance that had so excited our anxiety and alarm. In less perilous moments we probably would have regarded it as a beautiful phenomenon of nature, of which so many are to be witnessed through the pure atmosphere of the plains.

All were ordered to get ready to advance; not a word to officer or men was spoken above undertone. It began growing lighter in the east, and we moved forward toward the crest of the hill. Up to this time two of the officers and one of the Osages had remained on the hill overlooking the valley beyond, so as to detect any attempt at a movement on the part of the occupants of the village below. These now rejoined the troops. Colonel West's squadron was formed in line on the right, Captain Hamilton's squadron in line on the left, while Colonel Cook with his forty sharpshooters was formed in advance of the left, dismounted. Although the early morning air was freezing cold, the men were directed to remove their overcoats and haversacks, so as to render them free in their movements. Before advancing beyond the crest of the hill, strict orders were issued prohibiting the firing of a single shot until the signal to attack should be made. The other three detachments had been informed before setting out that the main column would attack promptly at daylight, without waiting to ascertain whether they were in position or not. In fact it would be impracticable to communicate with either of the first two until the attack began. The plan was for each party to approach as closely to the village as possible without being discovered, and there await the approach of daylight. The regimental band was to move with my detachment, and it was understood that the band should strike up the instant the attack opened. Colonel Myers, commanding the third party, was also directed to move one-half his detachment dismounted. In this order we began to descend the slope leading down to the village. The distance to the timber in the valley proved greater than it had appeared to the eye in the darkness of the night. We soon reached the outskirts of the herd of ponies. The latter seemed to recognize us as hostile parties and moved quickly away. The light of day was each minute growing stronger, and we feared discovery before we could approach near enough to charge the village. The movement of our horses over the crusted snow produced considerable noise, and would doubtless have led to our detection but for the fact that the Indians, if they heard it at all, presumed it was occasioned by their herd of ponies. I would have given much at that moment to know the whereabouts of the first two columns sent out. Had they reached their assigned positions, or had unseen and unknown obstacles delayed or misled them? These were questions that could not then be answered. We had now reached the level of the valley, and began advancing in line toward the heavy timber in which and close at hand we knew the village was situated.

Immediately in rear of my horse came the band, all mounted, and each with his instrument in readiness to begin playing the moment their leader, who rode at their head, and who kept his cornet to his lips, should receive the signal. I had previously told him to play "Garry Owen" as the opening piece. We had approached near enough to the village now to plainly catch a view here and there of the tall white lodges as they stood in irregular order among the trees. From the openings at the top of some of them we could perceive faint columns of smoke ascending, the occupants no doubt having kept up their feeble fires during the entire night. We had approached so near the village that from the dead silence which reigned I feared the lodges were deserted, the Indians having fled before we advanced. I was about to turn in my saddle and direct the signal for attack to be given—still anxious as to where the other detachments were—when a single rifle shot rang sharp and clear on the far side of the village from where we were. Quickly turning to the band leader, I directed him to give us "Garry Owen." At once the rollicking notes of that familiar marching and fighting air sounded forth through the valley, and in a moment were reëchoed back from the opposite sides by the loud and continued cheers of the men of the other detachments, who, true to their orders, were there and in readiness to pounce upon the Indians the moment the attack began. In this manner the Battle of the Washita commenced. The bugles sounded the charge, and the entire command dashed rapidly into the village. The Indians were caught napping; but realizing at once the dangers of their situation, they quickly overcame their first surprise and in an instant seized their rifles, bows, and arrows, and sprang behind the nearest trees, while some leaped into the stream, nearly waist deep, and using the bank as a rifle-pit, began a vigorous and determined defence. Mingled with the exultant cheers of my men could be heard the defiant war-whoop of the warriors, who from the first fought with a desperation and courage that no race of men could surpass. Actual possession of the village and its lodges was ours within a few moments after the charge was made, but this was an empty victory unless we could vanquish the late occupants, who were then pouring in a rapid and well-directed fire from their stations behind trees and banks. At the first onset a considerable number of the Indians rushed from the village in the direction from which Elliot's party had attacked. Some broke through the lines, while others came in contact with the mounted troopers and were killed or captured.

Before engaging in the fight, orders had been given to prevent the killing of any but the fighting strength of the village; but in a struggle of this character it is impossible at all times to discriminate, particularly when, in a hand-to-hand conflict, such as the one the troops were then engaged in, the squaws are as dangerous adversaries as the warriors, while Indian boys between ten and fifteen years of age were found as expert and determined in the use of the pistol and bow and arrow as the older warriors. Of these facts we had numerous illustrations. Major Benteen, in leading the attack of his squadron through the timber below the village, encountered an Indian boy, scarcely fourteen years of age; he was well mounted, and was endeavoring to makes his way through the lines. The object these Indians had in attempting this movement we were then ignorant of, but soon learned to our sorrow. This boy rode boldly toward the Major, seeming to invite a contest. His youthful bearing, and not being looked upon as a combatant, induced Major Benteen to endeavor to save him by making "peace signs" to him and obtaining his surrender, when he could be placed in a position of safety until the battle was terminated; but the young savage desired and would accept no such friendly concessions. He regarded himself as a warrior, and the son of a warrior, and as such he purposed to do a warrior's part. With revolver in hand he dashed at the Major, who still could not regard him as anything but a harmless lad. Levelling his weapon as he rode, he fired, but either from excitement or the changing positions of both parties, his aim was defective and the shot whistled harmlessly by Major Benteen's head. Another followed in quick succession, but with no better effect. All this time the dusky little chieftain boldly advanced, to lessen the distance between himself and his adversary. A third bullet was sped on its errand, and this time to some purpose, as it passed through the neck of the Major's horse, close to the shoulder. Making a final but ineffectual appeal to him to surrender, and seeing him still preparing to fire again, the Major was forced in self-defence to level his revolver and despatch him, although as he did so it was with admiration for the plucky spirit exhibited by the lad, and regret often expressed that no other course under the circumstance was left him.

As the Indians by this time had taken cover behind logs and trees, and under the banks of the stream that flowed through the centre of the village, from which stronghold it was impracticable to dislodge them by the use of mounted men, a large portion of the command was at once ordered to fight on foot, and the men were instructed to take advantage of the trees and other natural means of cover, and fight the Indians in their own style. Cook's sharpshooters had adopted this method from the first, and with telling effect. Slowly but

The Battle of the Wasmita

steadily the Indians were driven from behind the trees, and those who escaped the carbine bullets posted themselves with their companions who were already firing from the banks. One party of troopers came upon a squaw endeavoring to make her escape, leading by the hand a little white boy, a prisoner in the hands of the Indians, and who doubtless had been captured by some of their war parties during a raid upon the settlements. Who or where his parents were, or whether still alive or murdered by the Indians, will never be known, as the squaw, finding herself and prisoner about to be surrounded by the troops, and her escape cut off, determined, with savage malignity, that the triumph of the latter should not embrace the rescue of the white boy. Casting her eyes quickly in all directions, to convince herself that escape was impossible, she drew from beneath her blanket a huge knife and plunged it into the almost naked body of her captive. The next moment retributive justice reached her in the shape of a well-directed bullet from one of the troopers' carbines. Before the men could reach them life was extinct in the bodies of both the squaw and her unknown captive.

The desperation with which the Indians fought may be inferred from the following: Seventeen warriors had posted themselves in a depression in the ground, which enabled them to protect their bodies completely from the fire of our men, and it was only when the Indians raised their heads to fire that the troopers could aim with any prospect of success. All efforts to drive the warriors from this point proved abortive, and resulted in severe loss to our side. They were only vanquished at last by our men securing positions under cover and picking them off by sharpshooting as they exposed themselves to get a shot at the troopers. Finally the last one was despatched in this manner. In a deep ravine near the suburbs of the village the dead bodies of thirty-eight warriors were reported after the fight terminated. Many of the squaws and children had very prudently not attempted to leave the village when we attacked it, but remained concealed inside their lodges. All these escaped injury, although when surrounded by the din and wild excitement of the fight, and in close proximity to the contending parties, their fears overcame some of them, and they gave vent to their despair by singing the death song, a combination of weird-like sounds which were suggestive of anything but musical tones. As soon as we had driven the warriors from the village, and the fighting was pushed to the country outside, I directed Romeo, the interpreter, to go around to all the lodges and assure the squaws and children remaining in them that they would be unharmed and kindly cared for; at the same time he was to assemble them in the large lodges designated for that purpose, which were standing near the centre of the village. This was quite a delicate mission, as it was difficult to convince the squaws and children that they had anything but death to expect at our hands.

To our surprise we saw a small party of Indians collected on a knoll a little over a mile below the village, and in the direction taken by those Indians who had effected an escape through our lines at the commencement of the attack. My surprise was not so great at first, as I imagined that the Indians we saw were those who had contrived to escape, and having procured their ponies from the herd had mounted them and were then anxious spectators of the fight, which they felt themselves too weak in numbers to participate in. In the meantime the herds of ponies belonging to the village, on being alarmed by the firing and shouts of the contestants, had, from a sense of imagined security or custom, rushed into the village, where details of troopers were made to receive them. California Joe, who had been moving about in a promiscuous and independent manner, came galloping into the village, and reported that a large herd of ponies was to be seen nearby, and requested authority and some men to bring them in. The men were otherwise employed just then, but he was authorized to collect and drive in the herd if practicable. He departed on his errand, and I had forgotten all about him and the ponies, when in the course of half an hour I saw a herd of nearly three hundred ponies coming on the gallop toward the village, driven by a couple of squaws, who were mounted, and had been concealed nearby, no doubt; while bringing up the rear was California Joe, riding his favorite mule, and whirling about his head a long lariat, using it as a whip in urging the herd forward. He had captured the squaws while endeavoring to secure the ponies, and very wisely had employed his captives to assist in driving the herd. By this time the group of Indians already discovered outside our lines had increased until numbered upwards of a hundred. Examining them through my field glass, I could plainly perceive that they were all mounted warriors; not only that, but they were armed and caparisoned in full war costume, nearly all wearing the bright-colored war-bonnets and floating their lance pennants. Constant accessions to their numbers were to be seen arriving from beyond the hill on which they stood. All this seemed inexplicable. A few Indians might have escaped through our lines when the attack on the village began, but only few, and even these must have gone with little or nothing in their possession save their rifles and perhaps a blanket. Who could these new parties be, and from whence came they? To solve these troublesome questions I sent for Romeo, and taking him with me to one of the lodges occupied by the squaws, I interrogated one of the latter as to who were the Indians to be seen assembling on the hill below the village. She informed me, to a surprise on my part almost equal to that of the Indians at our sudden appearance at daylight, that just below the village we then occupied, and which was a part of the Cheyenne tribe, were located in succession the winter villages of all the hostile tribes of the southern plains with which we were at war, including the Arapahos, Kiowas, the remaining band of Cheyennes, the Comanches, and a portion of the Apaches; that the nearest village was about two miles distant, and the others stretched along through the timbered valley to the one furthest off, which was not over ten miles.

What was to be done?—for I needed no one to tell me that we were certain to be attacked, and that, too, by greatly superior numbers, just as soon as the Indians below could make their arrangements to do so; and they had probably been busily employed at these arrangements ever since the sound of firing had reached them the early morning, and been reported from village to village. Fortunately, affairs took a favorable turn in the combat in which we were then engaged, and the firing had almost died away. Only here and there where some warrior still maintained his position was the fight continued. Leaving as few men as possible to look out for these, I hastily collected and reformed my command, and posted them in readiness for the attack which we all felt was soon to be made; for already at different points and in more than one direction we could see more than enough warriors to outnumber us, and we knew they were only waiting the arrival of the chiefs and warriors from the lower villages before making any move against us. In the meanwhile our temporary hospital had been established in the centre of the village, where the wounded were receiving such surgical care as circumstances would permit. Our losses had been severe; indeed we were not then aware how great they had been. Hamilton, who rode at my side as we entered the village, and whose soldierly tones I heard for the last time as he calmly cautioned his squadron, "Now, men, keep cool, fire low, and not too rapidly," was among the first victims of the opening charge, having been shot from his saddle by a bullet from an Indian rifle. He died instantly. His lifeless remains were tenderly carried by some of his troopers to the vicinity of the hospital. Soon afterwards I saw four troopers coming from the front bearing between them, in a blanket, a wounded soldier; galloping to them, I discovered Colonel Barnitz, another troop commander, who was almost in a dying condition, having been shot by a rifle bullet directly through the body in the vicinity of the heart. Of Major Elliot, the officer second in rank, nothing had been seen since the attack at daylight, when he rode with his detachment into the village. He, too, had evidently been killed, but as yet we knew not where or how he had fallen. Two other officers had received wounds, while the casualties among the enlisted men were also large. The sergeant-major of the regiment, who was with me when the first shot was heard, had not been seen since that moment. We were not in as effective condition by far as when the attack was made, yet we were soon to be called upon to contend against a force immensely superior to the one with which we had been engaged during the early hours of the day. The captured herds of ponies were carefully collected inside our lines, and so guarded as to prevent their stampede or recapture by the Indians. Our wounded, and the immense amount of captured property in the way of ponies, lodges, etc., as well as our prisoners, were obstacles in the way of our attempting an offensive movement against the lower villages. To have done this would have compelled us to divide our forces, when it was far from certain that we could muster strength enough united to repel the attacks of the combined tribes. On all sides of us the Indians could now be seen in considerable numbers, so that from being the surrounding party, as we had been in the morning, we now found ourselves surrounded and occupying the position of defenders of the village. Fortunately for us, as the men had been expending a great many rounds, Major Bell, the quartermaster, who with a small escort was endeavoring to reach us with a fresh supply of ammunition, had by constant exertion and hard marching succeeded in doing so, and now appeared on the ground with several thousand rounds of carbine ammunition, a reinforcement greatly needed. He had no sooner arrived safely than the Indians attacked from the direction from which he came. How he had managed to elude their watchful eyes I never could comprehend, unless their attention had been so completely absorbed in watching our movements inside as to prevent them from keeping an eye out to discover what might be transpiring elsewhere.

Issuing a fresh supply of ammunition to those most in want of it, the fight soon began generally at all points of the circle. For such in reality had our line of battle become—a continuous and unbroken circle of which the village was about the centre. Notwithstanding the great superiority in numbers of the Indians, they fought with excessive prudence and a lack of that confident manner which they usually manifest when encountering greatly inferior numbers—a result due, no doubt, to the fate that had overwhelmed our first opponents. Besides, the timber and the configuration of the ground enabled us to keep our men concealed until their services were actually required. It seemed to be the design and wish of our antagonists to draw us away from the village; but in this they were foiled. Seeing that they did not intend to press the attack just then, about two hundred of my men were ordered to pull down the lodges in the village and collect the captured property in huge piles preparatory to burning. This was done in the most effectual manner. When everything had been collected the torch was applied, and all that was left of the village were a few heaps of blackened ashes. Whether enraged at the sight of this destruction or from other cause, the attack soon became general along our entire line, and pressed with so much vigor and audacity that every available trooper was required to aid in meeting these assaults. The Indians would push a party of well-mounted warriors close up to our lines in the endeavor to find a weak point through which they might venture, but in every attempt were driven back. I now concluded, as the village was off our hands and our wounded had been collected, that offensive measures might be adopted. To this end several of the squadrons were mounted and ordered to advance and attack the enemy wherever force sufficient was exposed to be a proper object of attack, but at the same time to be cautious as to ambuscades. Colonel Weir, who had succeeded to the command of Hamilton's squadron, Colonels Benteen and Myers with their respective squadrons, all mounted, advanced, and engaged the enemy. The Indians resisted every step taken by the troops, while every charge made by the latter was met or followed by a charge from the Indians, who continued to appear in large numbers at unexpected times and places. The squadrons acting in support of each other, and the men in each being kept well in hand, were soon able to force the line held by the Indians to yield at any point assailed. This being followed up promptly, the Indians were driven at every point and forced to abandon the field to us. Yet they would go no further than they were actually driven. It was now about three o'clock in the afternoon. I knew that the officer left in charge of the train and eighty men would push after us, follow our trail, and endeavor to reach us at the earliest practicable moment. From the tops of some of the highest peaks or round hills in the vicinity of the village I knew the Indians could reconnoitre the country for miles in all directions. I feared if we remained as we were then until the following day, the Indians might in this manner discover the approach of our train and detach a sufficient body of warriors to attack and capture it; and its loss to us, aside from that of its guard, would have proven most serious, leaving us in the heart of the enemy's country, in midwinter, totally out of supplies for both men and horses.

By actual count we had in our possession 875 captured ponies, so wild and unused to white men that it was difficult to herd them. What we were to do with them was puzzling, as they could not have been led had we been possessed the means of doing this; neither could we drive them as the Indians were accustomed to do. And even if we could take them with us, either the one way or the other, it was anything but wise or desirable on our part to do so, as such a large herd of ponies, constituting so much wealth in the eyes of the Indians, would have been too tempting a prize to the warriors who had been fighting us all the afternoon, and to effect their recapture they would have followed and waylaid us day and night, with every prospect of success, until we should have arrived at a place of safety. Besides, we had upwards of sixty prisoners in our hands, to say nothing of our wounded, to embarrass our movements. We had achieved a great and important success over the hostile tribes; the problem now was how to retain our advantage and steer safely through the difficulties that seemed to surround our position. The Indians had suffered a telling defeat, involving great losses in life and valuable property. Could they succeed, however, in depriving us of the train and supplies, and in doing this accomplish the killing or capture of the escort, it would go far to offset the damage we had been able to inflict upon them and render our victory an empty one

As I deliberated on these points in the endeavor to conclude upon that which would be our wisest course, I could look in neatly all directions and see the warriors at a distance collected in groups on the tops of the highest hills, apparently waiting and watching our next move that they might act accordingly. To guide my command safely out of the difficulties which seemed just then to beset them, I again had recourse to that maxim in war that teaches a commander to do that which his enemy neither expects nor desires him to do.

California Joe hiding his trail.

CHAPTER 6

After the Battle of Washita—California Joe Sent with Despatches—Our Move to Camp Supply—In the Saddle Again—Mrs. Morgan and Miss White in the Hands of the Indians— Mo-nah-se-tah or "Young Grass That Shoots in the Spring"

The close of the last chapter left my command on the Washita, still surrounded by a superior but badly defeated force of Indians. We were burdened with a considerable number of prisoners and quite a number of our own and the enemy's wounded, and had in our possession nearly nine hundred ponies which we had just captured from the enemy. We were far away—just how far we did not know—from our train of supplies, and the latter with its escort was in danger of capture and destruction by the savages if we did not act to prevent it. We felt convinced that we could not, in the presence of so large a body of hostile Indians, hope to make a long march through their country, the latter favorable to the Indian mode of attack by surprise and ambush, and keep with us the immense herd of captured ponies. Such a course would only encourage attack under circumstances which would almost ensure defeat and unnecessary loss to us. We did not need the ponies, while the Indians did. If we retained them they might conclude that one object of our expedition against them was to secure plunder, an object thoroughly consistent with the red man's idea of war. Instead, it was our desire to impress upon his uncultured mind that our every act and purpose had been simply to inflict deserved punishment upon him for the many murders and other depredations committed by him in and around the homes of the defenceless settlers on the frontier. Impelled by these motives, I decided neither to attempt to take the ponies with us nor to abandon them to the Indians, but to adopt the only measure left—to kill them. To accomplish this seemingly—like most measures of war—cruel but necessary act, four companies of cavalrymen were detailed dismounted, as a firing party. Before they reluctantly engaged in this uninviting work, I took Romeo, the interpreter, and proceeded to the few lodges near the centre of the village that we had reserved from destruction, and in which were collected the prisoners, consisting of upward of sixty squaws and children. Romeo was directed to assemble the prisoners in one body, as I desired to assure them of kind treatment at our hands, a subject about which they were greatly wrought up; also to tell them what we should expect of them, and to inform them of our intention to march probably all that night, directing them at the same time to proceed to the herd and select therefrom a suitable number of ponies to carry the prisoners on the march. When Romeo had collected them in a single group, he, acting as interpreter, acquainted them with my purpose in calling them together, at the same time assuring them that they could rely confidently upon the fulfillment of any promises I made them, as I was the "big chief." The Indians refer to all officers of a command as "chiefs," while the officer in command is designated as the "big chief." After I had concluded what I desired to say to them, they signified their approval and satisfaction by gathering around me and going through an extensive series of hand-shaking. One of the middle-aged squaws then informed Romeo that she wished to speak on behalf of herself and companions. Assent having been given to this, she began the delivery of an address which for wisdom of sentiment, and easy, natural, but impassioned delivery, might have been heard with intense interest by an audience of cultivated refinement. From her remarks, interpreted by Romeo, I gathered much—in fact, the first reliable information as to what band we had attacked at daylight, which chiefs commanded, and many interesting scraps of information. She began by saying that now she and the women and children about her were in the condition of captivity, which for a long time she had prophesied would be theirs sooner or later. She claimed to speak not as a squaw, but as the sister of the head chief of her band, Black Kettle, who had fallen that morning almost the moment the attack was made. He it was who was the first to hear our advance, and leaping forth from his lodge with rifle in hand, uttered the first war-whoop and fired the first shot as a rally signal to his warriors, and was almost immediately after shot down by the opening volley of the cavalry. Not a chief or warrior of the village in her belief survived the battle of the forenoon. And what was to become of all these women and children, bereft of everything and of every friend? True, it was just. The warriors had brought this fate upon themselves and their families by their unprovoked attacks upon the white man. Who was left to care for the women and children who still lived? Only last night, she continued, did the last war party return from the settlements, and it was to rejoice over their achievements that the entire village were engaged until a late hour dancing and singing. This was why their enemies were able to ride almost into their lodges before they were aroused by the noise of the attack. For several minutes she continued to speak, first upbraiding in the bitterest terms the chiefs and warriors who had been the cause of their capture, then bewailing in the most plaintive manner their sad and helpless condition. Turning to me she added, "You claim to be a chief. This man," (pointing to Romeo) "says you are the big chief. If this be true and you are what he claims, show that you can act like a great chief and secure for us that treatment which the helpless are entitled to."

After the delivery of this strongly melodramatic harangue there was introduced a little by-play, in which I was unconsciously made to assume a more prominent part than either my inclinations or the laws of society might approve. Black Kettle's sister, whose name was Mah-wis-sa, and whose address had just received the hearty approval of her companions by their earnest expression of "Ugh!" the Indian word intended for applause, then stepped into the group of squaws, and after looking earnestly at the face of each for a moment, approached a young Indian girl—probably seventeen years of age—and taking her by the hand conducted her to where I was standing. Placing the hand of the young girl in mine, she proceeded in the Indian tongue to the delivery of what I, in my ignorance of the language, presumed was a form of administering a benediction, as her manner and gestures corresponded with this idea. After concluding the main portion of the formalities, she engaged in what seemed an invocation of the Great Spirit, casting her eyes reverently upward, at the same time moving her hands slowly down over the faces of the young squaw and myself. By this time my curiosity got the better of my silence, and turning to Romeo, who stood near me, and who I knew was familiar with Indian customs, I quietly inquired, "What is this woman doing, Romeo?" With a broad grin on his swarthy face he replied, "Why, she's marryin' you to that young squaw!" Although never claimed as an exponent of the peace policy about which so much has been said and written, yet I entertained the most peaceable sentiments toward all Indians who were in a condition to do no harm nor violate any law. And while cherishing these friendly feelings and desiring to do all in my power to render our captives comfortable and free from anxiety regarding their future treatment at our hands, I think even the most strenuous and ardent advocate of that peace policy which teaches that the Indian should be left free and unmolested in the gratification of his simple tastes and habits, will at least not wholly condemn me when they learn that this last touching and unmistakable proof of confidence and esteem, offered by Mah-wis-sa and gracefully if not blushingly acquiesced in by the Indian maiden, was firmly but respectfully declined. The few reasons which forced me to deny myself the advantages of this tempting alliance were certain circumstances over which I then had no control, among which was a previous and already solemnized ceremony of this character, which might have a tendency to render the second somewhat invalid. Then, again, I had not been consulted in regard to my choice in this matter—a trifling consideration, but still having its due influence. I had not had opportunities to become acquainted with the family of the young damsel who thus proposed to link her worldly fate with mine. Her father's bank account might or might not be in a favorable condition. No opportunity had been given me to study the tastes, disposition, or character the young lady—whether she was fond of music, literature, or domestic duties. All these were questions with which I was not sufficiently familiar to justify me in taking the important step before me. I did not, however, like certain candidates for office, thrice decline by standing up, and with my hand pressed to my heart say, "Your husband I cannot be"; but through the intermediation of Romeo, the interpreter, who from the first had been highly entertained by what he saw was an excellent joke on the big chief, and wondering in his own mind how I would extricate myself without giving offence, I explained to Mah-wis-sa my due appreciation of the kindness intended by herself and her young friend, but that according to the white man's laws I was debarred from availing myself of the offer, at the same time assuring them of my high consideration, etc. Glad to get away to duties that called me elsewhere, I left with Romeo. As soon as we had turned our backs on the group, I inquired of Romeo what object could have been in view which induced Black Kettle's sister to play the part she did. "That's easy enough to understand; she knows they are in your power, and her object is to make friends with you as far as possible. But you don't believe anything she tells you, do you? Why, that squaw—give her the chance, and she'd lift your or my scalp for us and never wink. Lord, I've heerd 'em talk fine too often to be catched so easy. I've lived with them people too long not to know 'em —root and branch. When she was talkin' all that palaver to you 'bout protectin' 'em and all that sort of stuff, if she could 'a know'd that minute that these outside Injuns was 'bout to gobble us up she'd 'a been the very fust one to ram a knife smack into ye. That's the way they allus talk when they want anythin'. Do you know her game in wantin' to marry that young squaw to you? Well, I'll tell ye; ef you'd 'a married that squaw, then she'd 'a told ye that all the rest of 'em were her kinfolks, and as a nateral sort of a thing you'd 'a been expected to kind o' provide and take keer of your wife's relation. That's jist as I tell it to you—fur don't I know? Didn't I marry a young Cheyenne squaw and give her old father two of my best ponies for her, and it wasn't a week till every tarnal Injun in the village, old and young, came to my lodge, and my squaw tried to make me b'lieve they were all relations of hern, and that I ought to give 'em some grub; but I didn't do nothin' of the sort." "Well, how did you get out of it, Romeo?" "Get out of it? Why, I got out by jist takin' my ponies and traps, and the first good chance I lit out; that's how I got out. I was satisfied to marry one or two of 'em, but when it come to marryin' an intire tribe, 'scuse me."

At this point Romeo was interrupted by the officer in command of the men detailed to kill the ponies. The firing party was all ready to proceed with its work, and was only waiting until the squaws should secure a sufficient number of ponies to transport all the prisoners on the march. The troopers had endeavored to catch the ponies, but they were too wild and unaccustomed to white men to permit them to approach. When the squaws entered the herd they had no difficulty in selecting and bridling the requisite number. These being taken off by themselves, the work of destruction began on the remainder, and was continued until nearly eight hundred ponies were thus disposed of. All this time the Indians who had been fighting us from the outside covered the hills in the distance, deeply interested spectators of this strange proceeding. The loss of so many animals of value was a severe blow to the tribe, as nothing so completely impairs the war-making facilities for the Indians of the Plains as the deprivation or disabling of their ponies.

In the description of the opening of the battle in the preceding chapter, I spoke of the men having removed their overcoats and haversacks when about to charge the village. These had been disposed of carefully on the ground, and one man from each company left to guard them, this number being deemed sufficient, as they would be within rifle-shot of the main command; besides, the enemy as was then supposed would be inside our lines and sufficiently employed in taking care of himself to prevent any meddling on his part with the overcoats and haversacks. This was partly true, but we had not calculated upon Indians appearing in force and surrounding us. When this did occur, however, their first success was in effecting the capture of the overcoats and rations of the men, the guard barely escaping to the village. This was a most serious loss, as the men were destined to suffer great discomfort from the cold; and their rations being in the haversacks, and it being uncertain when we should rejoin our train, they were compelled to endure both cold and hunger. It was when the Indians discovered our overcoats and galloped to their capture, that one of my staghounds, Blucher, seeing them riding and yelling as if engaged in the chase, dashed from the village and joined the Indians, who no sooner saw him than they shot him through with an arrow. Several months afterward I discovered his remains on the ground near where the overcoats had been deposited on that eventful morning.

Many noteworthy incidents were observed or reported during the fight. Before the battle began, our Osage allies, in accordance with the Indian custom, dressed in their war costume, painting their faces in all imaginable colors, except one tall, fine-looking warrior, who retained his ordinary dress. Upon inquiring of the chief, Little Beaver, why this one did not array himself as the others had done, he informed me that it was in obedience to a law among all the tribes, under which any chief or warrior who has had a near relative killed by an enemy belonging to another tribe, is not permitted to don the war costume or put on war paint until he has avenged the murder by taking a scalp from some member of the hostile tribe. A war party of the Cheyennes had visited the Osage village the preceding summer, under friendly pretences. They had been hospitably entertained at the lodge of the warrior referred to by his squaw, he being absent on a hunt. When ready to depart they killed his squaw and destroyed his lodge, and until he could secure a scalp he must go on the war path unadorned by feathers or paint. After the battle had been waged for a couple of hours in the morning, I saw this warrior approaching, his horse urged to his highest speed; in his hand I saw waving wildly overhead something I could not distinguish until he halted by my side, when I perceived that it was an entire scalp, fresh and bleeding. His vengeance had been complete, and he was again restored to the full privileges of a warrior—a right he was not long in exercising, as the next time I saw him on the field his face was completely hidden under the stripes of yellow, black, and vermilion, the colors being so arranged apparently as to give him the most hideous visage imaginable.

Riding in the vicinity of the hospital, I saw a little bugler boy sitting on a bundle of dressed robes, near where the surgeon was dressing and caring for the wounded. His face was completely covered with blood, which was trickling down over his cheek from a wound in his forehead. At first glance I thought a pistol bullet had entered his skull, but on stopping to inquire of him the nature of his injury, he informed me that an Indian had shot him in the head with a steel-pointed arrow. The arrow had struck him just above the eye, and upon encountering the skull had glanced under the covering of the latter, coming out near the ear, giving the appearance of having passed through the head. There the arrow remained until the bugler arrived at the hospital, when he received prompt attention. The arrow being barbed could not be withdrawn at once, but by cutting off the steel point the surgeon was able to withdraw the wooden shaft without difficulty. The little fellow bore his suffering manfully. I asked him if he saw the Indian who wounded him. Without replying at once, he shoved his hand deep down into his capacious trousers pocket and fished up nothing more nor less than the scalp of an Indian, adding in a nonchalant manner, "If anybody thinks I didn't see him, I want them to take a look at that." He had killed the Indian with his revolver after receiving the arrow wound in his head.

After driving off the Indians who had attacked us from the outside, so as to prevent them from interfering with our operations in the vicinity of the village, parties were sent here and there to look up the dead and wounded of both sides. In spite of the most thorough search, Major Elliott and nineteen enlisted men had still not been discovered. Various commands were examined, but nothing was elicited from them except that Major Elliott had been seen about daylight charging with his command into the village. I had previously given him up as killed, but was surprised that so many of the men should be missing, and none of their comrades be able to account for them. All the ground inside of the advanced lines held by the Indians who attacked us after our capture of the village was closely and carefully examined, in the hope of finding the bodies of some if not all the absentees, but with no success. It was then evident that when the other bands attempted to reinforce our opponents of the early morning, they had closed their lines about us in such manner as to cut off Elliott and nineteen of our men. What had been the fate of this party after leaving the main command? This was a question to be answered only in surmises, and few of these were favorable to the escape of our comrades. At last one of the scouts reported that soon after the attack on the village began he had seen a few warriors escaping, mounted, from the village, through a gap that existed in our line between the commands of Elliott and Thomspon, and that Elliott and a small party of troopers were in close pursuit; that a short time after he had heard a very sharp firing in the direction taken by the Indians and Elliott's party, but that as the firing had continued for only a few minutes, he had thought nothing more of it until the prolonged absence of our men recalled it to his mind. Parties were sent in the direction indicated by the scout, he accompanying them; but after a search extending nearly two miles, all the parties returned, reporting their efforts to discover some trace of Elliott and his men fruitless. As it was now lacking but an hour of night, we had to make an effort to get rid of the Indians, who still loitered in strong force on the hills, within plain view of our position. Our main desire was to draw them off from the direction in which our train might be approaching, and thus render it secure from attack until under the protection of the entire command, when we could defy any force our enemies could muster against us. The last lodge having been destroyed, and all the ponies except those required for the pursuit having been killed, the command was drawn in and united near the village. Making dispositions to overcome any resistance that might be offered to our advance, by throwing out a strong force of skirmishers, we set out down the valley in the direction where the other villages had been reported, and toward the hills on which were collected the greatest number of Indians. The column moved forward in one body, with colors flying and band playing, while our prisoners, all mounted on captured ponies, were under sufficient guard immediately in rear of the advanced troops. For a few moments after our march began the Indians on the hills remained silent spectators, evidently at a loss at first to comprehend our intentions in thus setting out at that hour of the evening, and directing our course as if another night march was contemplated; and more than all, in the direction of their villages, where all that they possessed was supposed to be. This aroused them to action, as we could plainly see considerable commotion among them—chiefs riding hither and thither, as if in anxious consultation with each other as to the course to be adopted. Whether the fact that they could not fire upon our advance without endangering the lives of their own people, who were prisoners in our hands, or some other reason prevailed with them, they never offered to fire a shot or retard our movements in any manner. This was exactly the effect I desired, and our march was conducted with such appearance of determination and rapidity that this conclusion on their part was a most natural one. Leaving a few of their warriors to hover along our flanks and watch our progress, the main body of the Indians, able to travel much faster than the troops, soon disappeared from our sight in front. We still pushed on in the same direction, and continued our march in this manner until long after dark, by which time we reached the deserted villages, the occupants—at least the non-combatants and herds—having fled in the morning when news of our attack on Black Kettle's village reached them. We had now reached a point several miles below the site of Black Kettle's village, and the darkness was sufficient to cover our movements from the watchful eyes of the Indian scouts, who had dogged our march as long as the light favored them.

Facing the command about, it was at once put in motion to reach our train, not only as a measure of safety and protection to the latter, but as a necessary movement to relieve the wants of the command, particularly that portion whose haversacks and overcoats had fallen into the hands of the Indians early in the morning. By ten o'clock we reached the battle ground, but without halting pushed on, following the trail we had made in striking the village. The march was continued at a brisk gait until about two o'clock in the morning, when I concluded it would be prudent to allow the main command to halt and bivouac until daylight, sending one squadron forward without delay, to reinforce the guard with the train. Colonel West's squadron was detailed upon this duty. The main body of the troops was halted, and permitted to build huge fires, fuel being obtainable in abundance from the timber which lined the valley of the Washita—our march still leading us up the course of this stream.

At daylight the next morning we were again in our saddles and wending our way hopefully toward the train. The location of the latter we did not know, presuming that it had been pushing after us since we had taken our abrupt departure from it. Great was our joy and satisfaction, about ten o'clock, to discover the train safely in camp. The teams were at once harnessed and hitched to the wagons, and without halting even to prepare breakfast, the march was resumed, I being anxious to encamp at a certain point that night from where I intended sending scouts through with despatches to General Sheridan. Early in the afternoon this camp was reached; it was near the point where we had first struck the timbered valley, at the time not knowing that it was the valley of the Washita. Here men and horses were given the first opportunity to procure a satisfactory meal since the few hasty morsels obtained by them during the brief halt made between nine and ten o'clock the night we arrived in the vicinity of the village. After posting our pickets and rendering the camp secure from surprise by the enemy, horses were unsaddled, tents pitched, and every means taken to obtain as comfortable a night as the limited means at our disposal and the severities of the season would permit. After partaking of a satisfactory dinner, I began writing my report to General Sheridan.

First I sent for California Joe, and informed him that I desired to send a despatch to General Sheridan that night, and would have it ready by dark, so that the bearer could at once set out as soon as it was sufficiently dark to conceal his movements from the scouts of the enemy, who no doubt were still following and watching us. I told California Joe that I had selected him as the bearer of the despatch, and he was at liberty to name the number of men he desired to accompany him, as it was a most perilous mission on which he was going. The exact distance he would have to ride in order to reach General Sheridan's headquarters at Camp Supply could not be determined. The command had occupied four days in accomplishing it, but California Joe, with his thorough knowledge of the country, and the experience of our march, would be able to follow a much more direct route than a large command moving with a train.

He did not seem in the least disturbed when told of his selection for this errand, so full of danger. When informed that he might name the number of men to accompany him, I supposed he would say about twelve or more, under command of a good non-commissioned officer. Very few persons in or out of the military service would have cared to undertake the journey with much less than ten times that force, but he contented himself by informing me that before answering that question he would walk down to where the scouts were in camp and consult his "pardner." He soon returned saying, "I've just been talkin' the matter over with my pardner, and him and me both concludes that as safe and sure a way as any is for him and me to take a few extra rounds of ammunition and strike out from here together the very minnit it's dark. As for any more men, we don't want 'em; because yer see in a case of this 'ere kind thar's more to be made by dodgin' an' runnin' than thar is by fightin', an' two spright men kin do better at that than twenty; they can't be seen half as fur. Besides, two won't leave as much of a trail for the Injuns to find. If my pardner an' me kin git away from here as soon as it is plum dark, we'll be so fur from here by daylight to-morrer mornin' the Injuns never couldn't tetch hide nor har of us. Besides, I don't reckon the pesky varmints 'll be so overly keen in meddlin' with our business, seein' as how they've got their han's tolerable full settin' things to rights at home, owin' to the little visit we've jist made 'em. Wal, I'm goin' back to the boys to see if I can borrer a little smokin' tobacker. I may want to take a smoke on the way. Whenever you git yer dockiments ready jist send your orderly down thar, and me and my pardner will be ready. I'm mighty glad I'm goin' to-night, for I know Gineral Sheridan 'll be monstrous glad to see me back so soon."

Leaving California Joe to procure his "tobacker," I assembled all the officers of the command and informed them that as there was but an hour or two in which I was to write my report of the Battle of the Washita, I would not have time, as I should have preferred to do, to send to them for regular and formally written reports of their share in the engagement; but in order that I might have the benefit of their combined knowledge of the battle and its results, each officer in response to my request gave me a brief summary of some of the important points which his report would have contained if submitted in writing. With this information in my possession, I sat down in my tent and penned, in as brief manner as possible, a report to General Sheridan, up to the point from which my despatch was written, giving particularly the main facts of our discovery, attack, and complete destruction of the village of Black Kettle. It was just about dark when I finished this despatch and was about to send for California Joe, when that loquacious personage appeared at the door my tent. "I'm not so anxious to leave yer all here, but the fact is, the sooner me and pardner are off, I reckon the better it'll be in the end. I want to put at least fifty miles 'tween me and this place by daylight to-morrer mornin', so if yer'll jest hurry up yer papers, it'll be a lift for us."

On going outside the tent I saw that the "pardner" was the scout Jack Corbin, the same who had first brought the intelligence of Elliott's discovery of the trail to us at Antelope Hills. He was almost the antipodes of California Joe in regard to many points of character, seldom indulging in a remark or suggestion unless prompted by a question. These two scouts recalled to my mind an amicable arrangement said to exist between a harmonious married pair, in which one was willing to do all the talking and the other was perfectly willing he should. The two scouts, who were about to set out to accomplish a long journey through an enemy's country, with no guides save the stars, neither ever haying passed over the route they proposed to take, and much of the ride to be executed during the darkness of night, apparently felt no greater, if as great, anxiety as to the result of their hazardous mission than one ordinarily feels in contemplating a journey of a few hours by rail or steamboat. California Joe was dressed and equipped as usual. About his waist and underneath his cavalry greatcoat and cape he wore a belt containing a Colt revolver and hunting knife; these, with his inseparable companion, a long Springfield breech-loading rifle, composed his defensive armament. His "pardner," Jack Corbin, was very similarly arrayed except in equipment, his belt containing two revolvers instead of one, while a Sharps carbine supplied the place of a rifle, being more readily carried and handled on horseback. The mounts of the two men were as different as their characters, California Joe confiding his safety to the transporting powers of his favorite mule, while Corbin was placing his reliance upon a fine gray charger. Acquainting the men with the probable route we should pursue in our onward march toward Camp Supply, so that, if desirable, they might be able to rejoin us, I delivered my report to General Sheridan into the keeping of California Joe, who, after unbuttoning numerous coats, blouses, and vests, consigned the package to one of the numerous capacious inner pockets with which each garment seemed supplied, with the remark, "I reckon it'll keep dry thar in case of rain or accident." Both men having mounted, I shook hands with them, wishing them Godspeed and a successful journey. As they rode off in the darkness California Joe, irrepressible to the last, called out, "Wall, I hope an' trust yer won't have any scrimmage while I'm gone, because I'd hate mightily now to miss anything of the sort, seein' I've stuck to yer this fur."

After enjoying a most grateful and comparatively satisfactory night's rest, the demands of hunger on the part of man and beast having been bountifully supplied from the stores contained in our train, while a due supply of blankets and robes, with the assistance of huge campfires, enabled the men to protect themselves against the intense cold of midwinter, our march was resumed at daylight in the direction of Camp Supply. By easy marches we gradually neared Camp Supply, and had begun to descend the long slope leading down to the valley of Wolf Creek, the stream on which we had encamped three nights when we first set out from Camp Supply in search of Indians.

With two or three of the Osage guides and as many of the officers, I was riding some distance in advance of the column of troops, and could indistinctly see the timber fringing the valley in the distance, when the attention of our little party was attracted to three horsemen who were to be seen riding slowly along near the edge of the timber. As yet they evidently had not observed us, the troops behind us not having appeared in view. We were greatly at a loss to determine who the three horsemen might be; they were yet too distant to be plainly visible to the eye, and the orderly with my field glass was still in rear. While we were halting and watching their movements we saw that they also had discovered us, one of their number riding up to a small elevation nearby from which to get a better view of our group. After studying us for a few moments he returned at a gallop to his two companions, when all three turned their horses toward the timber and moved rapidly in that direction. We were still unable to determine whether they were Indians or white men, the distance being so great between us, when my orderly arrived with my field glass, by which I was able to catch a glimpse of them just as they were disappearing in the timber, when whose familiar form should be revealed but that of California Joe, urging his mule to its greatest speed in order to reach the timber before we should discover them. They had evidently taken us for Indians, and well they might, considering that two of our party were Osages and the others were dressed in anything but the regulation uniform. To relieve the anxious minds of California Joe and his companions, I put spurs to my horse and was soon bounding down the plains leading into the valley to join him. California Joe, after shading his eyes with his hand and looking for a few moments, raised his huge sombrero from his matted head, and waving it above him as a signal of recognition pressed his great Mexican spurs deep into the sides of his humble-looking steed, if a mule may receive such an appellation, and the three scouts were soon galloping toward us.

The joy at the meeting was great on both sides, only dampened somewhat on the part of California Joe by the fact that he and his comrades had taken to the timber so promptly when first they discovered us; but he explained it by saying, "I counted on it bein' you all the time when I fust got my eye on yer, until I saw two Injuns in the squad, an' forgettin' all about them Osages we had along, I jumped at the conclusion that if thar war any Injuns around, the comfortablest place I knowed for us three was to make fur the timber, and there make a stand. We war gettin' ready to give it to yer if jet turned out yer war all Injuns. Wal, I'm powerful glad to see yer agin, an' that's sure."

From his further conversation we were informed that Jack Corbin and himself had made their trip to General Sheridan's headquarters without hindrance or obstacle being encountered on their way, and that after delivering the despatches and being well entertained in the meantime, they, with one other scout, had been sent by the

General to endeavor to meet us, bringing from him a package of orders and letters.

While the column was overtaking us, and while California Joe, now in his element, was entertaining the attentive group of officers, scouts, and Osages who gathered around him to hear him relate in his quaint manner what he saw, heard, and told at General Sheridan's headquarters, I withdrew to one side and opened the large official envelope in which were contained both official and personal despatches. These were eagerly read, and while the satisfaction derived from the perusal of some of the letters of a private and congratulatory nature from personal friends at Camp Supply was beyond expression, the climax of satisfaction was reached when my eye came to an official-looking document bearing the date and heading which indicated department headquarters as its source. We had but little further to go before going into camp for that night, and as the command had now overtaken us, we moved down to the timber and there encamped; and in order that the approving words of our chief should be transmitted promptly to every individual of the command, the line was formed and Sheridan's order announced to the officers and men.

This order, containing as it did the grateful words of approval from our revered commander, went far to drown the remembrance of the hunger, cold, and danger encountered by the command, in the resolute and united effort made by it to thoroughly discharge its duty.

The last camp before we reached Camp Supply was on Wolf Creek, about ten miles from General Sheridan's headquarters. The weather had now moderated to the mildest winter temperature, the snow having melted and disappeared.

From this point I sent a courier to General Sheridan soon after going into camp, informing him of our whereabouts and the distance from his camp, and that we would reach the latter at such an hour in the forenoon, when the officers and men of my command would be pleased to march in review before him and his staff as we finished our return march from the opening of the winter campaign.

After marching in review, the troops were conducted across the plain to the border of Beaver Creek, about a quarter of a mile from General Sheridan's camp, where we pitched our tents and prepared to enjoy a brief period of rest.

Our sojourn at Camp Supply was to be brief. We arrived there on the 2nd of December, and in less than one week we were to be in the saddle with our numbers more than doubled by reinforcements, and again wending our way southward over the route we had so lately passed over.

Before setting out on the last expedition, I had stated to the officers in a casual manner that all parties engaged in the conduct of the contemplated campaign against the Indians must reconcile themselves in advance—no matter how the expedition might result—to becoming the recipients of censure and unbounded criticism; that if we failed to engage and whip the Indians—labor as we might to accomplish this—the people in the West, particularly along and near the frontier, those who had been victims of the assaults made by Indians, would denounce us in unmeasured terms as being inefficient or lukewarm in the performance of our duty; whereas if we should find and punish the Indians as they deserved, a wail would rise up from the horrified humanitarians throughout the country, and we would be accused of attacking and killing friendly and defenceless Indians. My predictions proved true; no sooner was the intelligence of the Battle of the Washita flashed over the country than the anticipated cry was raised.

In Camp Supply

The government, however, was in earnest in its determination to administer proper and deserved punishment to the guilty; and as a mark of approval of the opening event of the winter campaign, the following telegram from the Secretary of War was transmitted to us at Camp Supply:

LIEUTENANT-GENERAL SHERMAN, St. Louis, MO.

WAR DEPARTMENT, WASHINGTON CITY, December 2, 1868.

I congratulate you, Sheridan, and Custer on the splendid success with which your campaign is begun. Ask Sheridan to send forward the names of officers and men deserving of special mention.

(SIGNED)   J. M. SCHOFIELD, Secretary of War.

We had returned on the 30th of November from the campaign of the Washita, well satisfied with the result of our labors and exposures; but we were not to sit quietly in our tents or winter quarters and give way to mutual congratulations upon the success which had already rewarded our efforts.

In less than one week from the date of our arrival at Camp Supply, we were to be again in the saddle and wending our way southward toward the supposed winter haunts of our enemies—this time, however, with more than double our former numbers. So long had the thrifty and enterprising settlers upon the frontier of Kansas, particularly those who had selected homes in the fertile valleys of the Saline, Solomon, and Republican Rivers, been subjected to the depredations of the Cheyennes, Arapahos, Apaches, Kiowas, and Sioux, and so frequent had the murder and capture of settlers by these Indians become, that the citizens and the officials of the State felt forced to take measures in their own defence, and for the purpose of uniting with the forces of the General Government, in the attempt to give quiet and protection to life and property to the inhabitants of the border settlements. The last needed impulse to this movement on the part of the people of Kansas was given when the Indians, late in the preceding summer, made two raids upon the settlements in the Saline, Solomon, and Republican Valleys, and, after murdering many of the men and children, burning houses, and destroying or capturing a vast amount of stock, carried off into captivity two young women or girls, both belonging to highly respected families residing on the

Capture of Mrs. Morgan and Miss White

exposed border of the State. Although one of the captives was married, her marriage to a farmer having been celebrated less than one month prior to the day of her unfortunate capture by the Indians, yet neither of them could scarcely be said to have passed the line which separates girlhood from womanhood. Mrs. Morgan, the bride, was but nineteen, while her companion in misfortune, Miss White, was still her junior by a year or more. As they played no unimportant part in subsequent operations against the Indians, the principal events attending their capture may not be out of place. Neither knew the other, nor had they ever seen each other until they met as captives in an Indian village hundreds of miles from their frontier homes. One can readily imagine with what deep interest and mutual sympathy the acquaintance of these two helpless girls began. Miss White had been captured and carried to the Indian village about one month before the capture of Mrs. Morgan occurred. The brief story of the capture of the former is soon told. One day, her father being at work in the field, she and a younger sister were engaged in the garden, when she saw four Indians entering the house where her mother and the younger children of the family were. Her first impulse was to fly, but seeing an Indian on the opposite side of the garden she turned and entered the house. One or two of the Indians could speak broken English; all of them assumed a most friendly demeanor and requested something to eat. This request was met by a most prompt and willing response upon the part of Mrs. White and her children. With true Western hospitality they prepared for their unbidden guests as bountifully as the condition of the larder would permit. No depredations had been committed in that vicinity for some time, and as it was not an unusual occurrence for small parties of Indians when engaged on hunting excursions to visit the settlements, where they were invariably met with kind treatment at the hands of the settlers. It was hoped that after obtaining the desired meal the party would quietly withdraw without committing any depredations. Such, however, was not the intention of the savages. Already on that day their hands had been dipped in the white man's blood, and the peaceful procurement of something to appease their hunger was merely the dropping of the curtain between two acts of a terrible drama. Having satisfied the demands of their appetites, it was then time for them to throw aside the guise of friendship, under which they entered the house and been treated as favored guests, and to reveal the true object of their visit. Two stalwart warriors grasped Miss White in their arms and rushed toward the door. Neither her shrieks nor the feeble resistance she was able to offer retarded their movements. As she found herself being rapidly carried from the house the last glimpse she obtained of those within revealed her mother engaged in an unequal struggle with a powerful warrior, while another of the savages had felled a younger sister to the floor and was then engaged in destroying such articles of furniture or table ware as he could lay hands upon. Her two captors hurried her from the house, hastened to the spot where they had left their ponies, and after binding their captive upon the back of one of their ponies, and being joined by the others of the party, began their flight from the settlements, well knowing that the alarm would soon be given, and pursuit by the enraged settlers would be the result. Amid the terrible surroundings of her own situation, the anxieties of the fair captive to know the fate of the dear ones left behind must have been unspeakable. I can scarcely imagine a more deplorable fate than that to which this defenceless girl had become the victim. Torn from her home amid scenes of heartrending atrocities, distracted with anxious thoughts as to the fate that had befallen her mother and sister, she now found herself a helpless prisoner in the hands of the most cruel, heartless, and barbarous of human enemies.

With war parties returning from a foray upon the settlements, the first object is to place as long a distance as possible between themselves and any party which may be in pursuit. To accomplish this, as soon as they have completed the destruction and havoc of which the settlers are the victims, the entire party, usually numbering from fifty to one hundred warriors, collect at a point near the settlements previously agreed upon, and at once begin their flight toward their village, probably located at least two hundred miles from the scene of their attack. Being mounted, as all war parties are, upon the fleetest of Indian ponies with extra animals driven along, little or no rest for either pony or rider is taken during the first twenty-four hours, by which time it is no unusual feat for a war party to traverse a distance of one hundred miles.

During the early part of the flight every precaution is adopted to prevent leaving a heavy trail, or one easily to be followed; to this end, instead of moving, as is customary, in single file, thereby leaving a clearly defined path, each warrior moves independently of his fellows, until all danger from pursuit is safely passed, when the party falls into single file, and, with the chief at the head, moves along in an almost unbroken silence. If during an attack upon the frontier settlements the Indians should encounter unexpected and successful resistance, necessitating a premature withdrawal and flight on their part, they still resort to stratagem in order to secure their safety. In accordance with a plan previously formed and understood by each member of the party, and specially provided for an emergency, the war party finding themselves about to encounter successful resistance on the part of the frontiersmen beat a hasty retreat; but instead of taking their flight in a single direction and in one party, thereby leaving an unmistakable clue for their pursuers, the entire party breaks up into numerous smaller bands, each apparently fleeing in an independent direction, a few of the best mounted usually falling behind to attract the attention of the pursuers and give time to those of the party who are burdened with prisoners and captured stock to make good their escape. In such an emergency as this, a rendezvous for the entire party has been previously fixed upon. Then ensues a long and tiresome flight, until, having worn out or outwitted their pursuers, of whose movements they keep themselves thoroughly informed, they make their way in safety to the village. At the latter, lookouts are constantly kept on some prominent hill to watch the coming of the absent warriors and give notice of their approach. A war party returning from a successful raid into the settlements, and bringing with them prisoners and captured stock, is an event of the greatest importance to every occupant of the village. Having arrived within a few miles of the village, and feeling safe from all danger from pursuit, the chief in command of the war party causes a smoke signal to be sent up from some high point along the line of march, well knowing that watchful eyes near the village are on the alert and will not fail to observe the signal.

It is wonderful to what a state of perfection the Indian has carried this simple mode of telegraphing. Scattered over a great portion of the plains, from British America in the north almost to the Mexican border on the south, are to be found isolated hills, or, as they are usually termed, "buttes," which can be seen from a distance of twenty to more than fifty miles. These peaks are selected as the telegraphic stations. By varying the number of the columns of smoke different meanings are conveyed by the messages. The most simple as well as most easily varied mode, and resembling somewhat the ordinary alphabet employed in the magnetic telegraph, is arranged by building a small fire which is not allowed to blaze; then, by placing an armful of partially green grass or weeds over the fire, as if to smother it, a dense white smoke is created, which ordinarily will ascend in a continuous vertical column for hundreds of feet. This column of smoke is to the Indian mode of telegraphing what the current of electricity is to the system employed by the white man; the alphabet so far as it goes is almost identical, consisting as it does of long lines and short lines or dots. *But how formed?* is perhaps the query of the reader. By the simplest of methods. Having his current of smoke established, the Indian operator simply takes his blanket and by spreading it over the small pile of weeds or grass from which the column of smoke takes its source, and properly controlling the edges and corners of the blanket, he confines the smoke, and is in this way able to retain it for several moments. By rapidly displacing the blanket, the operator is enabled to cause a dense volume of smoke to rise, the length or shortness of which, as well as the number and frequency of the columns, he can regulate perfectly, simply by the proper use of the blanket. For the transmission of brief messages, previously determined upon, no more simple method could easily be adopted. As soon as the lookout near the village discerns the approach in the distance of the expected war party, Runners mounted upon fleet ponies are at once despatched to meet the returning warriors and gather the particulars of the expedition—whether successful or otherwise;

whether they are returning laden with scalps and plunder or come empty-handed. Have they brought prisoners and captured horses? and are their own numbers unbroken, or do their losses exceed their gains? These and similar questions are speedily solved when the runners hasten back to the village and announce the result, whereupon the occupants of the entire village, old and young, sally forth to meet the returning warriors. If the latter have been successful and have suffered no loss, they become the recipients of all the triumph that a barbarous and excited people are capable of heaping upon them. They advance toward the village painted and dressed in full war costume, singing their war songs, discharging their firearms, and uttering ever and anon the war-whoop peculiar to their tribe. Added to this, every soul in the village capable of uttering a sound joins in the general rejoicing, and for a time the entire population is wild with excitement. If, however, instead of returning in triumph, the war party has met with disaster and suffered the loss of one or more warriors, the scene witnessed upon their arrival at the village is as boisterous as the other, but even more horrible. The party is met as before by all the inhabitants of the village, but in a widely different manner; instead of the shouts and songs of victory, the war paint and bright colors give way to a deep black with which all the mourners and friends of the fallen warriors besmear their faces, while the members of the immediate family begin hacking and scarifying their faces, arms, and bodies with knives, and give way to lamentations the most piercing and horrible in sound. A not infrequent mode of disfiguring themselves, and one which I have often seen, is for the mourner, particularly if the one mourned is a wife or husband, to cut off the first joint of the little finger. This of course is done without the slightest regard for the rules of surgery, of which the Indians generally are wofully ignorant. The operation is simply performed by taking a knife, often of questionable sharpness, and cutting through the flesh and first joint of the little finger, leaving no "flap" of flesh to cover the exposed bone. As a result, in healing the flesh withdraws from the mutilated portion of the finger, and usually leaves nearly an inch of bone exposed, presenting of course a most revolting appearance.

The village to which Miss White's captors belonged was located at that time south of the Arkansas River, and distant from her home at least three hundred miles. How many girls of eighteen years of age possess the physical ability to survive a journey such as lay before this lonely captive? Unprovided with a saddle of any description, she was mounted upon an Indian pony, and probably required to accomplish nearly, if not quite, one hundred miles within the first twenty-four hours, and thus to continue the tiresome journey with but little rest or nourishment. Added to the discomforts and great fatigue of the journey was something more terrible and exhausting than either. The young captive, although a mere girl, was yet sufficiently versed in the perils attending frontier life to fully comprehend that upon her arrival at the village a fate awaited her more dreadful than death itself. She realized that if her life had been spared by her savage captors it was due to no sentiment of mercy or kindness on their part, but simply that she might be reserved for a doom far more fearful and more to be dreaded than death.

The capture of Mrs. Morgan occurred about one month later, and in the same section of country, and the story of her capture is in its incidents almost a repetition of that of Miss White. Her young husband was engaged at work in a field, not far from the house, when the crack of a rifle from the woods nearby summoned her to the door. She barely had time to see her husband fall to the ground when she discovered several Indians rushing toward the house. Her first impulse was to seek safety in flight, but already the Indians had surrounded the house, and upon her attempting to escape one of the savages felled her to the ground by a blow from his war club, and she lost all consciousness. When she recovered her senses it was only to find herself bound upon the back of a pony that was being led by a mounted warrior, while another warrior rode behind and urged the pony she was mounted upon to keep up the trot. There were about fifty warriors in the party, nearly all belonging to the Cheyenne tribe, the others belonging to the Sioux and Arapahos. As in the case of the capture of Miss White, a rapid flight immediately followed the capture.

It was the story oft repeated of outrages like these, but particularly of these two, that finally forced the people of Kansas to take up arms in their own defence. Authority was obtained from the General Government to raise a regiment of cavalry, whose services were to be accepted for a period of six months. So earnest and enthusiastic had the people of the frontier become in their determination to reclaim the two captives, as well as well as administer justly-merited punishment, that people of all classes and callings were eager to abandon their professions and take up arms against the traditional enemy of the frontier. The Governor of the State, Hon. S. J. Crawford, resigned the duties of the Executive of the State into the hands of the Lieutenant-Governor, and placed himself at the head of the regiment, which was then being organized and equipped for service during the winter campaign. After the return of the Seventh Cavalry from the Washita campaign, we were simply waiting the arrival at Camp Supply of the Kansas volunteers before again setting out to continue the campaign, whose opening had begun so auspiciously. Severe storms delayed the arrival of the Kansas troops beyond the expected time. They reached Camp Supply, however, in time for the 7th of December to be fixed upon as the date of our departure. My command, as thus increased, consisted of eleven companies of the Seventh United States Cavalry; ten companies of the Nineteenth Kansas Volunteer Cavalry, Colonel S. J. Crawford commanding; a detachment of scouts under Lieutenant Silas Pepoon, Tenth Cavalry; and between twenty and thirty whites, Osage and Kaw Indians, as guides and trailers. As our ultimate destination was Fort Cobb, Indian Territory, where we would obtain a renewal of our supplies after termination of our proposed march, and as General Sheridan desired to transfer his headquarters "in the field" to that point, he decided to accompany my command, but generously declined to exercise any command of the expedition, merely desiring to avail himself of this opportunity of an escort without rendering a detachment for that purpose necessary; and, as he remarked when announcing his intention to accompany us, he simply wished to be regarded as a "passenger."

The day prior to our departure I was standing in front of my tent when a young man, probably twenty-one or twenty-two years of age, accosted me and began a conversation by inquiring when I expected the expedition would move. Any person who has had much to do with expeditions in the Indian country knows how many and how frequent are the applications made to the commanding officer to obtain employment as scouts or guides. Probably one in fifty of the applicants is deserving of attention, and if employed would prove "worthy of his hire." Taking but a glance at the young man who addressed me, and believing him to be one of the numerous applicants for employment, my attention being at the time absorbed with other matters, I was in no mood to carry on a conversation that I believed would terminate in an offer of services not desired. I was disposed to be somewhat abrupt in my answers, but there was something in the young man's earnest manner, the eagerness with which he seemed to await my answers, that attracted and interested me. After a few questions on his part as to what portion of the country I expected to march through, what tribes I might encounter, and others of a similar nature, he suddenly said, "General, I want to go along with you." This only confirmed my first impression, although from his conversation I soon discovered that he was not one of the professional applicants for employment as a scout or guide, but more likely had been seized with a spirit of wild romance, and imagined the proper field for its display would be discovered by accompanying an expedition against the Indians. Many instances of this kind had previously fallen under my observation, and I classed this as one of them; so I simply informed him that I had already employed as many scouts and guides as were required, and that no position of that character, or any other in fact, was open to him. Not in the least discouraged by this decided refusal, he replied: "You do not understand me; I do not desire employment in your command, nor any position requiring pay. I only ask permission to accompany your expedition. I have neither arms nor horse; if you will furnish me these, and permit me to go with you, I will serve you in any capacity I can, and will expect no pay."

My curiosity was now excited; I therefore pressed him to explain his motive in desiring to accompany the expedition.

"Well, I'll tell you; it's a sad story. About four months ago, the Indians attacked my home, and carried off my only sister, a girl nineteen years of age. Since that day I have heard not a word as to what has become of her. I know not whether she is among the living or dead; but when I think of what must be her fate if among the living, I am almost tempted to wish she was quietly resting among the dead. I do not even know what tribe was engaged in her capture, but hearing of your expedition I thought it might afford me the means of getting some clue to my sister's fate. You may have a council with some of the chiefs, or some of the prisoners you captured at the battle of the Washita may tell me something of her; or if I can only learn where she is, perhaps you can exchange some of your prisoners for her; at any rate, the only chance I have to learn anything concerning her is by being permitted to accompany your expedition."

Of course he was permitted to accompany the expedition; not only that, but he was provided with a horse and arms, and appointed to a remunerative position. I asked him why he had not informed me at first as to his object in desiring to go with us. He replied that he feared that if it was known that he was in search of a lost sister, and we should afterward have interviews with the Indians, as we certainly would at Fort Cobb, he might not be as successful in obtaining information as if the object of his mission was unknown.

The name of this young man was Brewster, and the lost sister in whose search he was so earnestly engaged was Mrs. Morgan, whose capture has already been described. From him I learned that Mrs. Morgan's husband, although shot down at the first fire of the Indians, was in a fair way to recover, although crippled probably for life. But for his wounds, he too would have joined the brother in a search for the sister and for his bride, whose honeymoon had met with such a tragic interruption. Young Brewster remained with my command during the entire winter, accompanying it, and every detachment made from it, in the eager hope to learn something of the fate of his sister. In his continued efforts to discover some clue leading to her he displayed more genuine courage, perseverance, and physical endurance, and a greater degree of true brotherly love and devotion, than I have ever seen combined in one person.

It was decided to send the captives taken at the Washita to Fort Hays, Kansas, where they could not only be safely guarded, but also made far more comfortable than at Camp Supply. Before the expedition moved I suggested to General Sheridan that I should take with the expedition three of the squaws who were prisoners in our hands, with a view to rendering their services available in establishing communication with the hostile villages, if at any time this should become a desirable object. General Sheridan approved of the suggestion, and I selected three of the captives who were to accompany us. The first was Mah-wis-sa, the sister of Black Kettle, whose acquaintance the reader may have formed in the preceding chapter; the second was a Sioux squaw, probably fifty years of age, whom Mah-wis-sa expressed a desire to have accompany her, and who at times was disposed to be extremely communicative in regard to the winter resorts of the various tribes, and other matters connected with the purposes of the expedition. The third was the daughter of Little Rock, the chief second in rank to Black Kettle, who had been killed at the battle of the Washita. Little Rock's daughter was an exceedingly comely squaw, possessing a bright, cheery face, a countenance beaming with intelligence, and a disposition more inclined to be merry than one usually finds among the Indians. She was probably rather under than over twenty years of age. Added to bright, laughing eyes, a set of pearly teeth, and rich complexion, her well-shaped head was crowned with a luxuriant growth of the most beautiful silken tresses, rivalling in color the blackness of the raven, and extending, when allowed to fall loosely over her shoulders, to below her waist. Her name was Mo-nah-se-tah, which, anglicized, means "The young grass that shoots in the spring." Mo-nah-se-tah, although yet a maiden in years and appearance, had been given in marriage—or, more properly speaking, she had been traded in marriage, as an Indian maiden who should be so unfortunate as to be "given" away would not be looked upon as a very desirable match. In addition to her handsome appearance, both in form and feature, and to any other personal attraction which might be considered peculiarly her own, Mo-nah-se-tah, being the daughter of a chief high in rank, was justly considered as belonging to the cream of the aristocracy, if not to royalty itself; consequently the suitors who hoped to gain her hand must be prepared, according to the Indian custom, to pay handsomely for an alliance so noble.

Among the young warriors of the tribe there were many who would have been proud to call Mo-nah-se-tah to preside over the domestic destinies of their lodge, but the price to be paid for so distinguished an alliance was beyond the means of most of them. Among the number of young braves who aspired to the honor of her hand was one who, so far as worldly wealth was concerned, was eligible. Unfortunately, however, he had placed too much reliance upon this fact, and had not thought that while obtaining the consent of *paterfamilias* (the male head of the family) it would be well also to win the heart of the maiden; or perhaps he had, in seeking her hand, also attempted to gain her heart, but not meeting with the desired encouragement from the maiden of his choice, was willing to trust to time to accomplish the latter, provided only he could secure the first. According to Indian customs the consent of the bride to a proposed marriage, while it may be ever so desirable, is not deemed essential. All that is considered absolutely essential is that the bridegroom shall be acceptable to the father of the bride, and shall transfer to the possession of the latter ponies or other articles of barter, in sufficient number and value to be considered a fair equivalent for the hand of the daughter. When it is stated that from two to four ponies are considered as the price of the average squaw, and that the price for the hand of Mo-nah-se-tah, as finally arranged, was eleven ponies, some idea can be formed of the high opinion entertained of her.

It proved, however, so far as the young warrior was concerned, an unsatisfactory investment. The ponies were transferred to Little Rock, and all the formalities were duly executed which, by Indian law and custom, were necessary to constitute Mo-nah-se-tah the wife of the young brave. She was forced to take take up her abode in his lodge, but refused to acknowledge him as her husband, or to render him that obedience and menial service that the Indian husband exacts from his wife. Time failed to soften her heart, or to cause her to look kindly upon her self-constituted but unrecognized lord and master.

Here was a clear case of "incompatibility of disposition"; and within the jurisdiction of some of our State laws a divorce would have been granted almost unquestioned. The patience of the young husband having become exhausted, and he having unsuccessfully resorted to every measure of kindness deemed likely to win the love and obedience of his wife, he determined to have recourse to harsher measures—if necessary, to employ force. Again he mistook the character of her upon whose apparently obdurate heart neither threats nor promises had produced the faintest effect. Mo-nah-se-tah had probably been anticipating such a decision, and had prepared herself accordingly. Like most Indian women, she was as skillful in the handling and use of weapons as most warriors are; and when her husband, or rather the husband who had been assigned to her, attempted to establish by force an authority which she had persistently refused to recognize, she reminded him that she was the daughter of a great chief, and rather than submit to the indignities which he was thus attempting to heap upon her, she would resist even to the taking of life; and suiting the action to the word, she levelled a small pistol which she had carried concealed beneath her blanket and fired, wounding him in the knee and disabling him for life.

Little Rock, learning of what had occurred, and finding upon investigation that his daughter had not been to blame, concluded to cancel the marriage—to grant a divorce—which was accomplished simply by returning to the unfortunate husband the eleven ponies that had been paid for the hand of Mo-nah-se-tah, What an improvement upon the method prescribed in the civilized world! No lawyer's fees, no publicity nor scandal; all tedious delays are avoided, and the result is as nearly satisfactory to all parties as is possible.

Having sent a messenger to ask the three Indian women referred to to come to my tent, I acquainted them with my intention of taking them with the expedition when we moved in search of the hostile villages. To my surprise they evinced great delight at the idea, and explained it by saying that if they accompanied us they might be able to see or communicate with some of their people, while by remaining with the other prisoners, and becoming further separated from their own country and hunting grounds, they could entertain little or no hope of learning anything concerning the fate of other portions of their tribe. They gladly acceded to the proposition to accompany the troops. I then inquired of them in which mode they preferred to travel, mounted upon ponies, as was their custom, or in an ambulance. Much to my surprise, remembering how loath the Indian is to adopt any contrivance of the white man, they chose the ambulance, and wisely too, as the season was that of midwinter, and the interior of a closely covered ambulance was a much less exposed position than that to be found on the back of a pony.

Signaling on the march

CHAPTER 7

We Leave Camp Supply—We Revisit the
Washita Battleground—We Discover Major
Elliot's Command—Meeting the Chiefs—Son of
Satanta—The Kiowas Come In

Forage for the horses and mules, and rations for the men, sufficient
of both to last thirty days, having been loaded on the wagons, the

entire command, composed as previously stated, and accompanied by General Sheridan and staff, left Camp Supply early on the morning of December 7, and turning our horses' heads southward, we marched in the direction of the battleground of the Washita. Our march to the Washita was quiet and uneventful, if we except the loquacity of California Joe, who, now that we were once more in the saddle with the prospect of stirring times before us, seemed completely in his element, and gave vent to his satisfaction by indulging in a connected series of remarks and queries, always supplying the answer to the latter himself if none of his listeners evinced disposition to do so for him. His principal delight seemed to be in speculating audibly as to what would be the impression produced on the minds of the Indians when they discovered us returning with increased numbers both of men and wagons.

"I'd jist like to see the streaked count'nances of Satanta, Medicine Arrow, Lone Wolf, and a few others of 'em, when they ketch the fust glimpse of the outfit. They'll think we're comin' to spend an evenin' with 'em sure, and hev brought our knittin' with us. One look 'll satisfy 'em thar 'll be sum of the durndest kickin' out over these plains that ever war heern tell uv." In this interminable manner California Joe would pursue his semi-soliloquies, only too delighted if someone exhibited interest sufficient to propound an occasional question.

As our proposed route bore to the southeast after reaching the battlefield, our course was so chosen as to carry us to the Washita River a few miles below, at which point we encamped early in the day. General Sheridan desired to ride over the battleground, and we hoped by a careful examination of the surrounding country to discover the remains of Major Elliott and his little party, of whose fate there could no longer be the faintest doubt. With one hundred men of the Seventh Cavalry, under command of Captain Yates, we proceeded to the scene of the battle, and from there dispersed in small parties in all directions, with orders to make a thorough search for our lost comrades. We found the evidences of the late engagement much as we had left them. Here were the bodies, now frozen, of the seven hundred ponies which we had slain after the battle; here and there, scattered in and about the site of the former village of Black Kettle, lay the bodies of many of the Indians who fell during the struggle. Many of the bodies, however, particularly those of Black Kettle and Little Rock, had been removed by their friends. Why any had been allowed to remain uncared for could only be explained upon the supposition that the hasty flight of the other villages prevented the Indians from carrying away any except the bodies of the most prominent chiefs or warriors, although most of those remaining on the battleground were found wrapped in blankets and bound with lariats preparatory to removal and burial.

After riding over the ground in the immediate vicinity of the village, I joined one of the parties engaged in the search for the bodies of Major Elliott and his men. In describing the search and its result, I cannot do better than transcribe from my official report, made soon after to General Sheridan:

"After marching a distance of two miles in the direction in which Major Elliott and his little party were last seen, we suddenly came upon the stark, stiff, naked, and horribly mutilated bodies of our dead comrades. No words were needed to tell how desperate had been the struggle before they were finally overpowered. At a short distance from where the bodies lay could be seen the carcasses of some of the horses of the party, which had probably been killed early in the fight. Seeing the hopelessness of breaking through the line that surrounded them, and which undoubtedly numbered more than one hundred to one, Elliott dismounted his men, tied their horses together and prepared to sell their lives as early as possible. It may not be improper to add that in describing, as far as possible, the details of

We discover Major Elliot's command.

Elliott's fight I rely not only upon a critical and personal examination of the ground and attendant circumstances, but am sustained by the statement of Indian chiefs and warriors who witnessed and participated in the fight, and who have since been forced to enter our lines and surrender themselves up, under circumstances which will be made to appear in other portions of this report.

"The bodies of Elliott and his little band, with but a single exception, were found lying within a circle not exceeding twenty yards in diameter. We found them exactly as they fell, except that their barbarous foes had stripped and mutilated the bodies in the most savage manner.

"All the bodies were carried to camp. The latter was reached after dark. It being the intention to resume the march before daylight the following day, a grave was hastily prepared on a little knoll near our camp, and, with the exception of that of Major Elliott, whose remains were carried with us for interment at Fort Arbuckle, the bodies of the entire party, under the dim light of a few torches held by sorrowing comrades, were consigned to one common resting place.

"Before interment, I caused a complete examination of each body to be made by Dr. Lippincott, chief medical officer of the expedition, with direction to report on the character and number of wounds received by each, as well as to mutilations to which they had been subjected. The following extracts are taken from Dr. Lippincott's report:

"Major Joel H. Elliott, two bullet holes in head, one in left cheek, right hand cut off, left foot almost cut off. . . . deep gash in right groin, deep gashes in calves of both legs, little finger of left hand cut off, and throat cut.

"Sergeant-Major Walter Kennedy, bullet hole in right temple, head partly cut off, seventeen bullet holes in back, and two in legs.

"Corporal Harry Mercer, Troop E, bullet hole in right axilla, one in region of heart, three in back, eight arrow wounds in back, right ear cut off, head scalped, and skull fractured, deep gashes in both legs, and throat cut.

"Private Thomas Christer, Troop E, bullet hole in head, right foot cut off, bullet hole in abdomen, and throat cut.

"Corporal William Carrick, Troop H, bullet hole in right parietal bone, both feet cut off, throat cut, left arm broken.

"Private Eugene Clover, Troop H, head cut off, arrow wound in right side, both legs terribly mutilated.

"Private William Milligan, Troop H, bullet hole in left side of head, deep gashes in right leg. . . . left arm deeply gashed, head scalped, and throat cut.

"Corporal James F. Williams, Troop I, bullet hole in back; head and both arms cut off, many and deep gashes in back. . . .

"Private Thomas Dooney, Troop I, arrow hole in region of stomach, thorax cut open, head cut off, and right shoulder cut by a tomahawk.

"Ferrier Thomas Fitzpatrick, Troop M, bullet hole in left parietal bone, head scalped, arm broken. . . . throat cut.

"Private John Myres, Troop M, several bullet holes in head, scalped, nineteen bullet holes in body. . . . throat cut.

"Private Cal. Sharpe, Troop M, two bullet holes in right side, throat cut, one bullet hole in left side of head, one arrow hole in left side. . . . left arm broken.

"Unknown, head cut off, body partially destroyed by wolves.

"Unknown, head and right hand cut off. . . . three bullet and nine arrow holes in back.

"Unknown, scalped, skull fractured, six bullet and thirteen arrow holes in back, and three bullet holes in chest."

I have quoted these extracts in order to give the reader an insight of the treatment invariably meted out to white men who are so unfortunate as to fall within the scope of the red man's bloodthirsty and insatiable vengeance.

At daylight on the following morning the entire command started on the trail of the Indian villages, nearly all of which had moved down the Washita toward Fort Cobb, where they had good reason to believe they would receive protection. The Arapahos and remaining band of Cheyennes left the Washita Valley and moved across in the direction of Red River. After following the trail of the Kiowas and other hostile Indians for seven days, over an almost impassable country, where it was necessary to keep two or three hundred men almost constantly at work with picks, axes, and spades, before being able to advance with our immense train, my Osage scouts came galloping back on the morning of the 17th of December, and reported a party of Indians in our front bearing a flag of truce.

The only point to occasion surprise is how an officer possessing the knowledge of the Indian character, derived from an extensive experience on the frontier, which General Hazen could justly lay claim to, should be so far misled as to give the certificate of good conduct which follows. General Hazen had not only had superior opportunities for studying the Indian character, but had participated in Indian wars, and at the very time he penned the following note he was partially disabled from the effects of an Indian wound. The Government had selected him from the large number of intelligent officers of high rank whose services were available for the position, and had assigned him with plenary powers to the superintendency of the Southern Indian District, a position in which almost the entire control of all the southern tribes was vested in the occupant. If gentlemen of the experience and military education of General Hazen, occupying the intimate and official relation to the Indians which he did, could be so readily and completely deceived as to their real character, it is not strange that the mass of the people living far from the scene of operations, and only possessing such information as reaches them in scraps through the public press, and generally colored by interested parties, should at times entertain extremely erroneous impressions regarding the much-vexed Indian question. Now to the case in point:

With the Osage scouts who came back from the advance with the intelligence that a party of Indians were in front, also came a scout who informed me that a large party of Kiowa warriors, under Lone Wolf, Satanta, and other leading chiefs, were within less than a mile of my advance, and notwithstanding the above certificate regarding their friendly character, they had seized a scout, who accompanied the bearer of the despatch, disarmed him, and held him a prisoner of war. Taking a small party with me, I proceeded beyond our lines to meet the flag of truce. I was met by several of the leading chiefs of the Kiowas, including those above named. Large parties of their warriors could be seen posted in the neighboring ravines and upon the surrounding hilltops. All were painted and plumed for war, and nearly all were armed with one rifle, two revolvers, bow and arrow, some of their bows being strung, and their whole appearance and conduct plainly indicating that they had come for war. Their declarations to some of my guides and friendly Indians proved the same thing, and they were only deterred from hostile acts by discovering our strength to be far greater than they had imagined, and our scouts on the alert.

What were the facts? On the 27th of November, only twenty-one days prior to the date of the certificate, the same Indians, whose peaceable character was vouched for so strongly, had engaged in battle with my command by attacking it during the fight with Black Kettle. It was in their camp that the bodies of the murdered mother and child were found, and we had followed day by day the trail of the Kiowas and other tribes, leading us directly from the dead and mangled bodies of our comrades, slain by them a few days previous, until we were about to overtake and punish the guilty parties, when the above communication was received, some forty or fifty miles from Fort Cobb, in the direction of the Washita battleground

This, of itself, was conclusive evidence of the character of the tribes was were dealing with; but aside from these incontrovertible facts, had additional evidence been needed of the openly hostile conduct of the Kiowas and Comanches, and of their active participation in the battle of the Washita, it is only necessary to refer to the collected testimony of Black Eagle and other leading chiefs. This testimony was written, and was then in the hands of the agents of the Indian Bureau.

This evidence is all contained in a report made to the Superintendent of Indian Affairs, by one Philip McCuskey, United States interpreter for the Kiowa and Comanche tribes. This report was dated Fort Cobb, December 3, while the communication from General Hazen, certifying to the friendly disposition and conduct of these tribes, was dated the same place thirteen days later. Mah-wis-sa also confirmed these statements, and pointed out to me, when near the battleground, the location of Satanta's village. It was from her, too, that I learned that it was in Satanta's village that the bodies of the white women and child were found.

After meeting the chiefs, who with their bands had approached our advance under flag of truce, and compelling the release of the scout whom they had seized and held prisoner, we continued our march toward Fort Cobb, the chiefs agreeing to ride with us and accompany my command to that place. The chiefs only requested that they might send one of their number, mounted on a fleet pony, to the villages, in order to hasten their movement to Fort Cobb. How eager for peace were these poor, confiding sons of the forest is the mental ejaculation of some of my readers, particularly if they are inclined to be converts to the humanitarian doctrines supposed to be applicable in the government of Indians. If I am addressing any of this class, for whose kindness of heart I have the utmost regard, I regret to be compelled to disturb the illusion.

Peace was not included among the purposes which governed the chiefs who so freely and unhesitatingly proffered their company during our march to Fort Cobb. Nor had they the faintest intention of either accompanying us or directing their villages to proceed to the fort. The messenger whom they seemed so anxious to despatch to the village was not sent to hasten the movement of their villages toward Fort Cobb, as claimed by them, but to hasten their movement in a precisely opposite direction, viz., towards the head waters of Red River, near the northwestern limits of Texas. This sudden effusion of friendly sentiments rather excited my suspicions, but I was unable at first to divine the real intents and purposes of the chiefs. Nothing was to be done but to act so as to avoid exciting their suspicion, and trust to time to unravel the scheme. When we arrived at our camping ground, on the evening of that day, the chiefs requested permission to despatch another messenger to their people to inform them where we were encamped. To this proposition no objection was made. That evening I caused an abundant supply of provisions, consisting principally of beef, bread, coffee, and sugar, to be distributed among them. In posting my pickets that night for the protection of the camp, I arranged to have the reserve stationed within a short distance of the spot on which the chiefs were to encamp during the night, which point was but a few paces from my headquarters. Before retiring, I took Romeo, the interpreter, and strolled down to pay a visit to the chiefs. The latter, after the substantial meal in which they had just indulged, were seated, Indian fashion, around a small fire, enjoying such comfort as was to be derived from the occasional whiffs of smoke which each in proper turn inhaled from the long-stemmed pipe of red clay that was kept passing from right to left around the circle. Their greeting of me was cordial in the extreme, but, as in the play—of "Richelieu," I believe—they "bowed too low." Through Romeo I chatted on indifferent subjects with the various chiefs, and from nearly all of them received assurances of their firmly fixed resolution to abandon forever the dangers and risks of the war path, to live no longer at variance with their white brothers, to eschew henceforth all such unfriendly customs as scalp-taking, murdering defenceless women and children, and stealing stock from the settlers of the frontier. All this was to be changed in the future. It seemed strange, listening to these apparently "artless sons of nature," that men entertaining the ardent desire for repose which they professed, had not turned their backs on the war path long ago, and settled down to the quiet enjoyment of the blessings of peace. But better that this conclusion should be arrived at late than not at all. The curtain had fallen from their eyes, and they were enabled to see everything in its proper light. To adopt their own language, "their hearts had become good," and had now resolved to follow the white man's road, to adopt his mode of dress, till the soil, and establish schools for the education of their children, until in time the white man and the red man would not only be brothers in name, but would be found travelling the same road with interests in common.

Romeo was also told to inform the chiefs that after the camp had quieted down for the night, it would not be prudent for them to wander far from their campfire, as the sentries might mistake them for enemies and fire upon them. This I knew would make them hug their fire closely until morning. Before daylight we were again in the saddle and commencing the last march necessary to take us to Fort Cobb. Again did it become important, in the opinion of the chiefs, to despatch another of their number to hurry up the people of their villages, in order, as they said, that the villages might arrive at Fort Cobb at the same time we did. As the march progressed these applications became more frequent, until most of the chiefs had been sent away as messengers. I noticed, however, that in selecting those to be sent, the chiefs lowest in rank and importance were first chosen, so that those who remained were the highest. When their numbers had dwindled down to less than half the original party, I saw that instead of acting in good faith this party of chiefs was solely engaged in the effort to withdraw our attention from the villages, and, by an apparent offer on their part to accompany us to Fort Cobb, where we were encouraged to believe the villages would meet us, prevent us from watching and following the trail made by the lodges, which had already diverged from the direct route to Fort Cobb, the one the villages would have pursued had that fort been their destination. It became palpably evident that the Indians were resorting, as usual, to stratagem to accomplish their purpose, which of course involved our deception. Fortunately their purpose was divined in time to thwart it. As no haste was necessary, I permitted the remaining chiefs to continue the march with us, without giving them any grounds to suppose that we strongly doubted their oft-repeated assertions that their hearts were good and their tongues were straight. Finally, as our march for that day neared its termination and we were soon to reach our destination, the party of chiefs, which at first embraced upwards of twenty, had become reduced until none remained except the two head chiefs, Lone Wolf and Satanta, and these no doubt were laughing in their sleeves, if an Indian may be supposed to possess that article of apparel, at the happy and highly successful manner in which they had hoodwinked their white brethren. But had they known all that had been transpiring they would not have felt so self-satisfied. As usual, quite a number of officers and orderlies rode at the head of the column, including a few of General Sheridan's staff.

As soon as the scheme of the Indians was discovered, I determined to seize the most prominent chiefs as hostages for the fulfillment of their promises regarding the coming on of the villages; but as for this purpose two hostages were as valuable as twenty, I allowed all but this number to take their departure apparently unnoticed. Finally, when none but Lone Wolf and Satanta remained, and they no doubt were prepared with a plausible excuse to bid us in the most improved Kiowa *au revoir*, the officers just referred to, at a given signal, drew their revolvers, and Lone Wolf and Satanta were informed through Romeo that they were prisoners.

Not even the proverbial stoicism of the red man was sufficient to conceal the chagrin and disappointment recognizable in every lineament of the countenances of both Satanta and Lone Wolf when they discovered that all their efforts at deception had not only failed, but left them prisoners in our hands. Had we been in doubt as to whether their intention had really been to leave us in the lurch or not, all doubt would have been dispelled by a slight circumstance which soon after transpired. As I before stated, we had almost reached Fort Cobb, which was our destination for the time being. The chiefs who had already made their escape now became anxious in regard to the non-arrival in their midst of Satanta and Lone Wolf. The delay of the last two could not be satisfactorily accounted for. Something must have gone amiss.

Again was stratagem resorted to. We were marching along without interruption or incident to disturb our progress, such of us as were at the head of the column keeping watchful eyes upon our two swarthy prisoners, who rode sullenly at our sides, and whose past career justified us in attributing to them the nerve and daring necessary to induce an effort to secure their liberty should there be the slightest probability of success. Suddenly a mounted Indian appeared far away to our right, and approached us at a gallop until almost within rifle range, when halting his well-trained pony upon a little hillock which answered his purpose, he gracefully detached the scarlet blanket he wore, and began waving it in a peculiar but regular manner. Both chiefs looked anxiously in the direction of the warrior, then merely glanced toward me as if to see if I had also observed this last arrival; but too proud to speak or prefer a request, they rode silently on, apparently indifferent to what might follow. Turning to Romeo, who rode in rear, I directed him to inquire of the chiefs the meaning of the signals that the warrior was evidently endeavoring to convey to them. Satanta acted as spokesman, and replied that the warrior in sight was his son, and that the latter was signalling to him that he had something important to communicate, and desired Satanta to ride out and join him.

To have seen the innocent and artless expression of countenance with which Satanta made this announcement, one would not have imagined that the son had been sent as a decoy to cover the escape of the father, and that the latter had been aware of this fact from the first. However, I pretended to humor Satanta. Of course there was no objection to his galloping out to where his son awaited him, because, as he said, that son was, and for good reason perhaps, unwilling to gallop in to where his father was. But if Satanta was so eager to see and communicate with his son, there should be no objection to the presence of a small escort—not that there existed doubts in my mind as to Satanta's intention to return to us, because no such doubt existed. I was positively convinced that once safely beyond our reach, the place at the head of the column, which had known him for a few brief hours, would know him no more forever. I told Romeo to say to Satanta that he might ride across the plain to where his son was.

The most careless observer would have detected the air of vexation with which Satanta turned his pony's head, and taking me at my word started to meet his son. A brisk gallop soon brought us to the little hillock upon which Satanta's son awaited us. He was there, a tall, trimly built, warrior-like young fellow of perhaps twenty, and bore himself while in our presence as if he would have us to understand he was not only the son of a mighty chief, but some day would wear that title himself. What was intended to be gained by the interview did not become evident, as the presence of Romeo prevented any conversation between father and son looking to the formation of plans for escape. Questions were asked and answered as to where the village was, and in regard to its future movements, but nothing satisfactory either to Satanta or his captors was learned from the young warrior. Finally, I suggested to Satanta that as we only intended to proceed a few miles further, being then in the near vicinity of Fort Cobb, and would there encamp for an indefinite period, his son had better accompany us to camp, where Lone Wolf and Satanta would be informed what was to be required of them and their people, and then, after conferring with each other, the two chiefs could send Satanta's son to the village with any message that they might desire to transmit to their people. At the same time I promised the young warrior good treatment, with permission to go and come as he chose, and in no manner to be regarded or treated as a prisoner.

This proposition seemed to strike the Indians favorably, and much to my surprise, knowing the natural suspicion of the Indian, the young warrior readily consented to the plan, and at once placed himself in our power. Turning our horses' heads, we soon resumed our places at the head of the column, the three Indians riding in silence, brooding, no doubt, over plans looking to their freedom.

By way of a slight digression from the main narrative, I will here remark that during the prolonged imprisonment of the two chiefs, Satanta's son became a regular visitor to our camp, frequently becoming the bearer of important messages from the chiefs to their villages, and in time he and I, apparently, became firm friends. He was an excellent shot with the rifle, Satanta said he was the best in the tribe, and frequently, when time hung heavily on my hands, and I felt a desire for recreation, he and I took our rifles, and, after passing beyond the limits of camp, engaged in a friendly match at target practice, a much more agreeable mode of testing our skill as marksmen than by each other as a target.

Satanta had exhibited no little gratification when I first engaged to shoot with his son, and as the lodge in which he was kept a closely guarded prisoner was on my route in returning from target practice to my tent, I usually stopped a few moments in his lodge to exchange passing remarks. He was evidently disappointed when informed as to the result of the first trial with our rifles, that his son had come off only second best; and numerous were the explanations which his fertile mind suggested as the causes leading to this result—a result which in the eyes of the Indian assumed far greater importance than would ordinarily be attached to it by white men. As we had agreed to have frequent contests of this kind, Satanta assured me that his son would yet prove himself the better man. Each meeting, however, only resulted as the first, although by varying the distance every opportunity was given for a fair test. Finally, when all other explanations had failed, Satanta thought that I should offer the young warrior the use of my rifle, and that I should use his in the next match; a proposition which was at once accepted, and, as if to be better prepared to make an excellent score, my rifle was soon in his hands and undergoing the critical inspection and manipulation of trigger, sights, etc., which always suggest themselves the moment an experienced marksman finds a new rifle in his hands. The following day we engaged as usual in rifle practice, he with my rifle, I with his. I frankly confess that having entered into the contest from the first with as much zest and rivalry as even my dusky competitor could lay claim to, and having come off victor in the preceding contests, I was not entirely free from anxiety lest the change in rifles might also change the result, and detract, in the eyes of the Indians at least, from my former successes. On this occasion, as on all previous ones, we were alone, and consequently we were our own judges, umpire, and referee. Greatly to my satisfaction, my good fortune enabled me to make a better score than did my opponent, and this result seemed to settle his opinion finally as to our relative merits as marksmen. I attached no little importance to these frequent and friendly meetings between Satanta's son and myself. Any superiority in the handling or use of weapons, in horseback exercises, or in any of the recognized manly sports, is a sure steppingstone in obtaining for the possessor the highest regard of the red man.

Upon our arrival at Fort Cobb, the day of the seizure of the two chiefs, Lone Wolf and Satanta, we selected a camp with a view of remaining at that point during the negotiations which were to be conducted with the various tribes who were still on the war path. So far as some of the tribes were concerned, they were occupying that equivocal position which enabled them to class themselves as friendly and at the same time engage in hostilities. This may sound ambiguous, but is easily explained. The chiefs and old men, with the women and children of the tribe, were permitted to assemble regularly at the agency near Fort Cobb, and as regularly were bountifully supplied with food and clothing sufficient for all their wants; at the same time the young men, warriors, and war chiefs of the tribe were almost continually en-gaged in making war upon the frontier of northern Texas and south eastern Kansas. Indeed, we established the fact, while at or near Fort Cobb, that while my command was engaged in fighting the warriors and chiefs of certain tribes at the Battle of the Washita, the families of these same warriors and chiefs were being clothed and fed by the agent of the government then stationed at Fort Cobb.

Lone Wolf, head Chief of the Kiowas

Surprising as this may seem, it is not an unusual occurrence. The same system has prevailed during the past year. While my command was resisting the attacks of a large body of warriors on the Yellowstone River last summer, the families of many of these warriors, the latter representing seven tribes or bands, were subsisting upon provisions and clothed in garments issued to them at the regular Indian agencies by the government. But of this more anon.

The three tribes that became at that time the special objects of our attention, and with whom we were particularly anxious to establish such relations as would prevent in the future a repetition of the murders and outrages of which they had so long been guilty, were the Kiowas, Cheyennes, and Arapahos; and each tribe, dreading a repetition of the blow upon themselves, had removed their villages to remote points where they deemed themselves secure from further chastisement. Having Lone Wolf and Satanta, the two leading chiefs of the Kiowas, in our hands, we thought that through them the Kiowas could be forced to a compliance with the just and reasonable demands of the government, and with the terms of their treaty providing for the reservation system.

All demands upon the Kiowas were communicated by me to Lone Wolf and Satanta, under the instructions of General Sheridan, who, although on the ground, declined to treat directly with the faithless chiefs. The Kiowas were informed that unless the entire tribe repaired to the vicinity of the agency, then located not far from Fort Cobb, the war, which had been inaugurated with such vigor and effect at the Washita, would be renewed and continued until the terms of their treaty had been complied with. This proposition was imparted to Lone Wolf and Satanta, and by them transmitted to their tribe, through the son of the latter, who acted as a sort of diplomatic courier between the Kiowa village and our camp.

The Kiowas, while sending messages apparently in accord with the proposition, and seeming to manifest a willingness to come in and locate themselves upon their reservation, continued, after the manner of Indian diplomacy, to defer from time to time the promised movement. There was every reason to believe that, finding the military disposed to temporarily suspend active operations, and resort to negotiation, the Kiowas had located their village within a short distance of our camp, as Satanta's son, in going and coming with messages from one to the other, easily made the round journey in a single day; so that had they been so disposed, the Kiowas could have transferred their village to our immediate vicinity, as desired by the military authorities, in one day. The truth was, however, that while manifesting an apparent desire to conform to this requirement, as a precedent to final peace, they had not intended at any time to keep faith with the government, but, by a pretended acquiescence in the proposed arrangement, secure the release of the two head chiefs, Lone Wolf and Satanta, and then hasten, with the entire village, to join forces with the other two tribes, the Cheyennes and Arapahos, who were then represented as being located somewhere near the source of Red River, and on the border of the Llano Estacado, or Staked Plain, a region of country supposed to be impenetrable by civilized man. Every promise of the Kiowas to come in was always made conditional upon the prior release of Lone Wolf and Satanta.

Their efforts to procrastinate or evade a fulfillment of their part of the agreement finally exhausted the forbearance which thus far had prompted none but the mildest measures on the part of the military authorities, in the efforts of the latter to bring about a peaceful solution of existing difficulties. It had become evident that, instead of intending to establish relations of permanent peace and friendship with the whites, the majority of the tribe were only waiting the release of Lone Wolf and Satanta to resume hostilities, or at least two more firmly ally themselves with the extremely hostile tribes then occupying the head waters of Red River.

After hearing the oft-repeated excuses of the Kiowas, General Sheridan communicated his resolve to me in substance as follows: "Well, Custer, these Kiowas are endeavoring to play us false. Their object is to occupy us with promises until the grass enables them to go where they please and make war if they choose. We have given them every opportunity to come in and enjoy the protection of the government, if they so desired. They are among the worst Indians we have to deal with, and have been guilty of untold murders and outrages, at the same time they were being fed and clothed by the government. These two chiefs, Lone Wolf and Satanta, have forfeited their lives over and over again. They could now induce their people to come in and become friendly if they chose to exert their influence in that direction. This matter has gone on long enough, and must be stopped, as we have to look after the other tribes before spring overtakes us. You can inform Lone Wolf and Satanta that we shall wait until sundown tomorrow for their tribe to come in; if by that time the village is not here, Lone Wolf and Satanta will be hung, and the troops sent in pursuit of the village."

This might be regarded as bringing matters to a crisis. I proceeded directly to the lodge in which Lone Wolf and Satanta were prisoners, accompanied by Romeo as interpreter. I found the two chiefs reclining lazily upon their comfortable, if not luxurious couches of robes. Satanta's son was also present. After a few preliminary remarks, I introduced the subject which was the occasion of my visit, by informing the chiefs that I had just returned from General Sheridan's tent, where the question of the failure of the Kiowas to comply with their oft-repeated promises had been discussed, and that I had been directed to acquaint them with the determination that had been formed in regard to them and their people. At this announcement I could see that both chiefs became instantly and unmistakably interested in what was being said.

I had so often heard of the proverbial stoicism of the Indian character, that it occurred to me that this was a favorable moment for judging how far this trait affects their conduct. For it will be readily acknowledged that the communication which I was about to make to them was one likely, at all events, to overturn any self-imposed stolidity which was not deeply impregnated in their nature. After going over the subject of the continued absence of the Kiowas from their reservation, their oft-made promises, made only to be violated, I told them that they were regarded, as they had a right to be, as the two leading and most influential chiefs of the tribe; that although they were prisoners, yet so powerful were they among the people of their own tribe, that they had it in their power, by a single command, to cause a satisfactory settlement of existing difficulties to be made, yet so far they had failed utterly to exert an influence for peace between their people and the government. The announcement then to be made to them must be regarded as final, and it remained with them alone to decide by their action what the result should be. In as few words as possible I then communicated to them the fate which undoubtedly awaited them in the event of the non-appearance of their tribe. Until sunset of the following day seemed a very brief period, yet I failed to detect the slightest change in the countenance of either when told that that would be the extent of their lives if their tribe failed to come in. Not a muscle of their warrior-like faces moved. Their eyes neither brightened nor quailed; nothing in their action or appearance gave token that anything unusual had been communicated to them. Satanta's son alone of the three seemed to realize that matters were becoming serious, as could readily be told by watching his anxious glances, first at his father, then at Lone Wolf; but neither spoke.

Realizing the importance of time, and anxious to bring about a peaceful as well as satisfactory termination of our difficulties with the Kiowas, and at the same time to afford every facility to the two captive chiefs to save their oft-forfeited lives—for all familiar with their bloody and cruel career would grant that they merited death—I urged upon them the necessity of prompt action in communicating with their tribe, and pointed to Satanta's son, who could be employed for this purpose. Quickly springing to his feet, and not waiting to hear the opinions of the two chiefs, the young warrior rushed from the lodge, and was soon busily engaged in tightening the girths of his Indian saddle, preparatory to a rapid gallop on his fleet pony.

In the mean time Lone Wolf and Satanta began exchanging utterances, at first slow and measured, in tones scarcely audible. Gradually they seemed to realize how desperate was the situation they were in, and how much depended upon themselves. Then laying aside the formality which had up to that moment characterized their deportment, they no longer appeared as the dignified, reserved, almost sullen chiefs, but acted and spoke as would be expected of men situated as they were. In less time than I have taken to describe the action Satanta's handsome son appeared at the entrance of the lodge, mounted and in readiness for his ride. Although he seemed by his manner to incline toward his father as the one who should give him his instructions, it was soon apparent that a more correct understanding existed between the two captives. Lone Wolf was the head chief of their tribe, Satanta the second in rank. The occasion was too important to leave anything to chance. A message from Satanta might receive prompt attention; a command from the head chief could not be disregarded; hence it was that Satanta stood aside, and Lone Wolf stepped forward and addressed a few hasty but apparently emphatic sentences to the young courier, who was all eagerness to depart on his mission. As Lone Wolf concluded his instructions, and the young warrior was gathering up his reins and lariat, and turning his pony from the lodge in the direction of the village, Satanta simply added, in an energetic tone, "Hoodle-teh, hoodle-teh" (make haste, make haste); an injunction scarcely needed, as the young Indian and his pony were the next moment flying across the level plain.

No general commanding an army, who had transmitted his orders to his corps commanders, directing a movement at daylight the following morning, could have exhibited more confidence in the belief that his orders would be executed, than did this captive chief in the belief that, although a prisoner in the hands of his traditional enemies, his lodge closely guarded on all sides by watchful sentinels, his commands to his people would meet with a prompt and willing compliance. After a little further conversation with the two chiefs, I was preparing to leave the lodge, when Lone Wolf, true to the Indian custom, under which an opportunity to beg for something to eat is never permitted to pass unimproved, called me back, and said that the next day his principal chiefs would visit him, and although he was a prisoner, he would be glad to be able to entertain them in a manner befitting his rank and importance in the tribe, and therefore I was appealed to furnish the provisions necessary to provide a feast for a dozen or more hungry chiefs and their retainers; in reply to which modest request I made the heart of Lone Wolf glad, and called forth, in his most emphatic as well as delighted manner, the universal word, of approval, "How," by informing him that the feast should certainly be prepared if he only would supply the guests.

The next day was one of no little interest, and to none more than to the two chiefs, who expected to see the first step taken by their people that would terminate in their release from a captivity that had certainly become exceedingly irksome, not to mention the new danger that stared them in the face. Lone Wolf, however, maintained his confidence, and repeatedly assured me during the forenoon that Black Eagle and the other chiefs, whom he had sent for by name, would arrive no later than two o'clock that day. His confidence proved not to be misplaced. The sun had hardly marked the hour of one in the heavens, when a small cavalcade was seen approaching in the distance from the direction of the Kiowa village. The quick eye of Satanta was the first to discover it. A smile of haughty triumph lighted up the countenance of Lone Wolf when his attention was called to the approaching party, his look indicating that he felt it could not be otherwise: had he not ordered it?

On they came, first about a dozen chiefs, riding at a deliberate and dignified pace, they and their ponies richly caparisoned in the most fantastic manner. The chiefs wore blankets of bright colors, scarlet predominating, with here and there a bright green. Each face was painted in brilliant colors, yellow, blue, green, red, black, and combinations of all of them, no two faces being ornamented alike, and each new face seeming more horrible than its predecessor. These were warriors and confidential friends and advisers of the chiefs in whose train they rode. In rear of all rode a few meek-looking squaws, whose part in this imposing pageant became evident when the chiefs and warriors dismounted, giving the reins of their ponies to the squaws, who at once busied themselves in picketing the ponies of their lords, and, in every sense of the word, masters, wherever the grazing seemed freshest and most abundant. This being done, their part was performed, and they waited, near the ponies, the return of the chiefs and warriors. The latter, after forming in one group, and in similar order to that in which they rode, advanced toward the lodge outside of which, but within the chain of sentinels, stood Lone Wolf and Satanta. The meeting between the captive chiefs and their more fortunate comrades occasioned an exhibition of more feeling and sensibility than is generally accredited to the Indian. A bevy of school girls could not have embraced each other, after a twenty-four hours' separation, with greater enthusiasm and demonstrations of apparent joy than did these chieftains, whose sole delight is supposed to be connected with scenes of bloodshed and cruelty. I trust no gentle-minded reader, imbued with great kindness of heart, will let this little scene determine his estimate of the Indian character; for be it understood, not one of the chiefs who formed the group of which I am writing but had participated in acts of the most barbarous and wanton cruelty. It was a portion of these chiefs who had led and encouraged the hand that had subjected the Box family to such a horrible fate.

Immediately after greetings had been exchanged between the captives and their friends, I was requested, by a message from Lone Wolf, to repair to his lodge in order to hear what his friends had to say. As I entered the lodge, the entire party of chiefs advanced to meet me, and began a series of handshaking and universal "Hows," which in outward earnestness made up for any lack of real sincerity, and to an inexperienced observer or a tender-hearted peace commissioner might well have appeared as an exhibition of indubitable friendship if not affection. After all were seated, and the ever-present long red clay pipe had passed and repassed around the circle, each chief indulging in a few silent whiffs, Black Eagle arose, and after shaking hands with me, proceeded, after the manner of an oration, to inform me what I had reason to expect, and what the reader no doubt has also anticipated, that the entire Kiowa village was at that moment on the march, and would arrive in the vicinity of our camp before dark. No reference was made to the fact that this general movement on their part was one of compulsion, but on the contrary, to have heard Black Eagle, who was an impressive orator, one might well have believed that, no longer able to endure the separation from their brothers, the white men, who, as Black Eagle said, like themselves were all descended from one father, the Kiowas had voluntarily resolved to pack up their lodges, and when they next should put them down it would be alongside the tents of their white friends.

The Kiowas were now all located on their reservation except a single band of the tribe, led by a very wicked and troublesome chief, named Woman Heart, although his conduct and character were anything but in keeping with the gentleness of his name. He had taken his band and moved in the direction of the Staked Plains, far to the west of the Kiowa reservation.

However, the Indian question, so far as the Kiowas were concerned, was regarded as settled, at least for the time being, and it became our next study how to effect a similar settlement with the Cheyennes and Arapahos, who had fled after the battle of the Washita, and were then supposed to be somewhere between the Witchita Mountains and the western border of Texas, north of the head waters of Red River.

All the chiefs of that region who were interested in promoting peace between the whites and Indians were assembled at my head-quarters, when I informed them of the proposed peace embassy, and asked that some chief of prominence should volunteer as bearer of a friendly message to the Cheyennes and Arapahos. A well-known chief of the Apaches, named Iron Shirt, promptly offered himself as a messenger in the cause of peace. In reply to my inquiry, he said he could be ready to depart upon his commendable errand the following day, and estimated the distance such that it would be necessary to take provision sufficient to last him and his companion three weeks. Having arranged all the details of the journey, the assemblage of chiefs dispersed, the next step being to decide which of the three squaws should accompany Iron Shirt to her tribe. I concluded to state the case to them, and make the selection a matter for them to decide. Summoning Mah-wis-sa, Mo-nah-se-tah, and the Sioux squaw, their companion, to my tent, I, through Romeo, acquainted them with the desire of the government to establish peace with their people and with the Arapahos, and in order to accomplish this we intended despatching a friendly message to the absent tribes, which must be carried by some of their own people. After conferring with each other a few minutes, they concluded that Mah-wis-sa, the sister of Black Kettle, should return to her people. Every arrangement was provided, looking to the comfort of the two Indians who were to undertake this long journey. A bountiful supply of provisions was carefully provided in convenient packages, an extra amount of clothing and blankets being given to Mah-wis-sa in order that she should not return to her people empty-handed. To transport their provision and blankets a mule was given them to be used as a pack-animal. It was quite an event, sufficient to disturb the monotony of camp, when the hour arrived for the departure of the two peace commissioners. I had told Iron Shirt what he was to say to the chiefs of the tribes who still remained hostile, which was in effect that we were anxious for peace, and to that end invited them to come at once and place themselves and their people on the reservations, where we would meet and regard them as friends, and all present hostilities, as well as reckoning for past differences, should cease; but if this friendly proffer was not accepted favorably and at once, we would be forced to regard it as indicating their desire to prolong the war, in which event the troops would be sent against them as soon as practicable. I relied not a little on the good influence of Mah-wis-sa, who, as I have before stated, was a woman of superior intelligence, and was strongly impressed with a desire to aid in establishing a peace between her people and the white men. Quite a group, composed of officers, soldiers, teamsters, guards, and scouts, assembled to witness the departure of Iron Shirt and Mah-wis-sa, and to wish them Godspeed in their mission.

After Iron Shirt and Mah-wis-sa had seated themselves upon their ponies and were about to set out, Mah-wis-sa, suddenly placing her hand on the neat belt which secured her blanket about her, indicated that she was unprovided with that most essential companion of frontier life; a *mutch-ka* as she expressed it, meaning a hunting knife. Only those who have lived on the plains can appreciate the unpurchasable convenience of a hunting knife. Whether it is to carve a buffalo or a mountain trout, mend horse equipments, or close up a rent in the tent, there is a constant demand for the services of a good hunting knife. Mah-wis-sa smiled at the forgetfulness that had made her fail to discern this omission sooner, but I relieved her anxiety by taking from my belt the hunting knife that hung at my side and gave it to her. When all was ready for the start, Iron Shirt rode first, followed by the pack-mule, which he led, while Mah-wis-sa, acting as driver to the latter and well mounted, brought up the rear.

As they rode away amid the shower of good wishes that was bestowed upon them and their mission, many were the queries as to the probable extent of their journey, their return, and whether they would be successful. For upon the success or failure of these two Indians depended in a great measure on the question whether or not we were to be forced to continue the war; and among the hundreds who watched the departing bearers of the olive branch, there was not one but hoped earnestly that the mission would prove successful, and we be spared the barbarities that a further prosecution of the war would necessarily entail. Yet there are those who would have the public believe that the army is at all times clamorous for an Indian war. I have yet to meet the officer or man belonging to the army, who, when the question of war or peace with the Indians was being agitated, did not cast the weight of his influence, the prayers of his heart, in behalf of peace. When I next called Mah-wis-sa's attention to the *mutch-ka* (knife), it was far from the locality we then occupied, and under very different circumstances.

After the departure of Iron Shirt and Mah-wis-sa, we were forced to settle down to the dullest routine of camp life, as nothing could be done until their return. It was a full three weeks before the interest in camp received a fresh impetus, by the tidings, which flew from tent to tent, that Iron Shirt had returned. He did return, but Mah-wis-sa did not return with him. His story was brief. He and Mah-wis-sa, after leaving us and travelling for several days westward, had arrived at the Cheyenne and Arapaho villages. They delivered their messages to the chiefs of the two tribes, who were assembled in council to hear them, and after due deliberation thereon, Iron Shirt was informed that the distance was too great, the ponies in too poor condition, to permit the villages to return. In other words, these two tribes had virtually decided that rather than return to their reservation they preferred the chances of war. When asked to account for Mah-wis-sa's failure to accompany him back, Iron Shirt stated that she had desired to fulfill her promise and return with him, but the chiefs of her tribe would not permit her to do so.

The only encouragement derived from Iron Shirt was in his statement that Little Robe, a prominent chief of the Cheyennes, and Yellow Bear, the second chief of the Arapahos, were both extremely anxious to effect a permanent peace between their people and the government, and both had promised Iron Shirt that they would leave their villages soon after his departure and visit us, with a view to prevent a continuation of the war. Iron Shirt was rewarded for his journey by bountiful presents of provisions for himself and his people. True to their promises made to Iron Shirt, it was but a short time before Little Robe and Yellow Bear arrived at our camp and were well received.

They reported that their villages had under consideration the question of accepting our invitation to come in and live at peace in the future, and that many of their people were strongly in favor of adopting this course, but for the present it was uncertain whether or not the two tribes would come in. The two tribes would probably act in concert, and if they intended coming, would make their determination known by despatching couriers to us in a few days.

After waiting many long weary days for the arrival of the promised couriers from the two tribes, until even Little Robe and Yellow Bear were forced to acknowledge that there was no longer any reason to expect their coming, it occurred to me that there was but one expedient yet untried that furnished even a doubtful chance of averting war. This could only be resorted to with the approval of General Sheridan, whose tent had been pitched in our midst during the entire winter, and who evidently proposed to remain on the ground until the Indian question in that locality should be disposed of. My plan was as follows:

We had some fifteen hundred troops, a force ample to cope with all the Indians which could then, or since, be combined at any one point on the plains. But in the state of feeling existing among those Indians at that time, consequent upon the punishment which they had received at and since the Washita campaign, it would have been an extremely difficult if not impracticable matter to attempt to move so large a body of troops near their villages, and retain the latter in their places, so fearful were they of receiving punishment for their past offences. It would also have been impracticable to move upon them stealthily, as they were then, for causes already given, more than ever on the alert, and were no doubt kept thoroughly informed in regard to our every movement.

It was thus considered out of the question to employ my entire command of fifteen hundred men in what I proposed should be purely a peaceful effort to bring about a termination of the war, as so large a force would surely intimidate the Indians, and cause them to avoid our presence.

I believed that if I could see the leading chiefs of the two hostile tribes and convince them of the friendly desire of the government, they might be induced to relinquish the war and return to their reservation. I have endeavored to show that I could not go among them with my entire command, neither was I sufficiently orthodox as a peace commissioner to believe what so many of that order preach, but fail to practise, that I could take an olive branch in one hand, the plan of a schoolhouse in the other, and, unaccompanied by force, visit the Indian villages in safety. My life would certainly have been the price of such temerity. Too imposing a force would repel the Indians; too small a force would tempt them to murder us, even though our mission was a friendly one.

After weighing the matter carefully in my own mind, I decided that with General Sheridan's approval I would select from my command forty men, two officers and a medical officer, and, accompanied by the two chiefs, Little Robe and Yellow Bear, who regarded my proposition with favor, I would set out in search of the hostile camp, there being but little doubt that with the assistance of the chiefs I would have little difficulty in discovering the whereabouts of the villages; while the smallness of my party would prevent unnecessary alarm or suspicion as to our intentions. After discussing it fully, Sheridan gave his assent by saying that the character of the proposed expedition was such that he would not order me to proceed upon it, but if I volunteered to go, he would give me the full sanction of his authority and every possible assistance to render the mission a successful one; in conclusion urging me to exercise the greatest caution against the stratagems or treachery of the Indians, who no doubt would be but too glad to massacre my party in revenge for their recent well-merited chastisement. Returning to my tent, I at once set about making preparations for my journey, the extent or result of which now became interesting subjects for deliberation. The first thing necessary was to make up the party which was to accompany me.

As the number of men was to be limited to forty, too much care could not be exercised in their selection. I chose the great majority of them from the sharpshooters, men who, in addition to being cool and brave, were experienced and skillful marksmen. My standard-bearer, a well-tried sergeant, was selected as the senior non-commissioned officer of the party. The officers who were to accompany me were my brother Colonel Custer, Captain Robbins, and Dr. Renick, Acting Assistant Surgeon U.S. Army. As guide I had Neva, a Blackfoot Indian, who had accompanied General Fremont in his explorations, and who could speak a little English. Little Robe and Yellow Bear were also to be relied upon as guides, while Romeo accompanied us as interpreter. Young Brewster, determined to miss no opportunity of discovering his lost sister, had requested and been granted permission to become one of the party. This completed the personnel of the expedition. All were well armed and well mounted. We were to take no wagons or tents; our extra supplies were to be transported on pack-mules. We were to start on the evening of the second day, the intervening time being necessary to complete our preparations. It was decided that our first march should be a short one, sufficient merely to enable us to reach a village of friendly Apaches, located a few miles from our camp, where we would spend the first night and be joined by Little Robe and Yellow Bear, who at that time were guests of the Apaches. I need not say that in the opinion of many of our comrades our mission was regarded as closely bordering on the imprudent, to qualify it by no stronger term.

So confident did one of the most prudent officers of my command feel in regard to our annihilation by the Indians, that in bidding me good-by he contrived to slip into my hand a small pocket Derringer pistol, loaded, with the simple remark, "You had better take it, General; it may prove useful to you." As I was amply provided with arms, both revolvers and rifle, and as a pocket Derringer may not impress the reader as being a very formidable weapon to use in Indian warfare, the purpose of my friend in giving me the small pocket weapon may not seem clear. It was given me under the firm conviction that the Indians would overwhelm and massacre my entire party; and to prevent my being captured, disarmed, and reserved for torture, that little pistol was given me in order that at the last moment I might become my own executioner—an office I was not seeking, nor did I share in my friend's opinion.

Everything being ready for our departure, we swung into our saddles, waved our adieus to the comrades who were to remain in camp, and the next moment we turned our horses' heads westward.

Cheyenne way of life.

CHAPTER 8

Village of the Apaches—Guides Little Robe and Yellow Bear—Tidings of the Captured Girls—In Search of the Cheyennes—Daughter of Black Eagle—A Pipe Shared with Medicine Arrow—The Captive Girls Released

The Apache village had been represented as located only five or six miles from our camp, but we found the distance nearly twice as great; and although we rode rapidly, our horses being fresh, yet it was quite dark before we reached the first lodge, the location of the rest of the village being tolerably well defined by the apparently countless dogs, whose barking at our approach called forth most of the inhabitants of the village.

As our coming had been previously announced by Little Robe and Yellow Bear, our arrival occasioned no surprise. Inquiring of the first we saw where the stream of water was, as an Indian village is invariably placed in close proximity to water, we were soon on our campground, which was almost within the limits of the village. Our horses were soon unsaddled and picketed out to graze, fires were started by the men preparatory to the enjoyment of a cup of coffee, and every preliminary made for a good night's rest and early start in the morning. But here the officers of the party encountered their first drawback. From some unexplained cause, the pack-mule that carried our blankets had with his attendant failed thus far to put in an appearance. His head leader had probably fallen behind, and in the darkness lost the party. The bugler was sent to a neighboring eminence to sound signals with his bugle, in the hope that the absent man with his mule might make his way to us, but all to no purpose. We were soon forced to relinquish all hope of seeing either man, mule, or blankets until daylight, and consequently the prospect of enjoying a comfortable rest was exceedingly limited. Saddle blankets were in great demand, but I was even more fortunate. A large number of the Apaches had come from their lodges out of mere curiosity to see us, hoping no doubt too that they might secure something to eat. Among them was one with whom I was acquainted, and to whom I made known the temporary loss of my blankets. By promising him a pint of sugar and an equal amount of coffee on my return to my camp, he agreed to loan me a buffalo robe until morning. With this wrapped around me and the aid of a bright blazing campfire, I passed a most comfortable night among my less fortunate companions, as we all lay stretched out on the ground, using our saddles for pillows.

Early next morning (our pack animals having come up in the night) we were in our saddles, and on our way ready and eager for whatever might be in store for us. The route taken by the guides led us along the northern border of the Witchita Mountains, our general direction being nearly due west. As soon as it had become known in the main camp that the expedition of which I now write was contemplated, young Brewster, who had never relinquished his efforts or inquiries to determine the fate of his lost sister, came to me with an earnest request to be taken as one of the party—a request which I was only too glad to comply with.

After getting well on our way I began, through Romeo, conversing with the two chiefs Little Robe and Yellow Bear, who rode at my side, upon the topic which was uppermost in the minds of the entire party: When and where should we probably find their people? Before our departure they had given me to understand that the villages might be found on one of the small streams flowing in a southerly direction past the western span of the Witchita Mountains, a distance from our main camp not exceeding sixty or seventy miles; but I could easily perceive that neither of the chiefs spoke with a great degree of confidence. They explained this by stating that the villages would not remain long in one place, and it was difficult to say positively in what locality or upon what stream we should find them; but that when we reached the last peak of the Witchita Mountains, which commanded an unlimited view of the plains beyond, they would send up smoke signals, and perhaps be able to obtain a reply from the village.

In the evening we reached a beautiful stream of water, with abundance of wood in the vicinity; here we halted for the night. Our horses were fastened to the trees, while the officers and men spread their blankets on the ground, and in groups of twos and threes prepared for the enjoyment of a good night's rest. One sentry remained awake during the night, and in order that the loss of sleep should be as little as might be consistent with our safety, the relief, instead of being composed of three men, each of whom would have to remain on duty two hours for every four hours of rest, was increased in number so that each member thereof was required to remain on post but a single hour during the night. While I felt confidence in the good intentions of the two chiefs, I did not neglect to advise the guards to keep a watchful eye upon them, as we could not afford to run any avoidable risks. Long after we had sought the solace of our blankets, and I had dropped into a comfortable doze, I was awakened by an Indian song. There was, of course, no occasion for alarm from this incident, yet it was sufficient to induce me to get up and make my way to the small fire, around which I knew the three Indians and Romeo to be lying, and from the vicinity of which the singing evidently came. As I approached the fire I found Neva, the Blackfoot, replenishing the small flame with a few dried twigs, while Romeo and Yellow Bear were sitting nearby enjoying some well-broiled beef ribs. Little Robe was reclining, in a half-sitting position, against a tree, and, apparently oblivious to the presence of his companions, was singing or chanting an Indian melody, the general tenor of which seemed to indicate a lightness of spirits. Young Brewster—unable, perhaps, to sleep, owing to thoughts of his lost sister—had joined the group, and appeared an interested observer of what was going on. I inquired of Romeo why Little Robe had selected such an unreasonable hour to indulge in his wild smelodies. Romeo repeated the inquiry to Little Robe, who replied that he had been away from his lodge for a long time, and the thought of soon returning, and of being with his people once more, had filled his heart with a gladness with which could only find utterance in song.

Taking a seat on the ground by the side of young Brewster, I joined the group. As neither Little Robe nor Yellow Bear could understand a word of English, and Neva was busily engaged with his culinary operations, young Brewster, with unconcealed delight, informed me that from conversations with Little Robe, who appeared in a more communicative mood than usual, he felt cheered by the belief that at last he was in a fair way to whereabouts of his sister. Little Robe had admitted that the Cheyennes had two white girls as prisoners, the date of the capture of one of them and the personal description given by Little Robe closely answering to that of Brewster's sister. In the hope of gleaning other valuable information from time to time, I advised the young man not to acquaint the Indians with the fact that he had lost a sister by capture; else, becoming suspicious, the supply of information might be cut off.

The tidings in regard to the captured girls were most encouraging, and spurred us to leave no effort untried to release them from the horrors of their situation. Before daylight the following morning we had breakfasted, and as soon as it was sufficiently light to enable us to renew our march we set out, still keeping almost due west. In the afternoon of that day we reached the last prominent peak of the Witchita Mountains, from which point Little Robe and Yellow Bear had said they would send up a smoke signal.

I had often during an Indian campaign seen these smoke signals, on my front, on my right and left—everywhere, in fact—but could never catch a glimpse of the Indians who were engaged in making them, nor did I comprehend at the time the precise import of the signals. I was glad, therefore, to have an opportunity to stand behind the scenes, as it were, and not only witness the *modus operandi* (method of operation), but understand the purpose of the actors.

Arriving at the base of the mountain or peak, the height of which did not exceed one thousand feet, we dismounted, and leaving our horses on the plain below, owing to the rough and rocky character of the ascent, a small portion of our party, including of course, the two chiefs, climbed to the summit. After sweeping the broad horizon, which spread out before us, and failing to discover any evidence of the presence of an Indian village anywhere within the scope of our vision, the two chiefs set about to make preparations necessary to enable them to "call to the village," as they expressed it.

The sight of these two Indian chiefs so intently engaged in this simple but effective mode of telegraphing was to me full of interest. In our case, however, the picture was not so complete in its results. For strain our eager eyes as we might in every direction, no responsive signal could be discovered, and finally the chiefs were reluctantly forced

Yellow Bear, second chief of the Arapahoes

to acknowledge that the villages were not where they expected to find them, and that to reach them would probably involve a longer journey t to acknowledge that the villages were not where they expected to find han we had anticipated. Descending from the mountain, we continued our journey, still directing our course nearly due west, as the two chiefs felt confident the villages were in that direction. That day and the next passed without further incident.

After arriving at camp on the second evening, a conversation with the two Indian chiefs made it seem probable that our journey would have to be prolonged several days beyond the time which was deemed necessary when we left the main camp. And as our supply of provisions was limited to our supposed wants during the shorter journey, it was necessary to adopt measures for obtaining fresh supplies. This was the more imperative as the country through which we were then passing was almost devoid of game. Our party was so small in number that our safety would be greatly imperilled by any serious reduction, yet it was a measure of necessity that a message should be sent back to General Sheridan, informing him of our changed plans and providing for a renewal of our stores.

I acquainted the men of my command with my desire, and it was not long before a soldierly young trooper announced that he would volunteer to carry a despatch safely through. The gallant offer was accepted, and I was soon seated on the ground, pencil in hand, writing to General Sheridan a hurried account of our progress thus far and our plans for the future, with a request to forward to us a supply of provisions; adding that the party escorting them could follow on our trail, and I would arrange to find them when required. I also requested that Colonel Cook, who commanded the sharpshooters, should be detailed to command the escort, and that California Joe might also be sent with the party.

It was decided that the despatch bearer should remain in camp with us until dark and then set out on his return to the main camp. Being well mounted, well armed, and a cool, daring young fellow, I felt but little anxiety as to his success. Leaving him to make his solitary journey guided by the light of the stars, and concealing himself during the day, we will continue our search after what then seemed to us the two lost tribes.

Daylight as usual found us in our saddles, the country continually interesting but less rolling, and (we judge by appearances) less productive. We saw but little game along our line of march, and the importance of time rendered delays of all kinds undesirable. The countenances of Little Robe and Yellow Bear wore an anxious look, and I could see that they began to doubt their ability to determine positively the locality of the villages.

Yellow Bear finally encouraged us by stating that by noon the following day we would arrive at a stream, on whose banks he expected to find the Arapaho village, and perhaps that of the Cheyennes. Nothing occurred worthy of note until about noon next day, when Yellow Bear informed me that we were within a few miles of the stream to which he had referred the day before, and added that if the village was there his people would have a lookout posted on a little knoll which we would find about a mile from the village in our direction; and as the appearance of our entire force might give alarm, Yellow Bear suggested that he, with Little Robe, Romeo, Neva, myself, and two or three others, should ride some distance in advance.

Remembering the proneness of the Indians to stratagem, I was yet impressed not only with the apparent sincerity of Yellow Bear thus far, but by the soundness of the reasons he gave for our moving in advance. I assented to his proposition, but my confidence was not sufficiently great to prevent me from quietly slipping a fresh cartridge in my rifle, as it lay in front of me across my saddlebow, nor from unbuttoning the strap which held my revolver in place by my side. Fortunately, however, nothing occurred to make it necessary to displace either rifle or revolver.

After riding in advance for a couple of miles, Yellow Bear pointed out in the distance the little mound at which he predicted we would see something posted in the way of information concerning his tribe. If the latter was not in the vicinity a letter would no doubt be found at the mound, which now became an object of interest to all of us, each striving to be the first to discover the confirmation of Yellow Bear's prediction.

In this way we continued to approach the mound until not more than a mile of level plain separated us from it, and still nothing could be seen to encourage us, when, owing to my reason being quickened by the excitement of the occasion, thus giving me an advantage over the chiefs, or from other causes, I caught sight of what would ordinarily have been taken for two half-round stones or small boulders, just visible above the upper circle of the mound, as projected against the sky beyond. A second glance convinced me that instead of the stones, which they so closely resembled, they were neither more nor less than the upper parts of the heads of two Indians, who were no doubt studying our movements with a view of determining whether we were a friendly or war party.

Reassuring myself by the aid of my fieldglass, I announced my discovery to the chiefs and the rest of the party. Yellow Bear immediately cantered his pony a few yards to the front, when, freeing his scarlet blanket from his shoulders, he waved it twice or thrice in a mysterious manner, and waited anxiously the response. In a moment the two Indians, the tops of whose heads had alone been visible, rode boldly to the crest of the mound and answered the signal of Yellow Bear, who uttered a quick, oft-repeated whoop, and, at my suggestion, galloped in advance, to inform his people who we were, and our object in visiting them. Yellow Bear then despatched one of the Indians to the village, less than two miles distant, to give news of our approach.

It seemed that they had scarcely had time to reach the village, before young and old began flocking out to meet us, some on ponies, others on mules, and occasionally two full-grown Indians would be seen mounted on one diminutive pony. If any of our party had feared that our errand was attended with risk, their minds probably underwent a change when they looked around, and upon all sides saw armed warriors, whose numbers exceeded ours more than ten to one, and whose entire bearing and demeanor toward us gave promise of any but hostile feelings.

Not deeming it best to allow them to encircle us too closely, I requested Yellow Bear, in whose peaceable desires I had confidence, to direct his people to remain at some distance from us, so as not to impede our progress; at the same time to inform them that it was our purpose to pitch our camp immediately alongside of theirs, when full opportunity would be given for interchange of visits. This proposition seemed to meet with favor, and our route was left unobstructed.

I decided to cross the creek and bivouac on the right bank, opposite the lower end of the village, and within easy pistol range of the nearest lodge. This location may strike the reader with some surprise, and may suggest the inquiry why we did not locate ourselves at some point further removed from the village. It must be remembered that in undertaking to penetrate the Indian country with so small a force, I acted throughout upon the belief that if proper precautions were adopted, the Indians would not molest us. Indians contemplating a battle, either offensive or defensive, are always anxious to have their women and children removed from all danger thereof. By our watchfulness we intended to let the Indians see that there would be no opportunity for them to take us by surprise, but that if fighting was intended, it should not be all on one side.

But right, here I will do the Arapahos justice, by asserting that after the first council, which took place in my camp the same evening, and after they had an opportunity to learn the exact character and object of our mission, as told to them by me, and confirmed by the earnest addresses of Yellow Bear and Little Robe, they evinced toward us nothing but friendly feeling, and exhibited a ready willingness to conform to the only demand we made of them, which was that they should proceed at once, with their entire village, to our main camp, within their reservation, and then report to General Sheridan.

Little Raven, the head chief, spoke for his people, and expressed their gratification at the reports brought to them by Yellow Bear and Little Robe. They accepted with gladness the offer of peace, and promised to set out in three days to proceed to our main camp, near the site of Fort Sill.

Little Raven invited me to visit him the following day in his village, an invitation I promised to accept. Before the chiefs separated, I requested Little Raven to give notice through them to all his people, that after it became dark it would no longer be safe for any of them to approach our camp, as, according our invariable custom, guards would be posted about camp during the entire night; and as we could not distinguish friends from foes in the darkness, the sentries would be ordered to fire on every object seen approaching our camp. To this Little Raven and his chiefs promised assent. I then further informed him that during our stay near them we should always be glad, during the hours of daylight, to receive visits from him or from any of his people, but to prevent confusion or misunderstanding, not more than twenty Indians would be permitted to visit our camp at one time. This also was agreed to, and the chiefs, after shaking hands and uttering the customary "How," departed to their village. Yellow Bear remained only long enough to say that, his family being in the village, he preferred, of course, to be with them, but assured us that his people were sincere in their protestations of peace, and that we might sleep as soundly as if we were back among our comrades, in the main camp, with no fears of unfriendly interruption.

After tethering our horses and pack mules securely in our midst, and posting the guards for the night, each one of our little party, first satisfying himself that his firearms were in good order and loaded, spread his blanket on the ground, and, with his saddle for a pillow, the sky unobscured by tent or roof above him, was soon reposing comfortably on the broad bosom of mother earth, and yet we all, in seeking our lowly couches that night, felt that the chances were about even whether or not we should be awakened by the war whoop of our dusky neighbors. Nothing occurred, however, to disturb our dreams or break our slumber, save, perhaps, in my own case. From a greater sense of responsibility, perhaps, than rested on my comrades, but not greater danger, I awoke at different hours during the night, and to assure myself that all was well, rose up to a sitting posture on the ground, and, aided by the clear sky and bright starlight, looked about me, only to see, however, the dim outlines of my sleeping comrades as they lay in all manner of attitudes around me, wrapped in their blankets of gray, while our faithful horses, picketed in the midst of their sleeping riders, were variously disposed, some lying down, resting from the fatigues of the march, others nibbling the few tufts of grass which the shortness of their tether enabled them to reach. That which gave me strongest assurance of safety, however, as I glanced across the little stream, and beheld the conical forms of the white lodges of the Indians, was the silent picture of the sentry as he paced his lonely post within a few feet of where I lay. And when to my inquiry, in subdued tones, if all had been quiet during the night, came the prompt, soldierly response, "All quiet, sir," I felt renewed confidence, and again sought the solace of my equestrian pillow.

Breakfasting before the stars bade us good night, or rather good morning, daylight found us ready for the duties of the day. I asked Romeo and Neva to escort me to little Raven's lodge, the former as interpreter. I directed Captain Robbins, the officer next in rank, to cause all men to remain closely in camp during my absence, and to be careful not to permit more than the authorized number of Indians to enter; also to watch well the Indian village, not that I believed there would be an attempt at stratagem, but deemed it well to be on guard. To convince the Indians of my own sincerity, I left my rifle and revolver with my men, a measure of not such great significance as it might at first seem, as the question of arms or no arms would have exercised but little influence in determining my fate had the Indians, as I never for a moment believed, intended treachery.

Having Arrived at Little Raven's lodge, I found him surrounded by all his principal chiefs, a place being reserved by his side for me. After the usual smoke and the preliminary moments of silence, which strongly reminded me of the deep silence which is the prelude to religious services in some of our churches, Little Raven began a speech, which was mainly a review of what had been agreed upon the evening before, and closed with the statement that his people were highly pleased to see white men among them as friends, and that the idea of complying with my demand in regard to proceeding to our main camp had been discussed with great favor by all of his people, who were delighted with this opportunity of terminating the war. All questions affecting the Arapahos being satisfactorily disposed of, I now introduced the subject of the whereabouts of the Cheyenne village, stating that my purpose was to extend to them the same terms as had been accepted by the Arapahos.

To this I could obtain no decisive or satisfactory reply. The Cheyennes were represented to be moving constantly, hence the difficulty in informing me accurately as to their location; but all agreed that the Cheyennes were a long distance west of where we then were. Finally I obtained a promise from Little Raven that he would select two of his active young warriors, who would accompany me in my search for the Cheyenne village, and whose knowledge of the country and acquaintance with the Cheyennes would be of incalculable service to me. As the limited amount of provisions on hand would not justify us in continuing our search for the Cheyennes, I decided to await the arrival of Colonel Cook, who, I felt confident, would reach us in a few days.

In the meanwhile the day fixed for the departure of the Arapahos came, and the village was all commotion and activity, lodges being taken down and packed on ponies and mules; the activity, I might mention, being confined, however, to the squaws, the noble lords of the forest sitting unconcernedly by, quietly smoking their long red clay pipes. I was sorry to lose the services of Yellow Bear, but it was necessary for him to accompany his people, particularly as he represented the peace element. I gave him a letter to General Sheridan, in which I informed the latter of our meeting with the Arapahos, the council, and the final agreement. In view of the further extension of our journey, I requested a second detachment to be sent on our trail, with supplies, to meet us on our return. Everything being in readiness, the chiefs, commencing with Little Raven, gathered around me, and bade me good-by, Yellow Bear being the last to take his leave. This being ended the entire village was put in motion, and soon stretched itself into a long, irregular column.

After the excitement attending the departure of the Indians had passed, and the last glimpse of the departing village had been had, our little party seemed lonely enough, as we stood huddled together on the bank of Mulberry Creek. There was nothing to be done until the arrival of our expected supplies. Little Robe, impatient at the proposed delay, concluded to start at once in quest of his people, and if possible persuade them to meet us instead of awaiting our arrival. He evidently was anxious to have peace concluded with the Cheyennes, and thus enable his people to be placed on the same secure footing with the Arapahos. Instead of opposing, I encouraged him in the execution of his plan, although loath to part with him. The two young Arapahos were to remain with me, however, and by concert of plan between them and Little Robe we would be able to follow the trail.

It was agreed that if Little Robe should come up with his people and be able to induce them to return, he was to send up smoke signals each morning and evening, in order that we might receive notice of their approach and be able to regulate our march accordingly. Giving him a sufficient supply of coffee, sugar, and hard bread, we saw Little Robe set out on his solitary journey in the character of a veritable peace commissioner.

Three days after the departure of the Arapaho village, the lookout reported that parties were in sight some three or four miles in the direction taken by the village. This created no little excitement in camp. Fieldglasses were brought into immediate requisition, and after a careful examination of the parties, who could be plainly seen approaching us in the distance, we all came to the conclusion that what we saw must be the escort with our supplies. A few horses were soon saddled, and two of the officers, with some of the men, galloped out to meet the advancing party. It proved to be Colonel Cook, with California Joe and a dozen, men, bringing with them several pack animals loaded with fresh supplies.

The morning after my party had been reinforced by the arrival just described, we set out under guidance of Neva and the two young Arapaho warriors, and followed the direction in which Little Robe had gone. It being one of the winter months, the Indian ponies were still in unfit condition to make long or rapid marches; for this reason the two Arapahos had left their ponies with the village, and were accompanying or rather preceding us on foot; an undertaking which they seemed to have no difficulty in accomplishing. The grazing became more indifferent each day as we journeyed toward the West, until finally we ceased to rely upon it, but as a substitute for our horses upon the bark of the young cottonwood trees which are generally found fringing the borders of the streams. In spite, however, of our utmost care our horses and pack animals, having exhausted their supply of forage, began to fail in strength and condition under their cottonwood bark diet.

I therefore, after consultation with Neva and the two Arapahos, decided to recross to the north bank of Red River, and follow up its course until we should reach a small tributary coming in from the northwest, and which Neva informed me would furnish a good campground. In the meanwhile Neva, who was well-mounted on a hardy, active mule, was to take with him the two young Arapahos, and push on in advance in search of the Cheyenne village, the understanding being that I should follow in his direction until the stream referred to was reached, where I would await his return for three days. Should he fail to rejoin us in that time, we would commence our return march to the main camp.

When it was known that this plan had been definitely settled upon, young Brewster, who never for a moment had become discouraged as to his final success discovering his lost sister, came to me, and in the most earnest manner asked permission to accompany Neva in his search for the Cheyenne village. I did everything I could to dissuade him from so dangerous a project.

No arguments were of any avail. He felt satisfied that his sister was a prisoner in the Cheyenne village, and this his last and only opportunity to gain a knowledge of the fact; and even with the chances of death or torture staring him in the face he preferred to risk all, and learn the truth, rather than live longer in a state of horrible uncertainty. Against my judgment in the matter, I was forced by his importunate manner to grant him permission to accompany Neva.

Taking a suitable amount of supplies with them, the three Indians and young Brewster set out, Neva being the only one of the party mounted. After they had left us we moved in the same direction, with the intention of halting on the stream indicated by Neva, there to await their return. While the reader is also waiting their return, I will refer to an incident that should have appeared in an earlier part of this chapter. It was neither more nor less than what might, among fashionable notices in the Indian press—provided they had one—have been termed an elopement in high life.

One evening after we had gone into camp, many long weary miles from our point of starting, and when we supposed we had left all the Kiowas safely in camp awaiting the release of their two chiefs, Lone Wolf and Satanta, we were all surprised to see a young and handsome Kiowa warrior gallop into our midst accompanied by a young squaw, who certainly could not have reached the age that distinguishes the woman from the girl. In a few moments our little party gathered about these two wayfarers, eager to learn the cause of their sudden and unexpected visit. The girl was possessed of almost marvellous beauty, a beauty so remarkable that my companions of that march refer to her to this day as the most beautiful squaw they have ever seen. Her graceful and well-rounded form, her clearly-cut features, her dark expressive eyes, fringed with long silken lashes, cheeks rich with the color of youth, teeth of pearly whiteness occasionally peeping from between her full, rosy lips, added withal to a most bewitching manner, required not the romance of her story to make her an object of deep interest in the eyes of the gallants of our party. But to their story.

She was the daughter of Black Eagle, at that time the acting head chief of the Kiowas. The young warrior who rode at her side was somewhat of a young Lochinvar in disposition. It was the old, old story; not that the young warrior was objectionable, but unfortunately, as is but too often the case, he was poor, and could not offer in exchange for the hand of a chief's daughter the proper number of ponies. Black Eagle was inexorable—the lovers, constancy itself. There was but one thing for them to do, and they did it.

Aware of our proposed expedition in search of the Cheyennes and Arapahos, they timed their affairs accordingly. Giving us time to get two days the start, they slipped away from their village at dusk the evening of the second day after our departure, and hastening unperceived to a thicket nearby, where the lover had taken the precaution to conceal two of the fleetest ponies of the village already saddled, they were soon in their saddles and galloping for love and life away from the Kiowa village. I say galloping for life, for by the Indians law, if the father or relatives of the girl could overtake the lovers within twenty-four hours, the life of the young woman would pay the forfeit.

They followed our trail in order to avail themselves of our protection by travelling with us as far as our course might lead them in the direction of the Staked Plains, on the borders of which a straggling band of Kiowas, under the chief Woman Heart, was supposed to be, and which the lovers intended to join, at least until the rage of pater-familias should subside and they be invited to return. This in brief was their story. I need not add that they found a hearty welcome in our midst, and were assured that they need no longer fear pursuit.

That evening, after the campfires were lighted, the officers of our party, with Romeo as interpreter, gathered about the campfire of the bridal couple and passed a pleasant hour in conversation. Their happiness and exultation at their success in escaping from their village were too powerful to be restrained, and in many delicate little ways the bride—for by Indian law twenty-four hours' absence from the village with her lover made her a bride—plainly betrayed her exceeding fondness for him who had risked all to claim her as his own.

After my return to the main camp I met Black Eagle, and informed him that his daughter and her husband had been companions of our march. "Yes. Why did you not kill him?" was his reply, which upon inquiry he explained by saying that if some person had kindly put an end to the life of his son-in-law, it would have benefited him to the value of several ponies; his difficulty seeming to be in overcoming the loss of the ponies which should have been paid for his daughter's hand. I afterwards learned, however, that the haughty chief became reconciled to the wilful lovers, and invited them to return to his lodge, an invitation they were not tardy in accepting.

We pitched our camp at the point agreed upon between Neva and myself, and prepared to await the return of his party. Neva had been informed that our delay could not extend beyond three days, as our store of provisions and forage was almost exhausted, and this fact alone would force us to retrace our steps. I had hoped that during the time we were to spend in camp, hunting parties might be able to bring in a sufficient amount of game to satisfy our wants; but although parties were despatched in all directions, not an animal or bird could be found. So barren was the country as to offer no inducements that would attract game of any species.

Resort was had to cottonwood bark, to obtain which we cut down large numbers of the trees, and fed our horses upon the young bark of the branches. Knowing that in answer to my second request supplies of provisions both for men and horses must be on their way and probably near to us, I determined to begin our return march one day sooner than I had expected when Neva and his companions left us, as they would be able on finding our camp to follow our trail and overtake us.

We moved only a few miles, but even this short distance was sufficient to demonstrate how weak and famished our horses had become, one of them dying from starvation before we reached camp, the first day of our return march. This circumstance, however, was turned to our advantage. Much has been said and written in praise of the savoriness of horseflesh as a diet. Our necessities compelled us to put this question to practical test, and the animal had scarcely fallen, unable to rise again, when it was decided to prepare his carcass for food. That evening the men treated themselves to a bountiful repast made up of roasts, steaks, and broils, all from the flesh of the poor animal, whose death was attributable to starvation alone. Judging, however, from the jolly laughter that rang through camp at supper time, the introduction of this new article of diet met with a cordial reception.

Soon after finishing our supper, we discovered in the distance and following in our trail a horseman. We at once concluded that this must be Neva, a fact rendered conclusive by the aid of a fieldglass. Various were the surmises indulged in by the different members of our party as to the success of Neva's mission. What had become of his companions, particularly young Brewster? These and many other inquiries suggested themselves as we watched his approach. We could almost read the answer on Neva's face when he reached us as to the success of his search for the Cheyennes. Disappointment, hunger, and fatigue were plainly marked in his features as he dismounted and shook hands with us. Knowing that one of the characteristics of the Indian is to talk but little until the wants of the inner man have been fully attended to, I at once ordered him a steak. One of the party, however, fearing that if he knew the exact character of the diet offered him he might from some superstitious cause decline it, suggested that Neva be asked if he would like a nice buffalo steak, a deception which seemed somewhat justifiable under the circumstances. To this Neva returned a hearty affirmative, when one of the men placed before him a raw steak, whose dimensions would have amply gratified the appetites of an ordinary family of half a dozen. Having held the steak over the blazing fire until sufficiently done to suit his taste, Neva seated himself on the ground near by and began helping himself liberally to the dripping morsel. After he had indulged for some time in this pleasing entertainment, and having made no remark, one of the officers inquired of him if he was hungry.

"Yes," was his reply, but added in his very indifferent English, "Poor buffano, poor buffano." None of us ever informed him of the little deception that had been practised upon him.

His account of his journey was brief. He had travelled nearly due west, accompanied by Brewster and the two young Arapahos, and had discovered a trail of the Cheyenne village some two weeks old. Under these circumstances there was no course left to him but to return. The Arapahos decided to follow on and join the Cheyenne village. Neva and young Brewster began their return together, but the latter, being unable to travel as fast as Neva, fell behind. Neva, anxious to keep his promise and rejoin us at the time and place indicated, pushed forward as rapidly as possible. Young Brewster, however, manfully struggled along, and reached our camp a few hours after Neva's arrival.

The next morning we set out on our homeward or return march. During the night one of our horses strayed away from camp, and as one of the men thought he could find it before we made our start in the morning, he left camp with that purpose. Failing to rejoin us at the proper time, I sent parties in search of him, but they returned unsuccessful. We were compelled by our necessities to move without further delay. Weeks and months elapsed, and no tidings of the lost trooper reached us, when one day, while encamped near Fort Hays, Kansas, hundreds of miles from the locality of which I am now writing, who should step up to my tent but the man who was lost from us in northwestern Texas. He had become bewildered after losing sight of our camp, took the wrong direction, and was never able thereafter during his wanderings to determine his course. Fortunately he took a southerly route, and after nearly two months of solitary roaming over the plains of northern Texas, he arrived at a military post south of Red River in Texas, and by way of Galveston, the Gulf of Mexico, the Mississippi and Missouri Rivers, rejoined his regiment in Kansas.

As we gained the crest of the hill from which we obtained a view of the white tents that formed our camp, there was no one of our little party who did not enjoy a deep feeling of gratitude and thankfulness that our long and trying journey was about to end under happier auspices than many might have supposed when we began it. We had found the Arapahos, and succeeded in placing them on their reservation, where, from that date to the present time, they have remained, never engaging as a tribe in making war or committing depredations on the whites, so far as my knowledge extends.

We did not succeed so well with the Cheyennes, but we established facts regarding their location, disposition, and intentions as to peace, which were of invaluable service to us in determining future operations looking to the establishment of peace with them.

Our arrival in camp created a sensation among our comrades, who had seen us depart upon what they might well have considered an errand of questionable prudence. Leaving my companions of the march to answer the many queries of those who had not accompanied us, I galloped across the narrow plain that separated General Sheridan's tents from my camp, and was soon greeted by the General and staff in terms of hearty welcome. Repairing to the General's tent, I soon recounted the principal incidents of my expedition. I found that the Arapahos had kept their promise, made to me while I was in their village, and that the village was then located near our main camp.

The conduct of the Cheyennes, however, in declining our proffers of peace, left the Indian question in that section of country still unsettled; but this only rendered new plans necessary, plans which were quickly determined upon. Other events of great public importance rendered General Sheridan's presence necessary elsewhere at an early day.

It was therefore decided that he, accompanied by his escort of scouts under Lieutenant Pepoon, should proceed northward to Camp Supply, while I, with the Seventh Regulars and the Nineteenth Kansas Cavalry, and my Osage scouts, a force numbering about fifteen hundred men, should move westward in quest of the recalcitrant Cheyennes, and administer to them such treatment as their past conduct might merit and existing circumstances demanded. Satanta and Lone Wolf were still prisoners in our hands, a portion of their tribe having failed thus far to comply with the terms of the agreement by which they were to settle down peaceably on their reservation. As the greater portion of the tribe, however, was then encamped near us, and as both Satanta and Lone Wolf were loud in their protestations of peace, it was decided to release them. Accordingly, after conference with General Sheridan, I went to the lodge in which I kept the two chiefs closely guarded as prisoners, and informed them of the decision that had been arrived at in their behalf, the only response being a most hearty and emphatic "How" from the two robust chieftains.

General Sheridan had up to this time declined all their requests for an interview, but now deemed it best to see them and speak a few words of warning and caution as to their future conduct. No peace commissioners were ever entertained by promises of good behavior, peaceable intentions, and regrets for past offences, which smacked of greater earnestness and sincerity than those volunteered by Lone Wolf and Satanta when informed that they were free to rejoin their people. According to their voluntary representations, their love for their white brothers was unbounded; their desire for peace, their hatred of war, ungovernable; and nothing would satisfy them in future but to be permitted to lead their people down "the white man's road," by cultivating the soil, building school houses and churches, and forever eschewing a predatory or warlike life.

The winter of 1868–69 was rapidly terminating, acting as forcible reminder to us that if we hoped to operate in the field with any advantage over the Cheyennes, the movement must be made before the spring grass should make its appearance for the benefit of the Indian ponies. Accordingly, as soon as our arrangements were perfected, our camp at the present site of Fort Sill, Indian Territory, was broken up, and General Sheridan, accompanied by his staff and escort, set out for Camp Supply in the north, while my command faced westward and began its search for the Cheyennes, passing along the southern base of the Wichita Mountains.

On the morning of the first day after leaving the Wichita Mountains behind us, no little excitement was created throughout the command by the discovery of a column of smoke directly on our course, and apparently about fifteen or twenty miles in front of us. That Indians had originated the fire was beyond a doubt, as we all knew that beyond us, in the direction of the smoke, the country was inhabited by no human beings save hostile Indians. I at once decided to push on with the command to the point from which the smoke was ascending, and discover if possible some trace of the Indians.

Be it understood that neither I nor any members of my command supposed for one moment that when we arrived at the desired point we would find the Indians there awaiting our arrival, but we did hope to discover their trail. Of the many experienced frontiersmen embraced in the command, including of course California Joe, there were none who judged the distance that separated us from the smoke as greater than could be easily passed over by us before three or four o'clock that afternoon.

Our surmises proved correct. The fire had evidently been communicated to the dry winter grass from some Indian campfire. The Indians of course had gone; but where? As this was a question that could not be solved until daylight, and as all of us were glad enough of an opportunity to get a few hours' repose, the troops bivouacked in promiscuous order as they arrived.

Only those who have enjoyed similar experiences know how brief the preparation required for sleep. As for myself, as soon as the necessary directions had been given relating to the command, I unsaddled my horse, arranged my saddle for my pillow, tethered my horse within easy reach, and in less time than has been required to write these few lines, I was enjoying one of those slumbers which only come as the reward of a day of earnest activity in the saddle.

As soon as it was light enough for our purpose, we were in the saddle and searching in all directions for the trail left by the Indians who had fired the prairie. Our Osage scouts were not long in making the desired discovery. The trail led westward, following the general course of a small valley in which it was first discovered. The party was evidently a small one, numbering not more than fifteen persons, but the direction in which they were moving led me to hope that by following them carefully and with due caution to prevent discovery of our pursuit, we might be led to the main village.

Crossing a high ridge, or divide, the trail led us down into a beautiful open valley. After following up the course of the latter several miles, the freshness of the trail indicated that the Indians had passed over it that same day. As it was not our purpose to overtake them, but to follow as closely as prudence would allow, I determined to go into camp until the following morning. Soon after resuming the pursuit next day rain began to fall, at first slowly, but later in the day in copious showers. I knew the Indians would not travel in the rain if they could avoid it, unless they knew they were pursued, and of this fact I had reason to believe they were still ignorant, as evidences found all along the trail indicated that they were moving very leisurely.

To avoid placing ourselves in too close proximity to them, I ordered a halt about noon, and began preparation for camping for the night. Our wagons were still in rear. In the mean time the horses were all unsaddled and picketed out in the usual manner to graze. As was my usual custom upon halting for the night, I had directed the Osage scouts, instead of halting and unsaddling, to advance in the direction we were to follow next day, and examine the country for a distance of a few miles. We had barely completed the unsaddling of our horses and disposed of them over the grazing ground, when I discovered the Osage scouts returning over the ridge in front of us as fast as their ponies could carry them. Their story was soon told. Disliking to travel in the rain, the Indians whom we were pursuing had gone into camp also, and the Osage scouts had discovered them not more than a mile from us, the ridge referred to preventing the Indians from seeing us or being seen by us.

Quickly the command "Saddle up!" flew from mouth to mouth, and in a marvellously brief time officers and men were in the saddle and, under the guidance of the Osage scouts, were moving stealthily to surprise the Indian camp. Passing around a little spur of the dividing ridge, there before us, at a distance of but a few hundred yards, stood the half-erected lodges of the Indians, while scattered here and there in the immediate vicinity were to be seen the Indian ponies and pack animals, grazing in apparent unconsciousness of the close proximity of an enemy. At a given signal the cavalry put spurs to their steeds, drew their revolvers, and in a few moments were in possession of the Indian camp, ponies and all—no, not all, for not a single Indian could be discovered.

The troops were deployed at a gallop in all directions, but failed to find the trace of an Indian. Our capture was apparently an empty one. How the occupants of the Indian camp had first discovered our presence and afterwards contrived to elude us was a mystery that even puzzled our Osage scouts. This mystery was afterwards explained.

It seemed that during the haste and excitement attendant upon the discovery of the close proximity of the Indian camp to ours, two of our dogs, whether or not sharing in the bellicose humor of their masters, engaged in a quarrel, the noise of which reached the quick ears of the Indians nearly one mile distant. Comprehending the situation at once, the Indians, realizing the danger of delay, abandoned their camp and ponies and fled on foot, the better to effect concealment and elude pursuit.

On the following day we resumed the march. There being no longer any trail for us to follow, we continued in the same direction, believing that the small party we had been pursuing had been directing their course toward the location of the main village, which was somewhere westward of us. Day after day we travelled in this direction, hoping to discover some sign or trail that might give us a clue to the whereabouts of the Cheyenne village. Nearly all hope of discovering the Indians had vanished from the minds of the officers and men, when late in the afternoon the trail of a single lodge was discovered, leading in a southwesterly direction. The trail was nearly if not quite one month old; hence it did not give great encouragement. To the surprise of most of the command, I changed the direction of our march at once, and put the Osages on the trail, having decided to follow it.

Following our faithful Osages, who experienced no difficulty in keeping the trail, we marched until near sundown, when we arrived at the banks of a small stream upon which, and near a cool, bubbling spring, we discovered the evidences of an Indian camp, which must have not only included the lodge whose trail we had been following, but also about a dozen others. Here was a speedier confirmation of my hopes than I had anticipated. Here I determined to encamp until morning, and while the cavalry were unsaddling and pitching their tents, I asked Mo-nah-se-tah to examine the Indian camp minutely and to tell me how long a time had elapsed since its occupation by the Indians, how many constituted the party, and the character and probable indications of the latter.

No detective could have set about the proposed examination with greater thoroughness than did this Indian girl. The ashes of the camp fires were raked carefully away and examined with all the scrutiny of a chemical analysis. After many minutes spent in this examination, during which I accompanied her, a silent but far from disinterested spectator, she, apparently like a judge who had been carefully reviewing all the evidence, gave me her conclusions, communicating with me, through the medium of the sign language, with a grace characteristic of the Indian race, and which added to the interest of her statements.

Briefly summed up her conclusions were as follows: twelve lodges had encamped at that point, probably constituting the band of some petty chief, the different members of which, like the one whose trail we had that day discovered, had been separated for purposes of hunting, but had been called together at that point preparatory to joining the main village. The lodges had left this camp not to exceed two weeks previous to that date, and in all probability had moved to the rendezvous appointed for the main tribe, which would without doubt be found by other small bands from time to time, until the village would all be assembled at one point. Moving in this manner and at this early season of the year, when grass was scarce and no enemy known to be in the country, the Indians would make very short moves each day, passing merely from one stream to another, not accomplishing in one day a greater distance, probably, than the cavalry would in two or three hours.

This intelligence, of course, was most gratifying, and for encouragement was soon communicated to the individual members of the command. The trail was found to lead almost in a northerly direction, slightly inclining to the east. Perhaps no one of the command experienced such a feeling of hope and anxious suspense as the new discoveries gave rise to in the breast of young Brewster, who now more than ever believed, and with reason too, that he was soon to unravel or forever seal the fate of his lost sister, whose discovery and release had been the governing impulses of his life for months past.

With renewed interest the cavalry resumed the pursuit at daylight the following morning. We had marched but a few miles before we reached a second camping ground, which had been occupied not only by those whose trail we were then following, but the number of fires showed that the strength of the Indians had been increased by about twenty-five lodges, thus verifying the correctness of the surmises advanced by Mo-nah-se-tah.

Continuing our progress, we had the satisfaction of seeing still further accessions to the trail, until it was evident that at least one hundred lodges had united and passed in one body on the trail. As we marched in one day over the distance passed over in three by the Indians, and as the latter were moving unsuspicious of the presence of an enemy in that section of the country, the trail was becoming fresher as we advanced. It was reasonable, therefore, to suppose that we would come in contact with them that day, if not actually reach the village.

All our plans were made accordingly. The Osages, as usual, were kept in the advance, that their quick eyes might sooner discover the

Indians should they appear in our front. In order to avail myself of the earliest information, I, with Colonel Cook, accompanied the Osages. Two of the latter kept in advance of all, and as they neared a ridge or commanding piece of ground they would cautiously approach the crest on foot and peer beyond, to ascertain whether an enemy was in sight before exposing our party to discovery. This proceeding, a customary one with Indians, did not excite unusual attention upon the part of Colonel Cook and myself, until once we saw Hard Rope, the head warrior, who was in advance, slowly ascend a slight eminence in our front, and, after casting one glimpse beyond, descend the hill and return to us as rapidly as his pony could carry him.

In a few words Hard Rope informed us that less than a mile beyond the hill from which he had obtained a view, there was in plain sight a large herd of Indian ponies grazing, being herded and driven by a few Indian boys. As yet they had not seen us, but were liable to discover the column of troops further to the rear. To judge of the situation I dismounted, and, conducted by Hard Rope, advanced to the crest of the hill in front and looked beyond; there I saw in plain view the herd of ponies, numbering perhaps two hundred, and being driven in the opposite direction toward what seemed the valley of a stream, as I could see the tops of the forest trees that usually border the water courses.

The ponies and their protectors soon disappeared from view, but whether they had discovered us yet or not I was unable to determine. Sending a messenger back as rapidly as his horse could carry him, I directed the troops to push to the front, and to come prepared for action. I knew the village must be near at hand, probably in the vicinity of the trees seen in the distance. As the country was perfectly open, free from either ravines or timber capable of affording concealment to Indians, I took my orderly with me and galloped in advance in the direction taken by the Indians, leaving Colonel Cook to hasten and direct the troops as the latter should arrive.

After advancing about half way to the bluff overlooking the valley I saw about half a dozen Indian heads peering over the crest, evidently watching my movements; this number was soon increased to upwards of fifty. I was extremely anxious to satisfy myself as to the tribe whose village was evidently near at hand. There was but little doubt that it was the Cheyennes, for whom we had been searching. If this should prove true then the two white girls whose discovery and release from captivity had been one of my objectives was fast approaching. To effect their release unharmed then became my study, for I remembered the fate of the white woman and child held captive by a band of this same tribe at the Battle of the Washita. I knew that the first shot fired on either side would be the signal for the murder of the two white girls. While knowing the Cheyennes to be deserving of castigation, and feeling assured that they were almost in our power, I did not dare to imperil the lives of the two white captives by making an attack on the village, although never before or since have we seen so favorable an opportunity for administering well-merited punishment to one of the strongest and most troublesome of the hostile tribes. Desiring to establish a truce with the Indians before the troops should arrive, I began making signals inviting a conference. This was done by simply riding in a circle, and occasionally advancing toward the Indians on the bluff in a zigzag manner. Immediately there appeared on the bluffs about twenty mounted Indians; from this group three advanced toward me at a gallop, soon followed by the others of the party. I cast my eyes behind me to see if the troops were near, but the head of the column was still a mile or more in rear. My orderly was near me, and I could see Colonel Cook rapidly approaching about midway between the column and my position.

Directing the orderly to remain stationary, I advanced toward the Indians a few paces, and as soon as they were sufficiently near made signs to them to halt, and then for but one of their number to advance midway and meet me. This was assented to, and I advanced with my revolver in my left hand, while my right hand was held aloft as a token that I was inclined to be friendly. The Indian met me as agreed upon, and in response to my offer exchanged friendly greetings, and shook hands. From him I learned that the village of the entire Cheyenne tribe was located on the streams in front of us, and that Medicine Arrow, the head chief of the Cheyennes, was in the group of Indians then in view from where we stood. Little Robe, with his band numbering about forty lodges, was a short distance further down the stream. I asked the Indian to send for Medicine Arrow, as I desired to talk with the head chief. Calling to one of his companions, who had halted within hailing distance, the latter was directed to convey to Medicine Arrow my message, to do which he set off at a gallop.

At this juncture I perceived that the Indians, to the number of twenty or more, had approached quite near, while some of the party seemed disposed to advance to where I was. To this I had decided objections, and so indicated to the Indian who was with me. He complied with my wishes, and directed his companions to remain where they were. As a precaution of safety, I took good care to keep the person of the Indian between me and his friends. Medicine Arrow soon came galloping up accompanied by a chief.

While engaged in shaking hands with him and his companions, and exchanging the usual salutation, "How," with the new arrivals, I observed that the Indians who had been occupying a retired position had joined the group, and I found myself in the midst of about twenty chiefs and warriors. Medicine Arrow exhibited the most earnest desire to learn from me the number of troops following me. Whether this question was prompted by any contemplated act of treachery, in case my followers were few in number, or not, I do not know. But if treachery was thought of, the idea was abandoned when I informed him that my followers numbered fifteen hundred men, the advance guard being then in sight. Medicine Arrow then informed me that his village was alarmed by the approach of so large a body of troops. To give assurance to them he urged me to accompany him to his village in advance of the troops, and by my presence satisfy his people that no attack upon them would be made. This I consented to do.

By this time Colonel Cook had again joined me, also Dr. Lippincott. Leaving the doctor with directions for the troops, and taking Colonel Cook with me, I started with Medicine Arrow and a considerable party of his warriors to the village, Medicine Arrow urging us to put our horses to the gallop. The reader may regard this movement on my part as having been anything but prudent, and I will admit that viewed in the ordinary light it might seem to partake somewhat of a foolhardy errand. But I can assure them that no one could be more thoroughly convinced of the treachery and bloodthirsty disposition of the Indian than I am, nor would I ever trust life in their hands unless it was in their interest to preserve that life; for no class of beings act so much from self-interest as the Indian, and on this occasion I knew, before accepting the proposal of the chief to enter his village, that he and every member of his band felt it to be to their interest not only to protect me from harm, but treat me with every consideration, as the near approach of the troops and the formidable number of the latter would deter the Indians from any act of hostility, knowing as they did that in case of an outbreak of any kind it would be impossible for a great portion of the village, particularly the women and children, to escape. I considered all this before proceeding to the village.

As we were turning our horses' heads in the direction of the village, I caught sight of a familiar face in the group of Indians about me; it was that of Mah-wis-sa, the squaw whom I had sent as peace commissioner from our camp near Fort Sill, and who had failed to return. She recognized me at once, and laughed when I uttered the word "Mutah-ka," referring to the hunting knife I had loaned her as she was about to depart on her errand of peace. A brisk gallop soon brought us to the village.

Medicine Arrow hurried me to his lodge, which was located almost in the centre of the village, the latter being the most extensive I had ever seen. As soon as I had entered the lodge I was invited to a seat on one of the many buffalo robes spread on the ground about the inner circumfer ence of the lodge. By Medicine Arrow's direction the village crier, in a loud tone of voice, began calling the chiefs together in council. No delay occurred in their assembling. One by one they approached and entered the lodge, until fifteen of the leading chiefs had taken their seats in the circle within the lodge in the order of their rank. I was assigned the post of honor, being seated on the right of Medicine Arrow, while on my immediate right sat the medicine man of the tribe, official scarcely second in influence to the head chief.

The squaw of Medicine Arrow built a huge fire in the centre of the lodge. As soon as all the chiefs had assembled, the ceremonies, which were different from any I ever witnessed before or since, began. The chiefs sat in silence while the medicine man drew forth from a capacious buckskin tobacco pouch, profusely ornamented with beads and porcupine quills, a large red clay pipe, with a stem about the size of an ordinary walking stick. To this he added, in various amounts, dried leaves and herbs, with which he seemed well supplied. After thoroughly mixing these ingredients, he proceeded with solemn ceremony to fill the pipe with the mixture, muttering at times certain incantations, by which no doubt it was intended to neutralize any power or proclivity for harm I may have been supposed to possess.

To all of this I was a silent but far from disinterested spectator. My interest perceptibly increased when the medicine man, who was sitting close to me, extended his left hand and grasped my right, pressing it strongly against his body over the region of his heart, at the same time, and with complete devoutness of manner, engaging in what

Medicine Arrow and his squaw.

seemed to me a petition or prayer to the Great Spirit; the other chiefs from time to time ejaculating, in the most earnest manner, their responses, the latter being made simultaneously. To the Indians it was a most solemn occasion, and scarcely less impressive to me, who could only judge of what was transpiring by catching an occasional word, and by closely following their signs.

After the conclusion of the address or prayer by the medicine man, the latter released my hand, which up to this time had been tightly grasped in his, and taking the long clay pipe in both hands, it likewise was apparently placed under an imaginary potent spell, by a ceremony almost as long as that which I have just described. This being ended, the medicine man, first pointing slowly with the stem of the pipe to each of the four points of the compass, turned to me, and without even so much as saying, "Smoke, sir?" placed the mouthpiece of the long stem in my mouth, still holding the bowl of the pipe in his hand.

Again taking my right hand in his left, the favor or protecting influence of the Great Spirit was again invoked in the most earnest and solemn manner, the other chiefs joining at regular intervals with their responses. Finally, releasing my hand, the medicine man lighted a match, and applying it to the pipe made signs to me to smoke. I accordingly began puffing away with as great a degree of nonchalance as a man unaccustomed to smoking could well assume. Now being, as I have just stated, one of that class which does not number smoking among its accomplishments, I took the first few whiffs with a degree of confidence which I felt justified in assuming, as I imagined the smoking portion of the ceremony was to be the same as usually observed among Indians so devoted to the practice, in which each individual takes the pipe, enjoys half a dozen whiffs, and passes it to his next neighbor on his left. That much I felt equal to; but when, after blowing away the first half dozen puffs of smoke from my face, the medicine man still retained his hold of the pipe, with an evident desire that I should continue the enjoyment of this Indian luxury, I proceeded more deliberately, although no such rule of restraint seemed to govern the volubility of the medicine man, whose invocation and chants continued with unabated vigor and rapidity.

When the first minute had added to itself four more, and still I was expected to make a miniature volcano of myself, minus the ashes, I began to grow solicitous as to what might be the effect if I was subjected to this course of treatment. I pictured to myself the commander of an important expedition seated in solemn council with a score and a half of dusky chieftains, the pipe of peace being passed, and before it had left the hands of the aforesaid commander, he becoming deathly sick, owing to lack of familiarity with the noxious weed or its substitutes. I imagined the sudden termination of the council, the absurdity of the figure cut, and the contempt of the chiefs for one who must, under the circumstances, appear so deficient in manly accomplishments. These and a hundred similar ideas flashed through my mind as I kept pulling vigorously at the pipe, and wondering when this thing would terminate.

Fortunately for my peace of body as well as of mind, after a period which seemed to me equal to a quarter of an hour at least, I felt relieved by the medicine man taking the pipe from my mouth, and, after refilling it, handing it to the head chief, sitting on my left, who, drawing three or four long, silent whiffs, passed it to his next neighbor on his left; and in similar manner it made the circle of the chiefs, until it finally returned to the medicine man, who, after taking a few final whiffs, laid it aside, much to my relief, as I feared the consequences of a repetition of my former effort.

Romeo, the interpreter, having been mounted upon an indifferent animal, had fallen to the rear of the column during the march that day, and I was deprived of his services during my interview with the chief. Colonel Cook, during this time, was in an adjoining lodge, each moment naturally becoming more solicitous lest upon the arrival of the troops there should be a collision between the Indians and the excited volunteers. To the inquiries of the chiefs I explained the object of our march, without alluding to the two captive girls, the time not having arrived for discussing that subject. Having resolved to obtain the release of the captives, all other purposes were necessarily laid aside; and as I knew that the captives could not be released should hostilities once occur between the troops and Indians, I became for the time being an ardent advocate of peace measures, and informed the chiefs that such was my purpose at the time. I also requested them to inform me where I would find the most suitable camping ground in the vicinity of the village, to which request Medicine Arrow replied that he would accompany me in person and point out the desired ground.

When this offer was made I accepted it as a kindness, but when the chief conducted me to a camp ground separated from the village, and from all view of the latter, I had reason to modify my opinion of his pretended kindness, particularly when coupled with his subsequent conduct. My command soon came up, and was conducted to the camp ground indicated by Medicine Arrow, the distance between the camp and the village not exceeding three-fourths of a mile. I was still uncertain as to whether there were any grounds to doubt that the two white girls were captives in Medicine Arrow's village. I anxiously awaited the arrival of Mo-nah-se-tah, who could and would solve this question. She came with the main body of the troops, and I at once informed her whose village it was alongside of which we were located.

To my inquiry as to whether the two white girls were prisoners in Medicine Arrow's village, she promptly replied in the affirmative, and at the same time exhibited a desire to aid as far as possible in effecting their release. It was still early in the afternoon, and I did not deem it necessary, or even advisable, to proceed with undue haste in the negotiations by which I expected to bring about the release of the two captives. I felt confident that as soon as it was dark the entire village would probably steal away, and leave us in the lurch; but I proposed to make my demand for the surrender of the captives long before darkness should aid the Indians in eluding us.

From fifty to one hundred chiefs, warriors, and young men were assembled at my headquarters, or about the camp fire built in front of headquarters. Apparently they were there from motives of mere curiosity, but later developments proved they had another object in view. Finally Medicine Arrow came to my camp, accompanied by some of his head men, and after shaking hands with apparent cordiality, stated that some of his young men, desirous of manifesting their friendship for us, would visit our camp in a few minutes, and entertain us by a serenade. This idea was a novel one to me, and I awaited the arrival of the serenaders with no little curiosity.

Before their arrival, however, my lookouts reported unusual commotion and activity in the Indian village. The herd of the latter had been called in, and officers sent by me to investigate this matter confirmed the report, and added that everything indicated a contemplated flight on the part of the Indians. I began then to comprehend the object of the proposed serenade; it was to occupy our attention while the village could pack up and take flight. Pretending ignorance of what was transpiring in the village, I continued to converse, through Romeo, with the chiefs, until the arrival of the Indian musicians. These, numbering about a dozen young men, were mounted on ponies which, like themselves, were ornamented in the highest degree according to Indian fashion. The musicians were feathered and painted in the most horrible as well as fantastic manner. Their instruments consisted of reeds, the sounds from which more nearly resembled those of the fife than any other, although there was a total lack of harmony between the various pieces. As soon as the musicians arrived they began riding in a gallop in a small circle, of which circle our little group, composed of a few officers and the chiefs, composed the centre. The display of horsemanship was superb, and made amends for the discordant sounds given forth as music.

During all this time reports continued to come in, leaving no room to doubt that the entire village was preparing to decamp. To have opposed this movement by a display of force on the part of the troops would have only precipitated a terrible conflict, for which I was not yet prepared, keeping in mind the rescue of the white girls. I did not propose, however, to relinquish the advantage we then had by our close proximity to the village, and permit the latter to place several miles between us.

Knowing that the musicians would soon depart, and with them perhaps the chiefs and warriors then grouped about my camp fire, I determined to seize the principal chiefs then present, permit the village to depart if necessary, and hold the captured chiefs as hostages for the surrender of the white girls and the future good behavior of the tribe. This was a move requiring not only promptness but most delicate and careful handling, in order to avoid bloodshed. I quietly passed the word to a few of the officers who sat near, in such manner as not to attract the attention of the Indians. They proceeded to their companies and selected quickly some of their most reliable men, instructing the latter to assemble around and near my campfire, well armed, as if merely attracted there by the Indian serenade. The men thus selected were to come singly, appear as unconcerned as possible, and be in readiness to act promptly, but to do nothing without orders from me.

In this manner about one hundred of my men were, in an inconceivably short space of time, mingled with the Indians, who, to the number of forty or more, sat or stood about my camp fire, laughing in their sleeves (had they not been minus these appendages), no doubt, at the clever dodge by which they were entertaining the white men while their village was hastening preparations for a speedy flight. When the musicians had apparently exhausted their programme, they took their departure, informing us that later in the evening they would return and repeat the performance; they might have added, "with an entire change of programme."

After their departure the conversation continued with the chiefs until, by glancing about me, I saw that a sufficient number of my men had mingled with the Indians to answer my purpose. Of the forty or more Indians in the group, there were but few chiefs, the majority being young men or boys. My attention was devoted to the chiefs, and acting upon the principle that for the purposes desired half a dozen would be as valuable as half a hundred, I determined to seize the principal chiefs then present, and permit the others to depart. To do this without taking or losing life now became the problem. Indicating in a quiet manner to some of my men who were nearest to me to be ready to prevent the escape of three or four of the Indians whom I pointed out, I then directed Romeo to command silence on the part of the Indians, and to inform them that I was about to communicate something of great importance to them. This was sufficient to attract their undivided attention. I then rose from my seat near the fire, and unbuckling my revolver from my waist asked the Indians to observe that I threw my weapons upon the ground, as an evidence that in what I was about to do I did not desire or propose to shed blood unless forced to do so. I then asked the chiefs to look about them and count the armed men whom I had posted among and around them, completely cutting off every avenue of escape. They had attempted, under pretence of a friendly visit to my camp, to deceive me, in order that their village might elude us, but their designs had been frustrated, and they were now in our power. I asked them to quietly submit to what was now inevitable, and promised them that if they and their people responded in the proper manner to the reasonable demands which I intended to make, all would be well, and they would be restored to their people.

The reader must not imagine that this was listened to in tame silence by the thoroughly excited Indians, old and young. Upon the first intimation from me regarding the armed men, and before I could explain their purpose, every Indian who was dismounted sprang instantly to his feet, while those who were mounted gathered the reins of their ponies; all drew their revolvers or strung their bows, and for a few moments it seemed as if nothing could avert a collision, which could only terminate in the annihilation of the Indians, and an equal or perhaps greater loss on our part.

The powers of Romeo as interpreter were employed without stint, in repeating to the chiefs my urgent appeals to restrain their young men and avoid bloodshed. Even at this date I recall no more exciting experience with Indians than the occasion of which I now write. Near me stood a tall, gray-haired chief, who, while entreating his people to be discreet, kept his cocked revolver in his hand ready for use, should the emergency demand it. He was one of the few whom I had determined to hold. Near him stood another, a most powerful and forbidding-looking warrior, who was without firearms, but who was armed with a bow, already strung, and a quiver full of iron-pointed arrows. His coolness during this scene of danger and excitement was often the subject of remark afterward between the officers whose attention had been drawn to him. He stood apparently unaffected by the excitement about him, but not unmindful of the surrounding danger. Holding his bow in one hand, with the other he continued to draw from his quiver arrow after arrow. Each one he would examine as coolly as if he expected to engage in target practice. First he would cast his eye along the shaft of the arrow to see if it was perfectly straight and true. Then he would with thumb and finger gently feel the point and edge of the barbed head, returning to the quiver each one whose condition did not satisfy him.

In this manner he continued until he had selected perhaps half a dozen arrows, with which he seemed satisfied, and which he retained in his hand, while his quick eye did not permit a single incident about him to escape unnoticed. The noise of voices and the excitement increased until a movement began on the part of the Indians who were mounted, principally the young men and boys. If the latter could be allowed to escape and the chiefs be retained, the desired object would be gained. Suddenly a rush was made. But for the fact that my men were ordered not to fire, the attempt of the Indians would not have been successful. I, as well as the other officers near me, called upon the men not to fire. The result was that all but four broke through the lines and made their escape. The four detained, however, were those desired, being chiefs and warriors of prominence.

Forming my men about them in such impassable ranks that a glance was sufficient to show how futile all further efforts to escape would prove, I then explained to the four captive Indians that I knew the design under which they had visited our camp; that I also knew that in their village were held as captives two white girls, whose release the troops were there to enforce, and to effect their release, as well as to compel the Cheyennes to abandon the war path and return to their reservation, I had seized the four Indians as hostages. To prove my sincerity and earnest desire to arrange these matters amicably, and without resort to force, the Indians were told they might select one of their number, whom I would release and send as a messenger of peace to the village, the latter having left in indiscriminate flight as soon as the seizure of the chiefs was made.

It became a matter of great difficulty, without the employment of forces to induce the four Indians to give up their arms. I explained to them that they were prisoners, and it was one of our customs to disarm all men held as prisoners. I stated to them that a persistence in their refusal would compel me to summon a sufficient number of men to take the arms by force; and it was even necessary to parade, the men in front of them before the arms were finally given up. After a lengthy conference with each other, they announced that they had agreed upon one of their number who, in accordance with my promise, should be released and sent to the tribe as bearer of my demands, and of any messages they might desire to send to their people.

I accordingly caused bountiful presents of coffee and sugar to be given the one so chosen, returned to him his pony and arms, and intrusted him with verbal messages to his tribe, the substance of which was as follows: First, I demanded the unconditional surrender of the two white girls held captive in the village; hitherto surrenders of white captives by Indians had only been made on payment of heavy ransom. Second, I required the Cheyenne village, as an evidence of peaceable intentions and good faith on their part, to proceed at once to their reservation, and to locate near Camp Supply, reporting to the military commander at that station. Third, I sent a friendly message to Little Robe, inviting him to visit me with a view to the speedy settlement of the questions at issue, promising him unmolested transit coming and returning for him and as many of his people as chose to visit me. In case of failure to comply with the first two of my demands, hostilities would be continued, and my command would at once commence the pursuit of the village, which, considering its size and the poor condition of the ponies at that early season of the year, would be unable to escape from the cavalry.

The Indian who was to go as bearer of these demands was also invited to return, assured that whether the response of his people should prove favorable or not, he should be granted a safe conduct between the camp and the village. Inwardly congratulating himself, no doubt, upon the good fortune which gave him his liberty, the messenger of peace or war, as his tribe might elect, took his departure for his village. With him went the earnest wishes for success of every inmate of the camp; but if this was the feeling of the command generally, who can realize the intense interest and anxiety with which young Brewster now awaited the result of this effort to secure the freedom of his sister? And if the two forlorn, helpless girls knew of the presence of troops of their own race, what must have been the bitter despondency, the painful relinquishment of all hope as they saw the village and its occupants commencing a hasty flight, and no apparent effort upon the part of the troops to effect their release?

What comfort it would have been to these ill-fated maidens could they have known, before being hurried from the village, of the steps already taken to restore them to home and friends, or better still, if one of them could have known that almost within the sound of her voice, a brother was patiently but determinedly biding the time that should restore his sister to his arms.

Relying upon the influence which I believed Little Robe would exert upon his people, and knowing the pressure we were able to bring to bear through the three chiefs we held as hostages, I felt confident that sooner or later the Cheyennes would be forced to release the two white girls from their captivity. Placing a strong guard over the three chiefs, and warning them not to attempt to escape if they valued their lives, I returned to my tent after having ordered every comfort possible to be provided for our prisoners consistent with their position.

The following day was passed without incident in awaiting the arrival of tidings from the village. Early in the afternoon the pickets reported a small body of Indians in sight. Upon a nearer approach the party appeared to consist of about fifty mounted Indians. They rode steadily in the direction of the camp, with no apparent wish to conceal their movements, thus indicating that they were on an errand of peace. When within half a mile or less of camp the entire party dismounted, and after picketing their ponies out to graze, advanced on foot directly toward camp. So strange a proceeding, and at a time when the excitement regarding our relations with the Indians ran high, was sufficient to assemble nearly all the occupants of camp to watch the approach of this delegation of Indians. The latter were apparelled in their best and most highly colored clothes. As they came near, it was perceived that several paces in advance of the main group strode two chiefs, evidently leaders of the party; both advanced with uncovered heads. Suddenly I thought I detected a familiar face and form in the taller of the two chiefs in front, and on more careful scrutiny I recognized my former friend and guest Little Robe, who had thus quickly responded to my invitation to cast aside all doubts and come and visit me, with a view to bringing about more friendly relations between his people and the whites.

As soon as I recognized him I advanced to meet him. He grasped my hand and embraced me with what seemed to me real cordiality. Waiting until the other members of his party came up, I shook hands with each individual, and then invited them to my tent. As the tent would not accommodate the entire party, Little Robe designated about a dozen of the most important, who entered, while the others remained outside. I soon found that in Little Robe I had a hearty coadjutor in the work before me. He admitted that the white girls were held as captives in the Cheyenne village, which was the first positive evidence received of this fact. He also stated, what I had no reason to doubt, that he had at various times attempted to purchase them, with a view, if successful, of returning them to the nearest military post; but his efforts in this direction had always failed. He admitted the justice of my demands upon his people, and assured me that to bring about a satisfactory condition of affairs he would use every exertion and employ all the influence at his command. It was to assure me of this desire on his part that he had hastened to visit me.

Knowing that the surest and speediest way to establish a state of good feeling in an Indian is to provide liberally for the wants of his stomach, I ordered a beef to be killed and distributed among the followers of Little Robe; with this also were distributed the usual supplies of coffee, sugar, flour, etc., so that the recipients were not only prepared to regard us at least very kindly disposed, but I knew the effect on the village, when the result of the visit, and the treatment extended to our guests was described, would materially aid us in our negotiations with the tribe.

Little Robe, while earnest in his desire to see the white girls returned to us, frankly admitted that his influence was not supreme, and there were those who would object to their release, at least without compensation; and it might be that a satisfactory settlement of the question might be delayed for many days. After partaking of a bountiful repast, Little Robe and his party set out for the village, promising to send me word the following day as to his success. Another day was passed in waiting, when the chief who had accompanied Little Robe the previous day again visited us, but brought no decisive or satisfactory reply. The substance of the reply was that the Cheyennes desired us to release the three chiefs then held by us as hostages, after which they would be prepared to consider the question of the release of the two white girls. To this I sent back a reply that we would remain in the camp we then occupied until the following day, when, if a favorable answer should not have been received, we would follow on their trail and encamp nearer to the village, the great distance then separating us, about twelve miles, being a hindrance in the way of transmitting messages promptly from one to the other.

I knew that the village was in no condition for a rapid or extended flight, and could be overhauled by the cavalry whenever desired; at the same time, to allow as much freedom in their deliberations as possible, I had not been unwilling that a few miles should separate us. No reply was received; consequently we packed up and marched down the Sweetwater, on the trail of the village, about ten miles, and went into camp. Here I received another visit from the chief who had previously acted as diplomatic courier between the camp and village, but the response of the Cheyennes was still unsatisfactory, and exhibited a disinclination on their part to make any decided promises respecting the release of the captive white girls. They insisted as preliminary to such decision that the three chiefs held by us should be restored to liberty, after which we might discuss the question relating to the release of the girls.

I will not weary the reader by describing the various subterfuges resorted to by the Indians, by which they strove to avoid or delay the surrender of the white girls without first, as had been customary, receiving a ransom. Finally, after I had almost exhausted the patience of the troops, particularly of the Kansas regiment, which had been raised and organized mainly to effect the recapture of the white girls, or else avenge the outrage of which they had been the victims, I determined to force matters to an issue without further quibbling on the part of the Indians.

I sent for a delegation of chiefs from the Cheyenne village to receive my ultimatum. They came, and upon their arrival I assembled them in my tent, the three captured chiefs being also permitted to be present, as the conference, as will be seen, was to be of deep interest to them. After recounting to the chiefs the incidents of our pursuit of the village, their surprise at being overtaken, the stratagems by which they hoped to elude us, the steps we had already taken to obtain the release of the white girls, and the delays interposed by the Indians, I stated that I had but one other message to send to the village; and upon the chiefs of the latter would rest the responsibility of peace or war. Further delay would not be submitted to on our part. We knew they had two of our race captives in the village, and we were there to demand and enforce the demand for their release, cost what it might. I then informed them that if by sunset the following day the two white girls were not restored to our hands unharmed, the lives of the three chiefs would be forfeited, and the troops would resume active hostilities. At the same I called attention to the fact that in the famished condition of their ponies they could not expect to escape the pursuit of the cavalry. Every argument that might have weight in influencing a favorable decision was stated to them. The conference then broke up, and the three chiefs were remanded to the captain of the guard. The delegation from the village, after a brief interview with their captive comrades, took a hasty departure, and set out upon their return to the village, deeply impressed, apparently, with the importance of promptness in communicating to the chiefs at the village the decision which had been arrived at regarding the captives.

The terms given to the Indians soon became known to every individual in the command, and naturally excited the deepest interest. All hoped for a favorable issue, but no one regarded the events then transpiring with the intense interest and anxiety felt by young Brewster, who now saw that his long-cherished hope to recover his sister was either about to be realized, or forever sealed in disappointment.

The captive chiefs did not pretend to conceal their solicitude as to the part they were involuntarily made to play in the events then transpiring. I did not expect prompt action on the part of the chiefs in the village. I knew they would practise every delay conceivable before complying with our demands; but when the question was forced upon them as to whether they preferred to deliver up the white girls to us or to force by their refusal the execution of the three chiefs, their decision would be in favor of their people.

Three o'clock arrived, and no tidings from the village. By this time the officers and men of the command had assembled near headquarters, and upon the small eminences nearby, eagerly watching the horizon in the direction of the village, to catch the first glimpse of the messengers who must soon arrive to avert the execution of the three chiefs. Even the three chiefs became despondent as the sun slowly but surely approached the horizon, and no tidings from the village reached them. Finally Romeo came to me and stated that the three chiefs desired to see me. I repaired to their place of confinement at once, and was asked by the younger of the three if it was my firm purpose to make good my words in the event of the failure of their people to release the white girls. I replied in the affirmative. The chief then attempted a little Indian diplomacy, by assuring me that in the village and among his own people he was a man of great consequence, and could exert a wide influence; for this reason he requested me to release him, and he would hasten to the village, obtain the release of the two girls, and return in time to save his two companions.

When this proposition was first made I attributed it to fear that the chiefs in the village might decline to restore the two girls to liberty, and the lives of the three chiefs would be sacrificed thereby; but subsequent events proved that while this consideration may have had its influence, the principal motive that prompted the proposition was a desire to escape from our hands before the white girls should be restored to us, as the chief referred to had been a party to their capture and to the subsequent ill treatment they had received.

I replied to his proposal, that if he was of such importance in his tribe as he claimed to be, he was the most proper person for me to retain possession of, as his people would be more likely to accede to my demands to save his life than that of a person of less consequence.

The sun was perhaps an hour high when the dim outlines of about twenty mounted figures were discerned against the horizon, on a high hill, two or three miles to the west of us. Instantly all eyes were directed to the party, but the distance was too great to enable any of us to clearly define either the number or character of the group. Gradually, under the magnifying powers of the glass, I was able to make out the figures in sight. I could only determine at first that the group was, as might be imagined, composed of Indians, and began counting them audibly, when I discovered two figures mounted upon the same pony.

As soon as this was announced several of my companions at once exclaimed, "Can they be the girls?" I could detect nothing, however, in their appearance warranting such a conclusion, their dress apparently being the same as that of the other individuals of the group. While endeavoring to make out something more definite in regard to the party, I saw the two figures descend from the pony, and, leaving the rest of the group, advance toward us on foot. All this I reported to the anxious bystanders, who became now more than ever convinced that the two figures approaching must be the two girls. I began describing the appearance of the two as well as I could, with the aid of the glass: "One seems to have a short, heavy figure; the other is considerably taller and more slender." Young Brewster, who stood at my side, immediately responded, "The last one must be my sister; she is quite tall. Let me go and meet them; this anxiety is more than I can endure." But this I declined, fearing that should one of the two now approaching us prove to be his sister, seeing her in the forlorn condition in which she must be might provoke young Brewster beyond control, and induce him to attempt to obtain revenge in a manner not governed by either prudence or propriety. So I reluctantly declined to permit him to advance beyond our lines. But by this time the two figures had approached near enough to enable me clearly to determine that they were really of white complexion, and undoubtedly the two girls whose release we were so impatiently waiting for.

As the Kansas volunteers held left their homes and various occupations in civil life to accomplish, among other results, the release of the two girls who had been abducted from the frontier of their State, I deemed it appropriate that that regiment should be the first to welcome the two released captives to friends and freedom. Accordingly the three senior officers of the regiment were designated to proceed beyond our lines and conduct the two girls to camp—a duty whose performance carried its pleasure with it. The three officers advanced to meet the two figures (I use the term figures, as the dress was of that nondescript pattern which renders this term most appropriate). They had passed one fourth of the distance, perhaps, when young Brewster, whom I had detained at my side with difficulty, bounded away, and the next moment was running at full speed to greet his long-lost sister. Dashing past the three officers, he clasped in his arms the taller of the two girls. This told us all we had hoped for. We awaited their approach, and as they drew near to the little brook which flowed just beyond the point occupied by the group of officers around me, I stepped forward, and extending my hands to the two girls, bade them a hearty welcome to liberty. In a moment officers and men were struggling about them upon all sides, eager to take them by the hand,

and testify the great joy felt at their deliverance from a life of captivity.

Men whom I have seen face death without quailing found their eyes filled with tears, unable to restrain the deep emotion produced by this joyful event. The appearance of the two girls was sufficient to excite our deepest sympathy. Miss White, the younger of the two, though not beautiful, possessed a most interesting face. Her companion would have been pronounced beautiful by the most critical judge.

Their joy at their deliverance, however, could not hide the evidences of privation and suffering to which they had been subjected by their cruel captors. They were clothed in dresses made from flour sacks, the brand of the mills being plainly seen on each dress; showing that the Indians who had held them in captivity had obtained their provisions from the government at some agency. The entire dress of the two girls was as nearly like the Indian mode as possible; both wore leggings and moccasins; both their hair in two long braids, and as if to propitiate us, the Indians, before releasing them, had added to the wardrobe of the two girls various rude ornaments, such as are worn by squaws. About their wrists they wore coils of brass wire; on their fingers had been placed numerous rings, and about their necks strings of variously colored beads. Almost the first remark I heard young Brewster make after the arrival of the two girls was, "Sister, do take those hateful things off."

Fortunately they were not the only white women in camp. I had a white woman as cook, and to enable the two girls to improve their wardrobe a little before relating to us the history of their capture and captivity, they were conducted to the tent of the white woman referred to, from whose limited wardrobe they were able to obtain enough to replace the dresses made of flour sacks, and in a few minutes reappeared presenting a much more civilized appearance than when they first entered camp.

The story of their captivity was that of hundreds of other women and girls whose husbands, fathers, or brothers take their lives in their hands and seek homes on the frontier. There was much in their story not appropriate for these pages. They described how great their joy was at encountering each other for the first time as prisoners in the hands of the Indians. They had been traded repeatedly from the hands of one chief to those of another, the last transfer having been effected only two weeks prior to their release. Soon after their first meeting, it was their good fortune, comparatively, to become the property of one chief. This threw them into each other's society, and tended to lighten the horrors of their captivity.

The story of the two girls, containing accounts of wrongs and ill treatment sufficient to have ended the existence of less determined persons, is too long to be given here. Besides indignities and insults far more terrible than death itself, the physical suffering to which the two girls were subjected was too great almost to be believed. They were required to transport huge burdens on their backs, large enough to have made a load for a beast of burden. They were limited to barely enough food to sustain life; sometimes a small morsel of mule meat, not more than an inch square, was their allowance of food for twenty-four hours. The squaws beat them unmercifully with clubs whenever the men were not present. Upon one occasion one of the girls was felled to the ground by a blow from a club in the hands of one of the squaws. Their joy therefore at regaining their freedom after a captivity of nearly a year can be better imagined than described; while that of the brother who had struggled so long and determinedly to regain his sister could not be expressed in words.

After the momentary excitement consequent upon the safe arrival of the girls in camp had subsided, officers, particularly of the Kansas volunteers, came to me with the remark that when we first overtook the Cheyenne village and I failed to order an attack when all the chances were in our favor, they mentally condemned my decision as a mistake; but with the results accomplished afterwards they found ample reason to amend their first judgment, and frankly and cordially admit that the release of the two captives was far more gratifying than any victory over the Indians could have been if purchased by the sacrifice of their lives.

With this happy termination of this much of our negotiations with the Indians, I determined to march in the morning for Camp Supply, Indian Territory, satisfied that with the three chiefs in our possession, and the squaws and children captured at the Washita still held as prisoners at Fort Hays, Kansas, we could compel the Cheyennes to abandon the war path and return to their reservation. The three chiefs begged to be released, upon the ground that their people had delivered up the two girls; but this I told them was but one of the two conditions imposed; the other required the tribe to return to their reservation, and until this was done they need not hope for freedom; but in the meanwhile I assured them of kind treatment at our hands.

Before dark a delegation of chiefs from the village visited camp to like-wise urge the release of the three chiefs. My reply to them was the same as that I had given to the captives. I assured them, however, that upon complying with their treaty obligations and returning to their reservation, the three chiefs would be restored to their people, and we would return to them also the women and children captured at the Washita. Seeing that no modification of these terms could be obtained, they finally promised to accede to travel, but as soon as practicable they would surely proceed with their entire village to Camp Supply, and abandon the war path forever; a promise which, as a tribe, they have adhered to, from that day to this, with strict faith, so far as my knowledge extends.

I had not heard from General Sheridan since we separated at Fort Sill; he to set out for Camp Supply, and I with my command to begin my present movement. But when near Camp Supply, a courier met me with despatches from General Sheridann—who had been meanwhile summoned to Washington—informing me in regard to the arrangements made for my command upon its arrival at Camp Supply. The Kansas volunteers were to march to Fort Hays, and there be mustered out of the service. The Seventh Cavalry was also to proceed to the same point, and there await further orders, as the General in his note stated that he had concluded to draw in the Seventh and end the campaign.

Making a brief halt at Camp Supply to rest our animals and replenish our stores, my command continued its march to Fort Hays, crossing the Arkansas River at Fort Dodge, Kansas. Upon our arrival at Fort Hays we were met by the husband of young Brewster's sister, who had learned of her restoration to liberty from the published despatches that had preceded us to Fort Hays. He was still lame from the effects of the bullet wound received at the time the Indians carried off his bride, whom he had given up as dead or lost to him forever. The joy of their meeting went far to smooth over their late sorrow. They could not find language to express their gratitude to the troops for their efforts in restoring them to each other. As the Indians had robbed them of everything at the time of the attack, a collection was taken up among the troops for their benefit, which resulted in the accumulation of several hundred dollars, to be divided between the two captives. The time came for our guests to leave us, and rejoin their people, or such of them as had survived the attack of the Indians. Good-bys were spoken, and the two girls, so lately victims of the most heartless and cruel captivity, departed, with husband, brother, and friends, for their frontier homes, bearing with them the warm sympathies and cordial good wishes of every soldier in the command.

The events described in this chapter terminated my service in the field on what is known as the southern and middle plains, embracing all that portion of the plains south of the Platte River. From and after the Washita campaign the frontiers of Kansas have enjoyed comparative peace and immunity from Indian depredations. No general Indian war has prevailed in that part of the country, nor is it probable that anything more serious in this way than occasional acts of horse stealing will occur hereafter. Many of my friends have expressed surprise that I have not included some of the hunting scenes and adventures that have formed a part of my experience; but I feared the introduction of this new feature, although probably the pleasantest and in many respects most interesting of my recollections of border life, might prolong the series of articles far beyond the length originally assigned to them. I hope, however, at an early day to relate some of my experiences with the large game so abundant on the plains, and in this way fill up a blank in these articles which my friends who are lovers of sport have not failed to observe.

As I pen these lines, I am in the midst of scenes of bustle and busy preparation attendant upon the organization and equipment of a large party for an important exploring expedition, on which I shall start before these pages reach the publishers' hands. During my absence I expect to visit a region of country as yet unseen by human eyes, except those of the Indian—a country described by the latter as abounding in game of all varieties, rich in scientific interest, and of surpassing beauty in natural scenery.

CHAPTER 9

The Yellowstone Expedition Report, 1873

Headquarters Battalion Seventh Cavalry
Pompey's Pillar
Yellowstone River, Montana

August 15th, 1873

Acting Assistant Adjutant General
  Yellowstone Expedition

SIR: Acting under instructions of the Brevet Major General commanding, I proceeded at 5 o'clock on the morning of the 4th inst., with one squadron of my command numbering about ninety men to explore a route over which the main column could move. Having reached a point on the Yellowstone River, near the mouth of the Tongue River, and several miles in advance, and while waiting the arrival of the forces of the Expedition, six mounted Sioux dashed boldly into the skirt of the timber within which my command had halted and unsaddled, and attempted to stampede our horses. Fortunately our videttes discovered the approach of the Indians in time to give the alarm. A few well-directed shots soon drove the Indians to a safe distance where they kept up a series of yells, occasionally firing a few shots. As soon as the squadron could mount I directed Captain Moylan to move out in pursuit, at the same time I moved with the troop in advance commanded by 1st Lieut. T. W. Custer. Following the Indians at a brisk gait my suspicions became excited by the confident bearing exhibited by the six Sioux in our front whose course seemed to lead us near a heavy growth of timber which stood along the river bank above us. When almost within rifle range of this timber I directed the squadron to halt while I with two orderlies, all being well-mounted continued after the Sioux in order to develop their intentions. Proceeding a few hundred yards in advance of the squadron and keeping a watchful eye on the timber to my left, I halted. The six Indians in my front also halted as if to tempt further pursuit. Finding all efforts in this direction unavailing, their plans and intentions were quickly made evident as no sooner was it seen that we intended to advance no farther than with their characteristic howls and yells over three hundred well-mounted warriors dashed in perfect line from the edge of the timber and charged down upon Captain Moylan's squadron at the same time endeavoring to intercept the small party with me. As soon as the speed of the thoroughbred on which I was mounted brought me within hailing distance of Lieut. Custer's troop I directed that officer to quickly throw forward a dismounted line of troopers and endeavor to empty a few Indian saddles. The order was obeyed with the quickest alacrity, and as the Sioux came dashing forward expecting to ride down the squadron a line of dismounted cavalrymen rose from the grass and delivered almost in the faces of the warriors a volley of carbine bullets which broke and scattered their ranks in all directions, and sent more than one Sioux reeling from his saddle. This check gave us time to make our dispositions to resist the succeeding attacks which we knew our enemies would soon make upon us. The great superiority of our enemies in numbers, the long distance separating us from the main command, and the belief afterwards verified that the woods above us still concealed a portion of the savage forces—induced me to confine my movements at first strictly to the defensive. The entire squadron except the horse holders was dismounted and ordered to fight on foot. The Indians outnumbering us almost five to one were enabled to envelop us completely between their lines, formed a semicircle with the river which flowed at our backs. The little belt of timber in which we had been first attacked formed a very good cover for our lead horses while the crest of a second table of land conveniently located from the timber gave us an excellent line of defence. The length of our line and the numbers of the enemy prevented us from having any force in reserve. Every available officer and man was on the skirmish line which was in reality our line of battle, even the number of men holding horses had to be reduced one-half so that each horse holder held eight horses. Until the Indians were made to taste quite freely of our lead, they displayed unusual boldness frequently charging up to our line and firing with great deliberation and accuracy. Captain Moylan exercised command along the entire line. Lieut. Custer commanded the center. My Adjutant, Lieut. James Calhoun, commanded the right and Lieut. Charles A. Varnum the left. The first Indian killed was shot from his pony by "Bloody Knife," the Crow who acted as my guide and scout. Soon after Private Charles R. Miller of "A" Troop, 7th Cavalry, succeeded in sending a carbine bullet directly through the body of a chief who had been conspicuous throughout the engagement. At the same time it was known that our fire had disabled many of their ponies while owing to our sheltered position the only damage thus far inflicted upon us was one man and two horses wounded, one of the latter shot in three places. Finding their efforts to force back our line unavailing, the Indians now resorted to another expedient. By an evidently prescribed plan they set fire in several places to the tall grass that covered the ground in our front, hoping by this means to force us back to the river and there finish us at their pleasure. Fortunately for us there was no wind prevailing at the time while the grass was scarcely dry enough to burn rapidly. Taking advantage of the dense curtain of smoke which rose from the burning grass, the Indians by following the course of the flames could often contrive to obtain a shot at us at comparatively close range but my men observing that no damage was to be apprehended from the slowly advancing flames acted upon the hint given them by the savages, and by taking positions close to the flames could frequently catch an opportunity to send a shot through a break in the curtain of smoke and in this way surprised the Indians by the adoption of his own device.

The fight began at 11:30 AM and was waged without cessation until near three o'clock. All efforts of the Indians to dislodge us proving unsuccessful, the Indians had become extremely weary and had almost discontinued their offensive movements when my ammunition had run low. I decided to mount the squadron and charge the Indians with the intention of driving them from the field. Captain Moylan promptly had his men in the saddle and throwing forward twenty mounted skirmishers under Lieut. Varnum, the entire squadron moved forward at a trot. No sooner did the Indians discern our intention than despite their superior numbers they cowardly prepared for flight, in which preparation they were greatly hastened when Captain Moylan's squadron charged them and drove them "pell-mell" for three miles. Five ponies killed or badly wounded were left on the battleground along the line of their flight. So rapidly were they forced to flee that they abandoned and threw away breech-loading arms, saddle equipment, clothing, robes, lariats, and other articles comprised in an Indian outfit. Among the Indians who fought on this occasion were some of the identical warriors who committed the massacre at Fort Phil Kearney and they no doubt intended a similar programme when they sent the six warriors to dash up and attempt to decoy us into a pursuit past the timber in which the savages hoped to ambush us. Had we pursued the six warriors half a mile further, instead of halting, the entire band of warriors would have been in our rear, and all the advantage of position and numbers would have been with them. So far as the troops attacked were concerned, the Indians to offset their own heavy losses had been able to do us no damage except to wound one man and two horses, but unfortunately two noncombatants, Veterinary Surgeon John Honsinger, Seventh Cavalry, and Mr. Baliran of Memphis, Tennessee, in endeavoring to come from the main command to join the squadron in advance were discovered by the Indians during the attack and being unarmed were overtaken and killed almost within view of the battleground. Fortunately the Indians were so pressed as to not be able to scalp or otherwise mutilate the remains.

On the 8th inst. we discovered the trail of a large village, evidently that to which the party that attacked us on the 4th belonged. The course of the trail led up the Yellowstone, and apparently was not more than two days old. Acting under the authority of the Brevet Major General commanding, I ordered my command consisting of four squadrons of the

Seventh Cavalry in readiness to begin the pursuit that night. The Brevet Major General also directed the detachment of guides and Indian scouts under Lieut. Daniel H. Brush, Seventeenth Infantry, to report to me for tem-porary service. Leaving all tents and wagons behind, and taking with us rations for seven days we started in pursuit at 10 o'clock in the night of the 8th inst., having waited until that hour, until the moon should enable us to follow the trail. Following the trail as rapidly as the rough character of the country would permit, daylight next morning found us nearly thirty miles from our starting point. Concealing the horses and men in a ravine, a halt of three hours was ordered to enable the horses to graze and the men to obtain refreshment. Renewing the march at eight o'clock the pursuit was continued without halting until noon, when to avoid discovery as well as obtain needed rest for men and animals it was decided to conceal ourselves in the timber and await the cover of night to continue the pursuit. Starting out at 6 :30 PM, the trail was followed rapidly for six miles when to our disappointment we discovered that the Indians had taken to the river and crossed to the east side. In following their trail to this point it was evident that the movement of the Indians was one of precipitate flight, the result of the engagement on the 4th. All along their trail and in their camping places were to be found large quantities of what constituted Indian equipment such as lodge poles, robes, saddle equipment, arms, and cooking utensils—in hastily abandoned camp ground nearly two hundred axes besides a great many camp kettles and cups were found. My entire command was disappointed when the trail showed that the Indians had crossed to the other side, particularly as our rapid marching had carried us to the point of crossing the evening of the day on which the last of the Indians had crossed over, so that one more march would have enabled us to overhaul them. Bivouacking in a belt of timber on the river bank, we waited until daylight to begin an attempt to cross the command over the river, which at this point is about six hundred yards wide. At early dawn the entire command forded the river to an island located about the middle of the channel but our difficulties in the way of crossing—here began—as the volume of water and the entire force of the current were to be encountered between the island and the opposite bank. The current here rushes by at a velocity of about seven miles an hour, while the depth of the water was such that a horse attempting to cross would be forced to swim several hundred yards. Still, as we knew the Indians had not discovered our pursuit, and were probably located within easy striking distance of the river, it was most desirable that a crossing should be affected. To accomplish this Lieut. Weston, Seventh Cavalry, with three accomplished swimmers from the command, attempted to cross on a log raft, carrying with them a cable made of lariats. The current was so strong that Lieut. Weston's party was unable to effect a landing but were swept down the river nearly two miles, and then forced to abandon the raft and swim for shore. Lieut. Weston with characteristic perseverance and energy made repeated attempts afterward to carry the cable over, but although succeeding in reaching the opposite bank in person, was unable to connect the cable with the shore. Almost the entire day was spent in these unsuccessful efforts until finally a crossing in this manner had to be abandoned. I then caused some cattle to be killed and by stretching fresh hides over a kind of basket frame prepared by the Crow guide made what are known among the Indians as "bull boats." with these I hoped to be able to connect a cable with the opposite bank at daylight next morning, but just at sunset a small party of Indians were seen to ride down to the bank opposite us and water their ponies. They discovered our presence and at once hastened away. Of course it was useless now to attempt a surprise and the intention to cross the river the following morning was abandoned.

At early dawn the next day (the 11th inst.) the Indians appeared in strong force on the river bank opposite us, and opened a brisk fire upon us from their rifles. No attention was paid to them until encouraged by this. They had collected at several points in full view and within range of our rifles when about thirty of our best marksmen having posted themselves along the bank opened a well-directed fire upon the Indians and drove them back to cover. In the meantime strong parties of Indians were reported by our pickets to be crossing the river below and above us, their ponies and themselves being so accustomed to the river as to render this operation quite practicable for them. Capt. French commanding the right wing was directed to watch the parties crossing below, while Col. Hart commanding the left wing posted a force to discharge this duty with reference to parties crossing above. It would have been possible perhaps for us to have prevented the Indians from effecting a crossing, at least where they did, but I was not only willing, but anxious, that as many of them should come over as were so disposed. They were soon reported as moving to the bluffs immediately in rear of us from the river. Lieut. Brush was directed to employ his scouts in watching and reporting their movements, a duty they discharged in a thorough manner. While this was transpiring, I had mounted my command and formed it in line close under the bluffs facing from the river where we quietly waited the attack of the Indians in our front. The Indians having collected some of their best shots apparently armed with long range rifles, and were attempting to drive our men back from the waters edge. It was at this time that my standing orderly Private Tuttle of "E" Troop, Seventh Cavalry, one of the best marksmen in my command, took a sporting Springfield rifle and posted himself with two other men behind cover on the river bank and began picking off the Indians as they exposed themselves on the opposite bank. He had obtained the range of the enemy's position early in the morning and was able to place his shots wherever desired. It was while so engaged that he observed an Indian in full view near the river. Calling the attention of his comrade to the fact he asked him to "watch him drop that Indian," a feat which he succeeded in performing. Several other Indians rushed to the assistance of their fallen comrade when Private Tuttle by a skillful and rapid use of his breech-loading Springfield, succeeded in killing two other warriors. The Indians enraged no doubt at this rough handling directed their aim at Private Tuttle, who fell pierced through the head by a rifle bullet. He was one of the most useful and daring soldiers who ever served under my command. About this time Captain French who was engaged with the Indians who were attacking us from below succeeded by a shot from his rifle in shooting a warrior from his saddle, while several ponies were known to be wounded or disabled. The Indians now began to display a strong force on our front on the bluffs. Col. Hart was ordered to push a line of dismounted men to the crest and prevent the further advance of the enemy towards the river. This duty was handsomely performed by a portion of Capt. Yates squadron. Col. Hart had posted Lieut. Chas. Braden and twenty men on a small knoll which commanded our left. Against this party the Indians made their first determined onslaught. A mounted party of warriors numbering nearly two hundred rode boldly to within thirty yards of Lieut. Braden's position when the latter and his command delivered such a well-directed fire that the Indians were driven rapidly from that portion of the field after having evidently suffered considerable loss. Unfortunately Lieut. Braden received a rifle ball through the upper part of his thigh passing directly through the bone, but he maintained his position with great gallantry and coolness, until

he repulsed the enemy. Hundreds of Indians were now to be seen galloping up and down along our front, each moment becoming bolder
owing to the smallness of our force, which was then visible. Believing
the proper time had arrived to assume the offensive, orders to this effect were accordingly sent to Col. Hart and Capt. French the two wing
commanders. Lieut. Weston was directed to move his troop "L" up a
deep ravine on our left, which would carry him to the enemy's position,
and as soon as opportunity occurred he was to charge and pursue the
Indians with all the vigor practicable immediately after Capt. Owen
Hale directed to move his squadron consisting of "E" and "K" troops
in conjunction with Lieut. Weston's troop, and the three troops to
charge simultaneously. Similar dispositions were ordered in the center
and right. Lieut. T. W. Custer commdg. "B" Troop, was ordered to advance and charge the Indians in front of our center, while Capts. Yates
and Moylan moved rapidly forward in the same direction. Before this
movement began it became necessary to dislodge a large party of Indians posted in a ravine and behind rocks on our front, who were engaged in keeping up a heavy fire upon our troops while the latter were
moving. It was at this point that the horse of Lieut. Hiram H. Ketcham,
Acting Asst. Adjutant General of the Expedition, was shot from under
him. My own horse was also shot from under me, within a few paces of
the latter. The duty of driving the Indians engaged in sharpshooting
was entrusted to Lieut. Charles A. Varnum with a detachment of "A"
Troop, Seventh Cavalry, who soon forced the Indians back from their
cover. Everything being in readiness for a general advance, the charge
was ordered and the Squadrons took the gallop to the tune of "Garry
Owen," the band being immediately in rear of the skirmish line. The
Indians had evidently come out prepared to do their best and with no
misgivings as to their success as the mounds and high bluffs beyond the
river were covered with groups of squaws, old men, and children who
had collected there to witness our destruction. In this instance the proverbial power of music to sooth the savage breast utterly failed, for no
sooner did the band strike up the cheery notes of "Garry Owen" and
the squadrons advance to the charge than the Indians exhibited
unmistakable signs of commotion and their resistance became more
feeble, until finally satisfied of the earnestness of our attack they turned
their ponies heads and began a disorderly flight. The cavalry put spurs
to their horses and dashed forward in pursuit, the various troops and
squadron commanders vying with each other as to who should head the

advance. The appearance of the main command in sight down the valley at this moment enabled me to relieve Capt. French's command below us and he was ordered to join in the pursuit. Lieut. McIntosh, commanding "G" Troop, moved his command up the valley at a gallop and prevented many of the Indians from crossing. The chase was continued with the utmost vigor until the Indians were completely dispersed and driven a distance of nine miles from where the engagement took place, and they were here forced back across the Yellowstone. The last pony killed in the fight being shot fully eight miles from the point of attack. The number of Indians opposed to us has been estimated by the various officers engaged as from 800 to 1,000. My command numbered 450 officers and men. The Indians were made up of different bands of Sioux, principally the Uncpapas, the whole under command of "Sitting Bull," who participated in the second day's fight and who for once has been taught a lesson he will not soon forget. A large number of the Indians who fought us were fresh from their reservations on the Missouri River. Many of the warriors engaged in the fight on both days were dressed in complete suits of clothes issued at the agencies to Indians. The arms with which they fought us, several of which were captured in the fight, were of the latest improved pattern of breech-loading repeating rifles, and their supply of metallic rifle cartridges seemed unlimited as they were anything but sparing in its use. So amply have they been provided with breech-loading rifles and ammunition, that neither bows nor arrows were employed against us. As an evidence that these Indians, as least many of them, were recently from the Missouri River agencies, we found provisions such as coffee in their abandoned camps, and cooking and other domestic utensils such as only reservation Indians are supplied with. Besides our scouts conversed with them across the river for nearly an hour before the fight became general and satisfied themselves as to the identity of their foes. I only regret that it was impossible for my command to effect a crossing of the river before our presence was discovered and while the hostile village was located near at hand, as I am confident that we could have largely reduced the necessity for appropriation for Indian supplies the coming winter. Before closing this report I desire to bear testimony to the good conduct of every man connected with my command including officers, men, and scouts.

The loss of the Indians in ponies was particularly heavy, while we know that their loss in killed and wounded was beyond all proportion to that which they were enabled to inflict upon us. Our losses being one officer badly wounded, four men killed and three wounded, four horses killed and four wounded.

Careful investigation justifies the statement that including both days' battles, the Indians losses will number forty warriors, while their wounded on the opposite bank of the river may increase this number.

Respectfully Submitted,

/ s/ G. A. Custer

Lieutenant Colonel Seventh Cavalry

Brevet Major General U.S.A.

Commandg Battln.

Sitting Bull

APPENDIX

The Battle at Little Big Horn—Sitting Bull's Version

The following is Setting Bull's account, as related to a reporter of leading newspaper.

Through the intercession of Major Walsh, Sitting Bull was persuaded at nightfall to hold a special conference with me. It was explained to him that I was not his enemy, but that I was his good friend. He was told by Major Walsh that I was a great paper chief; one who talked with a million tongues to all the people in the world. Said the Major: "This man is a man of wonderful medicine; he speaks, and the people on this side and across the great water open their ears and hear him. He tells the truth; he does not lie. He wishes to make the world know what a great tribe is encamped here on the land owned by the White Mother. [This interview took place at Fort Walsh, on British Territory, and the 'White Mother' here mentioned is Queen Victoria.] He wants it understood that her guests are mighty warriors. The Long-Haired Chief (alluding to General Custer) was his friend. He wants to hear from you how he fought and whether he met death like a brave."

"Agh-howgh!" (It is well) said Sitting Bull.

He finally agreed to come, after dark, to the quarters which had been assigned to me, on the condition that nobody should be present except myself, his interlocutor, Major Walsh, two interpreters, and the stenographer I had employed for the occasion.

At the appointed time, half-past eight, the lamps were lighted, and the most mysterious Indian Chieftain who ever flourished in North America was ushered in by Major Walsh, who locked the door behind him. This was the first time that Sitting Bull had condescended, not merely to visit but to address a white man from the United States. During the long years of his domination he had withstood, with his hands, every attempt on the part of the U.S. government at a compromise of interests. He had refused all proffers, declined any treaty. He had never been beaten in a battle with U.S. troops; on the contrary, his warriors had been victorious over the pride of our army. Pressed hard, he had retreated, scorning the factions of his bands who accepted the terms offered them, with the same bitterness with which he scorned his white enemies.

Here he stood, his blanket rolled back, his head upreared, his right moccasin put forward, his right hand thrown across his chest.

I arose and approached him, holding out both hands. He grasped them cordially.

"How!" said he.

"How!"

And now let me attempt a better portrait of Sitting Bull. He is about five feet, ten inches high. He was clad in a black and white calico shirt, black cloth leggings and moccasins, magnificently embroidered with beads and porcupine quills. He held in his left hand a fox-skin cap, its brush drooping to his feet; with the dignity and grace of a natural gentleman he had removed it from his head at the threshold. His long, black hair hung far down his back, athwart his cheeks and in front of his shoulders. His eyes gleamed like black diamonds. His visage, devoid of paint, was noble and commanding; nay, it was something more. Besides the Indian character given to it by high cheekbones, a broad, retreating forehead, a prominent, aquiline nose, and a jaw like a bull dog's, there was about the mouth something of beauty, but more of an expression of exquisite, cruel irony. Such a mouth and such eyes as this Indian's, if seen in the countenance of a white man, would appear to denote qualities similar to those which animated the career of Mazarin and inspired the pen of Machiavelli.

Yet there was something fearfully sweet in his smile as he extended to me his hands.

Such hands! They felt as small and soft as a maiden's, but when I pressed them I could feel the sinews beneath the flesh quivering hard, like a wild animal's. I led him to a seat, a lounge set against the wall, on which he sank with indolent grace. Major Walsh, brilliant in red uniform, sat beside him, and a portable table was brought near. Two interpreters brought chairs and seated themselves, and at a neighboring desk the stenographer took his place. I afterward learned that two Sioux chiefs stood on guard outside the door, and that all the Indians in the fort had their arms ready to spring in case of a suspected treachery. On the previous night, two of the Indians had been taken suddenly ill, and their sickness had been ascribed by some warriors to poison. So restless and anxious were all the savages that nothing but the influence and tact of Major Walsh could have procured for me and for your readers the following valuable, indeed, historical, colloquy with the Sphinx of the Northwest.

I turned to the, interpreter and said:—

"Explain again to Sitting Bull that he is with a friend."

The interpreter explained.

"Banee!" said the chief, holding out his hand again and pressing mine.

Major Walsh here said: "Sitting Bull is in the best mood now that you could possibly wish. Proceed with your questions, and make them as logical as you can. I will assist you, and trip you up occasionally if you are likely to irritate him."

Then the dialogue went on. I give it literally.

"You are a great chief," said I to Sitting Bull, "but you live behind a cloud. Your face is dark, my people do not see it. Tell me, do you hate the Americans very much?"

A gleam as of fire shot across his face.

"I am no chief."

This was precisely what I expected. It will dissipate at once the erroneous idea which has prevailed, that Sitting Bull is either a chief or a warrior.

"What are you?"

"I am," said he, crossing both hands upon his chest, slightly nodding, and smiling satirically, "a man."

"What does he mean?" I inquired, turning to Major Walsh.

"He means," responded the Major, "to keep you in ignorance of his secret if he can. His position among his bands is anomalous. His own tribes, the Uncpapas, are not all in fealty to him. Parts of nearly twenty different tribes of Sioux, besides a remnant of the Uncpapas, abide with him. So far as I have learned, he rules over these fragments of tribes, which compose his camp of twenty-five hundred, including between eight hundred and nine hundred warriors, by sheer compelling force of intellect and will. I believe that he understands nothing particularly of war or military tactics, at least not enough to give him the skill or the right to command warriors in battle. He is supposed to have guided the fortunes of several battles, including the fight in which Custer fell. That supposition, as you will presently find, is partially erroneous. His word was always potent in the camp or in the field, but he has usually left to the war chiefs the duties appertaining to engagements. When the crisis came he gave his opinion, which was accepted as law."

"What was he then?" I inquired, continuing this momentary dialogue with Major Walsh. "Was he, is he, a mere medicine man?"

"Don't for the world," replied the Major, "intimate to him, in the questions you are about to ask him, that you have derived the idea from me, or from any one, that he is a mere medicine man. He would deem that to be a profound insult. In point of fact he is a medicine man, but a far greater, more influential medicine man than any savage I have ever known. He has constituted himself a ruler. He is a unique power among the Indians. His power consists in the universal confidence which is given to his judgment, which he seldom denotes until he is asked for an expression of it. It has been, so far, so accurate, it has guided his people so well, he has been caught in so few mistakes and he has saved even his ablest and oldest chiefs from so many evil consequences of their own misjudgment, that today his word among them all, is worth more than the united voices of the rest of the camp. He speaks. They listen and they obey. Now let us hear what his explanation will be."

"You say you are no chief?"

"No!" with considerable hauteur.

"Are you a head soldier?"

"I am nothing—neither a chief nor a soldier."

"What? Nothing?"

"Nothing."

"What, then, makes the warriors of your camp, the great chiefs who are here along with you, look up to you so? Why do they think so much of you?"

Sitting Bull's lips curled with a proud smile.

"Oh, I used to be a kind of a chief; but the Americans made me go away from my father's hunting ground."

"You do not love the Americans?"

You should have seen this savage's lips.

"I saw today that all the warriors around you clapped their hands and cried out when you spoke. What you said appeared to please them. They liked you. They seemed to think that what you said was right for them to say. If you are not a great chief, why do these men think so much of you?"

At this Sitting Bull, who had in the meantime been leaning back against the wall, assumed a posture of mingled toleration and disdain.

"Your people look up to men because they are rich; because they have much land, many lodges, many squaws?"

"Yes."

"Well, I suppose my people look up to me because I am poor. That is the difference."

In this answer was concentrated all the evasiveness natural to an Indian.

"What is your feeling toward the Americans now?"

He did not even deign an answer. He touched his hip, where his knife was.

I asked the interpreter to insist on an answer.

"Listen," said Sitting Bull, not changing his posture, but putting his right hand out upon my knee. "I told them today what my notions were—that I did not want to go back there. Every time that I had any difficulty with them they struck me first. I want to live in peace."

"Have you an implacable enmity to the Americans? Would you live with them in peace if they allowed you to do so; or do you think that you can only obtain peace here?"

"The White Mother is good."

"Better than the Great Father?"

"Howgh!"

And then after a pause, Sitting Bull continued. "They asked me today to give them my horses. I bought my horses, and they are mine. I bought them from men who came up the Missouri in mackinaws. They do not belong to the government, neither do the rifles. The rifles are also mine. I bought them; I paid for them. Why I should give them up I do not know. I will not give them up."

"Do you really think, do your people believe, that it is wise to reject the proffers that have been made to you by the United States Commissioners? Do not some of you feel as if you were destined to lose your old hunting grounds? Don't you see that you will probably have the same difficulty in Canada that you have had in the United States?"

"The White Mother does not lie."

"Do you expect to live here by hunting? Are there buffaloes enough? Can your people subsist on the game here?"

"I don't know; I hope so."

"If not, are any part of your people disposed to take up agriculture? Would any of them raise steers and go to farming?"

"I don't know."

"What will they do, then?"

"As long as there are buffaloes, that is the way we will live."

"But the time will come when there will be no more buffaloes."

"Those are the words of an American."

"How long do you think the buffaloes will last?"

Sitting Bull arose. "We know," said he, extending his right hand with an impressive gesture, "that on the other side the buffaloes will not last very long. Why? Because the country there is poisoned with blood—a poison that kills all the buffaloes and drives them away. It is strange," he continued, with his peculiar smile, "that the Americans should complain that the Indians kill buffaloes. We kill buffaloes, as we kill other animals, for food and clothing, to make our lodges warm. They kill buffaloes—for what? Go through your country. See the thousands of carcasses rotting on the Plains. Your young men shoot for pleasure. All they take from a dead buffalo is his tail, or his head, or his horns, perhaps, to show they have killed a buffalo. What is this? Is it robbery? You call us savages. What are they? The buffaloes have come North. We have come North to find them, and to get away from a place where the people tell lies."

To gain time, and not to dwell importunately on a single point, I asked Sitting Bull to tell me something of his early life. In the first place, where he was born?

"I was born on the Missouri River; at least I recollect that somebody told me so—I don't know who told me or where I was told of it."

"Of what tribe are you?"

"I am an Uncpapa."

"Of the Sioux?"

"Yes; of the great Sioux Nation."

"Who was your father?"

"My father is dead."

"Is your mother living?"

"My mother lives with me in my lodge."

"Great lies are told about you. White men say that you lived among them when you were young; that you went to school; that you learned to write and read from books; that you speak English; that you know how to talk French?"

"It is a lie."

"You are an Indian?"

(Proudly) "I am a Sioux."

Then, suddenly relaxing from his hauteur, Sitting Bull began to laugh. "I have heard," he said "of some of these stories. They are all strange lies. What I am I am," and here he leaned back and resumed his attitude and expression of barbaric grandeur.

"I am a man. I see. I know. I began to see when I was not yet born; when I was not in my mother's arms. It was then I began to study about my people. I studied about many things. I studied about the smallpox, that was killing my people—the great sickness that was killing the women and children. I was so interested that I turned over on my side. The God Almighty must have told me at that time [and here Sitting Bull unconsciously revealed his secret], that I would be the man to be the judge of all the other Indians—a big man, to decide for them in all their ways."

"And you have since decided for them?"

"I speak. It is enough."

"Could not your people, whom you love so well, get on with Americans?"

"No!"

"Why?"

"I never taught my people to trust Americans. I have told them the truth—that the Americans are great liars. I have never dealt with the Americans. Why should I? The land belonged to my people. I say I never dealt with them—I mean I never treated them in a way to surrender my people's rights. I treated with them, but I always gave full value for what I got. I never asked the U.S. Government to make me presents of blankets or cloth, or anything of that kind. The most I did was to ask them to send me an honest trader that I could trade with, and I proposed to give him buffalo robes and elk skins, and other hides in exchange for what we wanted. I told every trader who came to our camps that I did not want any favors from him—that I wanted to trade with him fairly and equally, giving him full value for what I got, but the traders wanted me to trade with them on no such terms. They wanted to give little and get much. They told me if I did not accept what they give me in trade they would get the government to fight me. I told them I did not want to fight."

"But you fought?"

"At last, yes; but not until I had tried hard to prevent a fight. At first my young men, when they began to talk bad, stole five American horses. I took the horses away from them and gave them back to the Americans. It did no good. By and by we had to fight."

It was at this juncture that I began to question the great savage before me in regard to the most disastrous, most mysterious Indian battle of the century—Custer's encounter with the Sioux on the Big Horn—the Thermopylæ of the Plains. Sitting Bull, the chief genius of his bands, has been supposed to have commanded the Sioux forces when Custer fell.

That the reader may understand Sitting Bull's statements, it will be necessary for him to read the following preliminary sketch. It should be understood, moreover, that, inasmuch as every white man with Custer perished, and no other white man, save one or two scouts, had conferred carefully with Sitting Bull or any of his chiefs since that awful day, this is the first authentic story of the conflict which can possibly have appeared out of the lips of a survivor. It has the more historical value, since it comes from the chief among Custer's and Reno's foes.

Custer, on the 22nd of June, started up the Rosebud, with the following order from General Terry in his pocket:—

"Lieutenant-Colonel Custer, Seventh Cavalry.

"COLONEL: The brigadier-general commanding directs that as soon as your regiment can be made ready for the march, you proceed up the Rosebud in pursuit of the Indians whose trail was discovered by Major Reno a few days since. It is, of course, impossible to give definite instructions in regard to this movement, and, were it not impossible to do so, the department commander places too much confidence in your zeal, energy, and ability, to wish to impose upon you precise orders which might hamper your action when nearly in contact with the enemy. He will, however, indicate to you his own views of what your action should be, and he desires that you should conform to them unless you shall see sufficient reason for departing from them. He thinks that you should proceed up the Rosebud until you ascertain definitely the direction in which the trail above spoken of leads. Should it be found, as it appears to be almost certain that it will be to turn toward the Little Big Horn, he thinks that you should still proceed southward, perhaps as far as the headquarters of the Tongue, and then turn toward the Little Big Horn, feeling constantly, however, toward your left, so as to preclude the possibility of the escape of the Indians to the south or southeast by passing around your left flank. The column of Colonel Gibbon is now in motion for the mouth of the Big Horn. As soon as it reaches that point it will cross the Yellowstone and move up at least as far as the parks of the Big and Little Big Horn. Of course, its future movements must be controlled by circumstances as they arise; but it is hoped that the Indians, if upon the Little Big Horn, may be so nearly enclosed by two columns that their escape will be impossible. The department commander desires that on your way up the Rosebud you should thoroughly examine the upper part of Tulloch's Creek, and that you should endeavor to send a scout through to Colonel Gibbon's column with information of the result of your examination. The lower part of this creek will be examined by a detachment of Colonel Gibbon's command. The supply steamer will be pushed up the Big Horn as far as the forks of the river are found to be navigable for that space, and the department commander, who will accompany the column of Colonel Gibbon, desires you to report to him there not later than the expiration of the time for which your troops are rationed, unless in the meantime you receive further orders.

Respectfully,

"E. W. SMITH,

Captain Eighteenth Infantry, Acting Assistant Adjutant-General."

With these tentative instructions, General Custer proceeded on his way. Hearing of the Indians, he found that he had a great opportunity to strike them. He touched their trail and followed it. He laid his plans, with what lack of success we know. But shall we not also inquire what was the real cause of his untimely, unnecessary failure?

General Custer had been chided for a division of his troops. In point of fact he never attacked an Indian camp when he had more than a company, without so separating his command as to encompass, bewilder, and capture it. We shall presently see whether it was the fault of his dispositions on this occasion which lost him his last battle. Here is Reno's account of the way in which the commands respectively, under Custer, himself, and Benteen, started into action:—

"The regiment left the camp at the mouth of Rosebud River, after passing in review before the department commander, under command of Brevet Major General G. A. Custer, Lieutenant-Colonel, on the afternoon of the 22nd of June, and marched up the Rosebud twelve miles and encamped. On the 23rd, marched up the Rosebud, passing many old Indian camps, and following a very large lodge-pole trail, but not fresh, making thirty-three miles. On the 24th, the march was continued up the Rosebud, the trail and signs freshening with every mile, until we had made twenty-eight miles, and we then encamped and waited for information from the scouts. At 9:25 PM Custer called the officers together and informed us that, beyond a doubt, the village was in the valley of the Little Big Horn, and that to reach it was necessary to cross the divide between the Rosebud and Little Big Horn, and that it would be impossible to do so in the daytime without discovering our march to the Indians; that we would prepare to move at 11 PM This was done, the line of march turning from the Rosebud to the right, up one of its branches, which headed near the summit at the divide.

"About 2 PM of the 25th, the scouts told him that he could not cross the divide before daylight. We then made coffee and rested three hours, at the expiration of which time the march was resumed, the divide crossed, and about 8 AM, the command was in the valley of one of the branches of the Little Big Horn. By this time the Indians had been seen, and it was certain that we could not surprise them, and it was determined to move at once to the attack.

"Previous to this no division of the regiment had been made since the order was issued on the Yellowstone annulling wing and battalion organizations. General Custer informed me he would assign commands on the march. I was ordered by Lieut. W. W. Cook, adjutant, to assume command of Companies M, A, and G Capt. Benteen of Companies H, D, and K; Custer retaining C, E, F, I, and L under his immediate command; and Company B, Capt. McDougall, in rear of the pack train. I assumed command of the companies assigned to me, and without any definite orders moved forward the rest of the column and well to its left. I saw Benteen moving further to the left, and as they passed he told me he had orders to move well to the left and sweep everything before him. I did not see him again until about 2:30 PM. The command moved down the creek toward the Little Big Horn Valley, Custer, and five companies, on the right bank, myself and three companies on the left bank, and Benteen further to the left and out of sight."

It appears to have been about the middle of the forenoon when Custer thus subdivided his column. Reno goes on to say that at half-past twelve Lieut. Cook, Custer's adjutant, came to him, told him that the village was only two miles away, and ordered him to move forward rapidly and charge it. Other evidence likewise shows that this order was given about that time, and that Reno was urged not to let up on the Indians. The Indian village, consisting of camps of Cheyennes, Ogallalas, Minneconjous, and Uncpapas, was nearly three miles long. Reno crossed the Little Big Horn, formed his first line just south of the crossing, and charged. He says:—

"I deployed, and, with the Ree scouts at my left charged down the valley with great ease for about two and a half miles."

Reno, instead of holding the ground thus gained, retreated, being hard pressed. He made a temporary stand in a bunch of timber, but finally retreated back over the valley, and across the Little Big Horn and up the bluffs, on the summit of which he entrenched himself late the afternoon.

Custer's march to the ford, where he attempted to cross the Little Big Horn and attack the Indians in their rear, was much longer than Reno's march; consequently Custer's assault was not made until after Reno's. Custer's intention was to sandwich, as it were, the main body of the Indians between Reno's and his own forces. He hoped by thus pressing them on two sides—Reno constantly fighting them and he himself constantly fighting them—to disconcert them and crush them at last. His plan is thus seen to have been that of a general. It relieves him from the aspersion of rashness. It must, in this connection, be remembered that Custer had fought Indians many times and had never been beaten by them, although on several occasions he had encountered more than three times the number of his own troops. He trusted in this instance to the fealty of his own officers, the bravery of his soldiers, and his own genius to overcome the mere weight of numbers, as he had so often done before.

The testimony of Sitting Bull which I am about to give, is the more convincing and important from the very fact of the one erroneous impression he derived as to the identity of the officer in command of the forces which assailed his camp. He confounds Reno with Custer. He supposes that one and the same general crossed the Little Big Horn where Reno crossed, charged as Reno charged, retreated as Reno retreated back over the river, and then pursued the line of Custer's march, attacked as Custer attacked, and fell as Custer fell.

"Did you know the Long Haired Chief?" I asked Sitting Bull.

"No."

"What! Had you never seen him?"

"No. Many of the chiefs knew him."

"What do they think of him?"

"He was a great warrior."

"Was he brave?"

"He was a mighty chief"

"Now, tell me. Here is something I wish to know. Big lies are told about the fight in which the Long Haired Chief was killed. He was my friend. No one has come back to tell the truth about him, or about that fight. You were there; you know. Your chiefs know. I want to hear something that forked tongues do not tell—the truth."

"It is well."

Here I drew forth a map of the battlefield and spread it out across Sitting Bull's knees and explained to him the names and situations as represented on it, and he smiled.

"We thought we were whipped," he said.

"Ah! Did you think the soldiers were too many for you?"

"Not at first; but by-and-by, yes. Afterwards, no."

"Tell me about the battle. Where was the Indian camp first attacked?"

"Here" (pointing to Reno's crossing on the map).

"About what time in the day was that?"

"It was some two hours past the time when the sun is in the centre of the sky."

"What white chief was it who came over there against your warriors?"

"The Long Hair."

"Are you sure?"

"The Long Hair commanded."

"But you did not see him?"

"I have said that I never saw him."

"Did any of the chiefs see him?"

"Not here, but there," pointing to the place where Custer charged and was repulsed, on the north bank to the Little Big Horn.

"Why do you think it was the Long Hair who crossed first and charged you here at the right side of the map?"

"A chief leads his warriors."

"Was there a good fight here, on the right side of the map? Explain it to me?"

"It was so," said Sitting Bull, raising his hands. "I was lying in my lodge. Some young men ran into me and said: 'The Long Hair is in the camp. Get up. They are firing in the camp.' I said, all right, and jumped up and stepped out of my lodge."

"Where was your lodge?"

"Here, with my people," answered Sitting Bull, pointing to the group of Uncpapa lodges, designated as "abandoned lodges" on the map.

"So the first attack was made, then, on the right side of the map, and upon the lodges of the Uncpapas?"

"Yes."

"Here the lodge are said to have been deserted?"

"The old men, the squaws, and the children were hurried away."

"Toward the other end of the camp?"

"Yes. Some of the Minneconjou women and children also left their lodges when the attack began."

"Did you retreat at first?"

"Do you mean the warriors?"

"Yes, the fighting men."

"Oh, we fell back, but it was not what warriors call a retreat; it was to gain time. It was the Long Hair who retreated. My people fought him here in the brush [designating the timber behind which the

Indians pressed Reno] and he fell back across [placing his finger on the line of Reno's retreat to the northern bluffs]."

"So you think that was the Long Hair whom your people fought in that timber and who fell back afterwards to those heights?"

"Of course."

"What occurred afterward? Was there any heavy fighting after the retreat of the soldiers to the bluffs?"

"Not then; not there."

"Where, then?"

"Why, down here," and Sitting Bull indicated with his finger the place where Custer approached and touched the river. "That," said he, "was where the big fight was fought a little later. After the Long Hair was driven back to the bluffs he took this road [tracing with his finger the line of Custer's march on the map], and went down to see if he could not beat us there."

(Here the reader should pause to discern the extent of Sitting Bull's error, and to anticipate what will presently appear to be Reno's misconception or mistake. Sitting Bull, not identifying Reno in the whole of this engagement, makes it seem that it was Custer who attacked, when Reno attacked in the first place, and afterward moved down to resume the assault from a new position. He thus involuntarily testifies to the fact that Reno's assault was a brief, ineffectual one before his retreat to the bluffs, and that Reno, after his retreat, ceased on the bluffs from aggressive fighting.)

"When the fight commenced here," I asked, pointing to the spot where Custer advanced behind the Little Big Horn, "what happened?"

"Hell!"

"You mean, I suppose, a fierce battle?"

"I mean a thousand devils."

"The village was by this time thoroughly aroused?"

"The squaws were like flying birds; the bullets were like humming bees."

"You say that when the first attack was made off here on the right of the map, the old men and squaws and children ran down the valley toward the left. What did they do when this second attack came from up here toward the left?"

"They ran back again to the right, here and there," answered Sitting Bull, placing his swarthy fingers on the words "Abandoned Lodges."

"And where did the warriors run?"

"They ran to the fight—the big fight."

"So that in the afternoon, after the first fight, on the right hand side of the map, was over, and after the big fight on the left-hand side began, you say the squaws and children all returned to the right-hand side, and that the warriors, the fighting men of all the Indian camps, ran to the place where the big fight was going on?"

"Yes."

"Why was that? Were not some of the warriors left in front of these entrenchments on the bluffs, near the right side of the map? Did not you think it necessary,—did not your war chiefs think it necessary—to keep some of your young men there to fight the troops who had retreated to these entrenchments?"

"No."

"Why?"

"You have forgotten."

"How?"

"You forget that only a few soldiers were left by the Long Hair on those bluffs. He took the main body of his soldiers with him to make the big fight down here on the left."

"So there were no soldiers to make a fight left in the entrenchments on the right-hand bluff?"

"I have spoken. It is enough. The squaws could deal with them. There were none but squaws and pappooses in front of them that afternoon."

This startling assertion of Sitting Bull involves the most terrible charge which has been brought against Reno. It amounts to an assertion, that Reno, having made his assault, been beaten and retreated, stayed there on the bluffs without renewing the attack for which General Custer, who had by this time come down with his horsemen on the rear of the Sioux camp from the north, vainly awaited —how hopelessly!

"Well, then," I inquired of Sitting Bull, "did the cavalry, who came down and made the big fight, fight?"

Again Sitting Bull smiled.

"They fought. Many young men are missing from our lodges. But is there an American squaw who has her husband left? Were there any Americans left to tell the story of that day?"

"No."

"How did they come on to the attack?"

"I have heard that there are trees which tremble."

"Do you mean the trees with trembling leaves?"

"Yes."

"They call them in some parts of the Western country Quaking Asps; in the eastern part of the country they call them Silver Aspens."

"Hah? A great white chief, whom I met once, spoke these words, 'Silver Aspens,' trees that shake; these were the Long Hair's soldiers."

"You do not mean that they trembled before your people because they were afraid?"

"They were brave men. They were tired. They were too tired."

"How did they act? How did they behave themselves?"

At this Sitting Bull again arose. I also arose from my seat, as did the other persons in the room, except the stenographer.

"Your people," said Sitting Bull, extending his right hand, "were killed. I tell no lies about dead men. These men who came with the Long Hair were as good men as ever fought. When they rode up their horses were tired and they were tired. When they got off from their horses they could not stand firmly on their feet. They swayed to and fro—so my young men have told me—like the limbs of cypresses in a great wind. Some of them staggered under the weight of their guns. But they began to fight at once; but by this time, as I have said, our camps were aroused, and there were plenty of warriors to meet them. They fired with needle guns. We replied with magazine guns— repeating rifles. It was so [and here Sitting Bull illustrated by patting his palms together with the rapidity of a fusillade]. Our young men rained lead across the river and drove the white braves back."

"And then?"

"And then they rushed across themselves."

"And then?"

"And then they found that they had a good deal to do."

"Was there at that time some doubt about the issue of the battle, whether you would whip the Long Hair or not?"

"There was so much doubt about it that I started down there [here again, pointing to the map] to tell the squaws to pack up the lodges and get ready to move away."

"You were on that expedition, then, after the big fight had fairly begun?"

"Yes."

"You did not personally witness the rest of the big fight? You were not engaged in it?"

"No; I have heard of it from the warriors."

"When the great crowds of your young men crossed the river in front of the Long Hair, what did they do? Did they attempt to assault him directly in his front?"

"At first they did, but afterward they found it better to try and get around him. They formed themselves on all sides of him, except just at his back."

"How long did it take them to put themselves around his flanks?"

"As long as it takes the sun to travel from here to here" (indicating some marks upon his arm, with which, apparently, he is used to gauge the progress of the shadow of his lodge across his arm, and probably meaning half an hour. An Indian has no more definite way than this to express the lapse of time).

"The trouble was with the soldiers," he continued; "they were so exhausted, and their horses bothered them so much, that they could not take good aim. Some of their horses broke away from them and left them to stand and drop and die. When the Long Hair, the General, found that he was so outnumbered and threatened on his flanks, he took the best course he could have taken. The bugle blew. It was an order to fall back. All the men fell back fighting and dropping. They could not fire fast enough, though. But from our side it was so," said Sitting Bull, and here he clapped his hands rapidly, twice a second, to express with what quickness and continuance the balls flew from the Henry and Winchester rifles wielded by the Indians. "They could not stand up under such a fire," he added.

"Were any military tactics shown? Did the Long Haired Chief make any disposition of his soldiers, or did it seem as though they retreated altogether, helter-skelter, fighting for their lives?"

"They kept in pretty good order. Some great chief must have commanded them all the while. They would fall back across a *coulie*, and make a fresh stand beyond, on higher ground. The map is pretty nearly right. It shows where the white men stopped and fought before they were all killed. I think that is right—down there to the left, just above the Little Big Horn. There was one party driven out there, away from the rest, and there a great many men were killed. The places marked on the map are pretty nearly the places where all were killed."

"Did the whole command keep on fighting until the last?"

"Every man, so far as my people could see. There were no cowards on either side."

Cowards! One would think not. The best testimony, from one who has examined the battlefield and the line of Custer's retreat, is as follows:—

"From this point [the north bank of the Little Big Horn, where Custer was forced back by overpowering numbers] he was driven back to make successive stands on the higher ground. His line of retreat stretches from the river to the spot indicated on the map as that where he fell. On the line of retreat, Calhoun's company seems to have been thrown across it to check the Indians. At a distance of about three-quarters of a mile from the river, the whole of Calhoun's company lay dead in an irregular line, Calhoun and Crittenden in place in the rear. About a mile beyond this, on the ridge parallel to the stream, still following the line of retreat indicated on the map, Keogh's company was slaughtered in position, his right resting on the hill where Custer fell, and which seems to have been held by Yates' company. On the most prominent part of the ridge Custer made his last desperate stand. Here, with Captain Yates, Colonel Cook, Captain Custer, Lieutenant Riley, and others, and thirty-two men of Yates' command, he went down, fighting heroically to the last, against the tremendous odds which assailed them on all sides. It is believed by some that, finding the situation a desperate one, they killed their horses for a barricade. From the point where Custer fell, the line of retreat again doubles back toward the river through a ravine, and along this line in the ravine twenty-three bodies of Smith's company were found. Where this terminates, near the river, are found the dead men and horses of Captain Custer's company, commingled with Smith's, and the situation of the dead indicates that some desperate attempt was made to make a stand near the river, or to gain the woods."

I inquired of Sitting Bull: "How long did this big fight continue?"

"The sun was there," he answered, pointing to within two hours from the western horizon.

I went on to interrogate Sitting Bull:—

"This big fight, then, extended through three hours?"

"Through most of the going forward of the sun."

"Where was the Long Hair the most of the time?"

"I have, talked with my people; I cannot find one who saw the Long Hair until just before he died. He did not wear his hair long as he used to wear it. His hair was like yours," said Sitting Bull, playfully touching my forehead with his fingers. "It was short, but it was of the color of the grass when the frost comes."

"Did you hear from your people how he died? Did he die on horseback?"

"No; none of them died on horseback."

"All were dismounted?"

"Yes."

"And Custer, the Long Hair?"

"Well, I have understood that there were a great many brave men in that fight, and that from time to time, while it was going on, they were shot down like pigs. They could not help themselves. One by one, the officers fell. I believe the Long Hair rode across once from this place down here [meaning the place where Tom Custer's and Smith's companies were killed], to this place up here [indicating the spot on the map where Custer fell], but I am not sure about this. Anyway it was said that up there, were the last fight took place, where the last stand was made, the Long Hair stood like a sheaf of corn with all the ears fallen around him."

"Not wounded?"

"No."

"How many stood by him?"

"A few."

"When did he fall?"

"He killed a man when he fell. He laughed."

"You mean he cried out?"

"No, he laughed; he had fired his last shot."

"From a carbine?"

"No, a pistol."

"Did he stand up after he first fell?"

"He rose up on his hands and tried another shot, but his pistol would not go off."

"Was any one else standing up when he fell down?"

"One man was kneeling, that was all. But he died before the Long Hair. All this was far up on the bluffs, far away from the Sioux encampment. I did not see it. It was told to me. But it is true."

"The Long Hair was not scalped?"

"No; my people did not want his scalp."

"Why?"

"I have said he was a great chief."

"Did you at any time," I persisted, "during the progress of the fight, believe that your people would get the worst of it?"

"At one time, as I have told you, I started down to tell squaws to strike the lodges. I was then on my way up to right end of the camp, where the first attack was made upon us. But before I reached that end of the camp, where the Minneconjou and Uncpapa squaws and children were, and where some of the other squaws—Cheyennes and Ogallalas—had gone, I was overtaken by one of the young warriors, who had just come from the fight. He called out to me. He said: 'No use to leave camp; every white man is killed.' So I stopped and went no further. I turned back, and by-and-by I met the warriors returning."

"But in the meantime," I asked, "were there no warriors occupied up here at the right end of the camp? Was nobody left, except the squaws and the children and the old men, to take care of that end of the camp? Was nobody ready to defend it against the soldiers in those entrenchments up there?"

"Oh," replied Sitting Bull again, "there was no need to waste warriors in that direction. There were only a few soldiers in those entrenchments, and we knew they wouldn't dare to come out."

This finished the interview, and with a few more "How! How"'s, the wily chieftain withdrew.